Taught to Kill

RELATED TITLES FROM POTOMAC BOOKS

A Mind in Prison: The Memoir of a Son and Soldier of the Third Reich,
by Bruno Manz

My Hitch in Hell: The Bataan Death March, by Lester I. Tenney

Strike and Hold: A Memoir of the 82nd Airborne in World War II,
by T. Moffatt Burriss

The Forgotten Soldier, by Guy Sajer

Wake Island Pilot: A World War II Memoir, by Brig. Gen. John F.
Kinney, USMC (Ret.) with James M. McCaffrey

An AUSA Book

Taught to Kill

AN AMERICAN BOY'S WAR FROM THE ARDENNES TO BERLIN

John B. Babcock

Potomac Books, Inc.
Washington, D.C.

First paperback edition published 2007
Copyright © 2005 by Potomac Books, Inc.

Published in the United States by Potomac Books, Inc. (formerly Brassey's, Inc.).
All rights reserved. No part of this book may be reproduced in any manner
whatsoever without written permission from the publisher, except in the case of
brief quotations embodied in critical articles and reviews.

Library of Congress Cataloging-in-Publication Data

Babcock, John B., 1922–
    Taught to kill : an American boy's war from the Ardennes to Berlin /
John B. Babcock.—1st ed.
      p. cm.
    ISBN 1-57488-799-8 (alk. paper)
    1. Babcock, John B., 1922– 2. United States. Army. Division, 78th—
Biography. 3. World War, 1939–1945—Campaigns—Western Front.
4. World War, 1939–1945—Personal narratives, American. 5. Soldiers—
United States—Biography. I. Title.

D769.378th .B33   2005
940.54'21'092—dc22   2004022589

ISBN 1-57488-799-8 (hardcover)
ISBN 978-1-57488-800-3 (paperback)

Printed in Canada on acid-free paper that meets the
American National Standards Institute Z39-48 Standard.

Potomac Books, Inc.
22841 Quicksilver Drive
Dulles, Virginia 20166

First Edition

10 9 8 7 6 5 4 3 2 1

CONTENTS

FOREWORD
by
Rick Atkinson

The best war stories are always less about battles than about the men who fight them. The extravagant stress of combat is a great revealer of character, refracting a soldier's elemental traits the way a prism refracts light. We see the man's mettle, for good and for ill. Writing well about war can never ennoble combat, but it can redeem those forced to wage war by affirming their humanity. We sense the skull beneath the helmet, the boy behind the rifle, the heart beating under the olive-drab field jacket.

Nearly sixty years after serving as an infantryman in Europe during the last months of World War II, John B. Babcock has written a memoir that is compelling, authentic, and deeply human. He reminds us that the war, like all truly epic stories, is bottomless; there is more to write, and there will always be more to write. His perspective is from the lip of a slit trench, the mud-spackled view of a junior sergeant in a mortar section. Larger military and political issues rarely intrude. We never see the big arrows on the map, barely even know what division the writer is in.

This allows us to experience the war as Sergeant Babcock saw it, smelled it, heard it, felt it. He bears witness well, with irony and sardonic humor and a flinty refusal to take refuge in retrospective sentimentality. He remembers the "rye bread and grease smell" of German prisoners tramping toward their cages; the "flick-of-a-whip swish" that precedes a mortar round detonating; the twitching of the mortally wounded; the smell of GI soap and GI socks, of Cosmoline and flea powder, of "pine pitch from freshly severed branches." He remembers how the dead become part of the landscape, even serving as landmarks for those giving directions, as in: "come up the street to the guy with the hole in his head, and turn right." He remembers the terror of the first near-miss from an artillery shell; the fumbling search of enemy corpses for spare lighter flints; the difficulty of hugging the ground for a mortarman wearing a canvas bib stuffed with a dozen shells.

Sergeant Babcock will not, cannot avert his eyes. The war he remembers includes friendly fire and fragging, looting and rape, and the execution of prisoners. He records these "shabby transgressions," but also valor, and hilarity, and infantrymen rubbing each others' frozen feet to ward off trench foot, a poignant image of mutual devotion that tells us much about comradeship.

This is a thoroughly modern combat memoir, one that enriches the genre. If occasionally crude and often haunting, it is always vivid. Just like war.

INTRODUCTION
TIME TO LOOK BACK

Brisk wind out of the northwest hurried bursts of slanting sleet across a shallow trench in the middle of a snowy, thirty-acre cornfield. Through tinted shooting glasses, reluctant dawn gradually illuminated the icy spew and scudding clouds as I lay in that raw hole, eyes and ears tuned for the arrival of the magnificent Canadian goose.

Fingers gnarled by arthritis and time were warm and dry in roomy mittens, each containing a chemical warming device. The receiver of my .12-gauge Winchester "21" shotgun was protected under a generous coat flap. Despite the cold gusts and wet clay walls, the rest of my arthritic joints were snug, so relaxed that I was drifting off. I wasn't used to rising at four in the morning to stumble in the dark over frozen hills of corn stubble, set out life-like plastic goose decoys, and dig a hunting blind; I was ready by dawn for my usual midday nap.

A sponge rubber mat was spread between the cold, cold ground and me. Tender and once frostbitten feet were warmly ensconced in bulbous Mickey Mouse snowmobile boots. Camouflaged, wool-lined overalls covered miracle-fiber longjohns. A roomy undershirt, virgin wool sports shirt, and cashmere sweater were layered under a generous, down-filled camo jacket that reached almost to my knees. The goose coat and the overalls were protected by special Gortex mesh. Body-generated moisture filtered out; cold water could not get in.

Through half-closed eyes, I watched insects crawling on the loose corn stalks and leaves scattered over my trench to conceal me from incoming geese. I recalled that it had been in a foxhole in Germany that I had first noticed that there were bugs and insects moving about outdoors in winter. What was a self-respecting bug doing out in cold like this?

For that matter, what the hell was a nice old duffer like me doing out on a day like this? Sleepily, I recalled a pledge made during winter combat in the European theater of operations during the Second World War: When the war was over, never, swore I, would I ever, ever spend a single avoidable minute shivering outside on a raw winter day.

If the foxholes I dug that winter in Germany had been laid end to end, they would have reached from Rochester to Albany; so I had sworn also, that never would I ever, ever hand-shovel another hole out of the frozen earth.

Yet, here I was, lured as I had been several times over the years, to hunt geese in the dead of a Northeast winter. Digging a blind was the dues one paid for the hunt. What other empty pledges had I broken since the end of infantry combat in Germany?

Well, I never did set up that 60mm mortar out on the front lawn so I could pee in it every day. Nor had I fixed a bayonet to an M1 rifle and stuck it in a concrete base by the back door so my faithful dog could raise a hind leg on it while I contentedly watched it rust away.

Over the years the hate and hostility that motivate a soldier to kill his mortal enemy had slowly dissipated. I had friends with German names. I took my second trip to the Rhine, this time aboard a luxury riverboat. We passed Remagen, where only the stone towers (one a museum) marked where I had in terror scrambled across the Ludendorf Bridge that pitch-black March night. Sauerbraten, sweet beer, oohm-pa-pa music. It got easier and easier to let bygones be bygones.

My forgiving spirit seems unfair to the fifty-some comrades from my infantry company who were snuffed out before most of them were old enough to vote. Here I was, hale and hearty, several of their shortened life spans later. For many years I had paused on Memorial Day to read from the battalion history book that long list of killed in action from my old outfit. Some had been close as brothers; others died so soon I couldn't place a face with the name. Finally, an old service pal who blew the bugle that echoed taps at our hometown Memorial Day graveside services died. I stopped attending that event and let slip the ritual of re-reading the casualty list.

Slumbering memories of ground combat lie always near the surface for surviving infantrymen. Ex-dogfaces seldom talk to others about their real war experiences. It seems like only we who have been deeply into it can swap among ourselves combat memories and not have them sound like flyboys bragging about missions of derring-do. We all have a collection of tales we feel comfortable in spinning: humorous garrison life episodes, weekend pass adventures, difficult travel experiences, irritating military chickenshit, etc. The really disturbing battle memories are relegated to occasional sleepless hours at night. Many of us still wrestle with the phenomenon of just how often and how close we were to being corpses.

Those who are curious about the big war that took place before they were born are treated to fuzzy, black-and-white film chronicles on public television. Lots of airplanes. Naval guns blazing in the distance. Equipment-laden troops boarding ships. Rifle-toting soldiers marching. Closer to combat, the boom-boom of tanks and artillery, the guns pitched at such high angles as to suggest that the recorded fire mission was far from any real fighting. There's a little footage of riflemen dashing house-to-house in unnamed villages, and to bring the horror "home," a few quick takes of fallen soldiers, ours, but mostly theirs.

So, lying in that goose blind, I decided for the first time since the big, "Good War," to examine my own records of that era, and with the perspective of decades, to see if I could put in words just what infantry combat meant to kids back then—in my instance, a college-age lad from a northeastern farm. I wanted more to examine its impact and effect on us than to reconstruct some new record for specific battles of World War II.

My reveries in the cornfield ditch were interrupted by the call: "Geese at three o'clock. Take 'em!"

I tossed aside the cornstalks, sat up as fast as I could, pulled off the warmed mittens, and mounted my side-by-side. By then the geese were wheeling back downwind and fast disappearing. I snapped off the safety, clicked the barrel selector to the full-choke tube, and let fly, remembering to pick a target goose and not shoot at the flock. The rest of the hunt was history. Tall tales. A shot of brandy in black coffee. Home by 9:00 a.m. Roast goose for dinner that night.

As I hung up my modern-age hunting clothes, I marveled that we had survived the German winter weather of 1944–45. Starting with non-breathable, dubbin-impregnated leather shoes that were coffins for healthy, pink feet, we were ill equipped for Arctic weather. The miracle fibers and materials that we now take for granted in the field had not yet been invented. We were wet, cold, miserable, ravaged by frostbite and trench foot. It was a hopeless, endless, destitute, bleak future we faced on the cruel German snowscape. The mere thought of it induced a chilly shudder.

After a hot shower, I dressed and went directly to a basement room that the family had labeled "Dad's Sports Closet." Here were my guns, shells, fishing gear, outdoor clothing, decoys, tin boxes of souvenirs, and, object of my present search, a cardboard transfer file filled with war memorabilia.

On top of the box were division and battalion history books put together by enterprising publishers who had obviously churned out similar chronicles for other military organizations. Next, my hardback copy of *All Quiet on the Western Front* by Erich Maria Remarque. On down was a stack of newsletters circulated among us division veterans, including personal accounts of battle experiences, reports of reunions, inquiries about lost buddies, reproductions of old overseas snapshots.

Deeper in the box was a large stack of letters, those I had written to my parents, brother, sister, even some mailed to friends and passed along to my family. There were reduced, gray photocopies, and V-Mail forms with words cut out by the company censor. Others bore letterheads from Service Clubs, USOs, camps, forts, hotels. Hundreds of letters. Those to my folks had been painstakingly copied by my mother on an old L.C. Smith typewriter.

At the bottom of the box, undisturbed for five decades, were ninety pages of single-spaced, no-margin typing: a personal account to myself of my memories, reactions, and thoughts about the war just concluded. Using the privilege of my final rank as first sergeant, I had commandeered a comfortable room and appropriated a German typewriter. Ordering that I remain undisturbed, I used my own hunt-and-peck technique and a week of Army time to create a record that I deliberately mothballed for later consumption.

I hadn't planned that so many years would pass before I reviewed my own words. Perhaps I sensed that there were confessionals and inner thoughts that I would not want to be reminded of, nor share with anyone else. Maybe that had kept me from probing the bottom of the box these many decades.

A lot of the pages were typed on the reverse side of the confiscated letterhead of a German physician. Typical of European paper stock during that period, the sheets were thin, almost transparent. They had yellowed far more than other paper I had scrounged. I was careful not to tear or fracture the fragile pages.

I started to page through the passionate words of a twenty-three-year-old, small-town American college kid, transformed at age twenty-one, by government edict, into a foreign-soil combat soldier.

As I riffled through the old pages, my inquiry was arrested temporarily by a passage that started: "What will I say when people ask me what an artillery barrage is really like?" We never could describe it to each other in any satisfactory manner. On a smudged mailing form, I had jotted down what two of us in a foxhole had agreed, between barrages, 88mm German artillery was like, and this is what we came up with:

> The ear-splitting shriek grows in intensity as 88s come closer and closer. Incoming mail comes to ground with an earth-shaking, tooth-jarring thud. A nearby hit is overwhelmingly loud. A near-

direct hit leaves you helpless, riding the crest of a huge, trembling shock wave. The reverberation lingers in your head well after the actual sound rumbles on. An 88 explosion is brain-shaking, tear-generating, throat-paralyzing, palate-drying, memory-destroying, piss-provoking, asshole-tightening, fingernail-breaking, toe-curling, sweat-making, hope-extinguishing, breath-shortening, dreaded hell. The only shell more terrible than the last one is the next one.

War bends all fighting men and breaks some. The term "shell-shock" of World War I was broadened to "battle fatigue" for World War II. Fifty years after World War II, "post-traumatic stress disorder treatment counseling and rehabilitation" is prescribed for military personnel who serve beyond our borders, whether they get shot at or not.

The difference between infantry training and actual combat? The ordered world we knew was replaced by cataclysm, chaos, profound shock, and terror. Calendar dates were obscured by bruised memory. There were no hours in a day, days in a week, weeks in a month. We had been dumped thousands of miles from home in a dark forest populated by hostile soldiers. Until published in military history books, there were few geographic benchmarks. We did not know the names of towns, the dates we attacked them, or where they were on maps we never saw. Only antitank barriers (dragon teeth) and huge concrete pillboxes told us we were invading Germany from someplace along the Belgium border. All incoming artillery was "88s," to us, despite the fact that much of the enemy fire originated from 75mm, 105mm, and larger caliber artillery. Enemy tanks were all Tigers, strafing planes were all Messerschmitts. Could such confusion prevail for four months? We had no choice.

There have been campaigns involving hundreds of thousands of United States troops that incurred total battle casualties fewer in number than were suffered in our little World War II infantry company of 193 men, where for every individual killed, three others were evacuated for wounds or freezing flesh . No battle death should go unheralded. There persists for World War II combat veterans a feeling that our grievous losses have been conveniently wrapped in some fuzzy, warm myth of freeing the world from oppression.

An individual account of any World War II event lacks perspective or objectivity. It's a small chip of a broad mosaic. At many a veterans' gathering, one man's description of an old battle typically draws the response: "No, that's not how it went. Here's what happened." To which a third voice would enjoin: "You're both nuts. This is what really happened." All three versions are earnest, but flawed by the overwhelming confusion, tension, and fear that are companion to kill-or-be-killed combat.

My account relies on records written back then, and indelible memories. Combat action was experienced personally, or happened nearby. To avoid embarrassment to others in some cases, I often avoid reference to dates, places, even my actual military unit in the Seventy-eighth Division. For convenience, I elected to call us A Company. Fictitious names are invented, some taken from the roster of my Uncle Charlie's Civil War letters. More often than not, I simply did not know the exact date or location of the battle and often suspected errors in written historical accounts.

Advanced preparation for ground combat focused on weapons instruction, mock battle maneuvers, and intense physical conditioning. These exercises honed the mental discipline required for effective combat performance and individual survival. The highest skills and resolve were no ticket to immortality, but they beat the hell out of the complete lack of preparation for the teenage replacements who, scant weeks out of high school, became the real cannon fodder of infantry warfare during that final winter of 1944–45.

Returning GIs were faceless, undistinguished, and indistinguishable from the sorry cartoon figure we left to mark our passing during combat: "Kilroy was here," scratched on foreign walls along with name, unit, and date. He was our substitute for a granite or bronze obelisk commemorating our achievements and honoring our dead at each battle site.

Maybe because there were so many millions of us in uniform, the deeds and the effects on us combat warriors suffered unique anonymity. There are many more living Unknown Soldiers from World War II than those whose graves bear that label. Every combat soldier suffers indescribable trials. The most resolute veteran experiences moments of shame. Merely to have lived through World War II was perhaps our single shared glory.

CHAPTER **1** | # PREPARING FOR WAR

Lay That Pistol Down, Babe

Half my three-year World War II military indenture, from 1943 to 1946, was served at camps or forts that trained infantry replacements. All ten million Americans who were in the service during World War II went through "basic," "boot camp," or some sort of military orientation. For many, it was a harsh and cruel transition from life back home. Only combat itself justified the rigors and discipline of being taught to serve as a foot soldier. The lessons were strict, the rewards few.

Infantry basic took place in "camps," if the facilities were constructed especially for use during the war, and "forts" if they were permanent military installations. I yearned to serve in a more hospitable arm, and bucked for transfer to several safe-haven noncombatant services such as the quartermaster or signal corps. I finally escaped replacement-training camps only to end up in a rifle company in an infantry division designated for overseas duty. I had "out-clevered" myself with all my maneuvering.

Regularly stripped of newly trained men shipped out as replacements in various war theaters, several infantry divisions, including mine, the Seventy-eighth, started to rebuild permanent combat rosters of fresh candidates qualified to serve in battle. The

3

nation's manpower pool of top-quality physical and mental specimens had been depleted as priorities grew for a European campaign that started on D-Day, June 6, 1944. The United States was finding the enemy very stingy about giving up ground, hedgerows, and villages as our troops came ever closer to the fatherland.

Exacting physical or mental qualifications for combat candidates gave way to expediency. One sardonic T-5 medic told us that the doctor he worked for looked down a man's throat while he, the medic, looked up his ass. Only if they could see each other was the man rejected.

I had been called up in April 1943 from Voluntary Enlisted Reserve status to active duty. Initial routine basic training was followed by selection to participate in the Army Specialized Training Program (ASTP). The Army determined that some privileged college students should be earmarked for further training. Many of us were sent to accredited colleges for advanced study. Some were accepted in special programs to become air corps or signal corps officers. Others engaged in studies to repair equipment, operate motor pools, even become cooks and bakers. Then, in mid-April 1944 came the abrupt termination of academic privilege. All trainees were "washed out" and sent to the infantry, with the purpose of providing fresh leadership and high intelligence to the combat commands. We were suddenly destined to be tomorrow's cannon fodder.

Most bitter were the Army air force cadets, who were washed out even though they were competent and well into flight training. There were quite a few men with a "T" below their corporal's or sergeant's stripes indicating that they were specially trained technicians in the signal corps, cooks' and bakers' school, or mechanical repair disciplines. Now they were all simple soldiers: infantry riflemen.

The bottom of the barrel had been scraped to include marginal-behavior incorrigibles, perennial AWOLs, and the woefully illiterate who signed their names with an X. By combining the brightest and best with the teenagers and deadbeats, the Army sought a mix that could become a cohesive fighting unit with potential leadership blood in its ranks. We were taught infantry tactics by old Regular Army noncoms (cadre) who had long ago dismissed all thought of actually practicing in real war what they taught in peace. We were consistently abused, bullied, and demeaned.

Our first sergeant, an old-timer, was the most miserable prick I was to meet in the service, and that's going some! I am not sure I knew his proper name even back then, for we called him either Sergeant, Top, or, behind his back, Slewfoot. He looked like a battle-scarred veteran, if his facial contours were any indication. It looked like his lower jaw had been shot away, leaving above it a beak-like nose over a drooping upper lip that was adequate to cover both upper and lower teeth. Although he had the look of an experienced combat leader, he had never heard a shot fired in anger. He resembled an almost comical, cartoon likeness, except that his deep-set, piggy eyes and that droopy lip revealed a mean, angry, and implacable disposition that sure didn't fit the funny papers.

The name Slewfoot had been bestowed in recognition of his size fourteen triple-A shoes, which resembled containers for some obscene sausage. Whether his feet could have carried him where ours were forced to march was never known. Slewfoot didn't go in the field with the men; he showed up at evening formation, seething with rancor and ill will, reeking of 3.2 beer. What Army beer lacked in alcoholic content could be made up by quantity. Slewfoot was living proof.

The growing tension between our imperious first sergeant and us downtrodden troops was inevitable. Subtle resistance fueled his habitual anger. There developed a new ingredient for Slewfoot to cope with: insolence. Heretofore, he had consistently and deftly crushed any but fleeting resistance to his overbearing, threatening management style. His subjects in past training groups had been easily dominated, cowed into submission. But there were some yardbirds in this final training bunch who were different: They simply didn't give a shit. They were hard-time losers.

On an overnight field exercise, Slewfoot came up by jeep to occupy the tent the company clerk had erected for him. Next morning his shoes had been stolen. Seething, but unable to exercise a choice disciplinary option in the field, Slewfoot was driven away in the jeep; it was two days before he showed up again for company formation. Every single man in the company took note of his new, shiny, custom triple-As.

During advanced combat training in the early fall of 1944, Slewfoot demonstrated his capacity for unfair, cruel, and relentless treatment of his men, practices commonly referred to as "chickenshit." This time, chickenshit harrassment met with resolute unruliness. At one o'clock on a Monday morning I was awakened, along with others, when my bunk was tipped over. The guy above me took quite a tumble. Slewfoot was raging up and down the barrack, pulling men out of the sack, ordering them to fall-the-hell-out in the company street, "toot sweet." I grabbed my fatigue jacket, pulled on pants, and jammed sockless feet into unlaced shoes before being rudely shoved toward the stairs and down to the street.

No one knew what the story was. Under our breaths we took Slewfoot's name in vain as we formed up in the dark. It was raining, but we were too shocked to react to cold or wet.

"Now who the gaddam hell was that singing off the back porch? One of you don't speak up, I'll run all your damned asses right straight to hell. And, believe me, I guaran-goddamn-tee you I kin do it!"

"What we here for, Top?" whined a voice from a rear rank.

"You shut you Gaddam mouth, Watkins. I'll tell ya when you kin talk. What I'm asking, and I'm asking it right now: Who was that singing 'Pistol Packin' Mama' off the back porch? They was a guard out there with a prisoner, and he's mighty pissed. Somebody 'fess up, and Watkins, you git to the supply room and come back pronto with a long-handle shovel. Teach you not to talk in ranks or sass me."

It was a song popular at the moment, "Pistol Packin' Mama." It went: "Lay that pistol down, babe, Lay that pistol down. Pistol packin' mama, Lay that pistol down." That refrain followed verses about the red hot mama and her cabaret. Everyone knew and sang the words. I had to admit it was pretty funny, a drunk on the back steps singing it to some poor bastard guarding a GI prisoner with an empty .45 caliber automatic pistol (in Stateside training, no one packed live ammo, except on firing ranges).

Whoever did the singing may have had a few drinks, but nothing like Slewfoot. He'd been off the base and had a snoot full. Noncom club 3.2 beer made him surly. Liquor made him crazy. The noncom club was closed Sundays, so he'd been into the real sauce.

We'd been at attention the better part of an hour, watching Watkins shovel mud out of the deep streetside ditch that ran in front of our tarpaper two-story barrack. Water started to trickle down the insides of our fatigues into our unlaced shoes. Watkins's buddy Private Shannon broke ranks and started for the building entrance.

"Fuck this noise, guys. I ain't gonna stand out here with this asshole any longer. You guys do what you want. I'm goin' to bed," said Shannon, head down, in full stride. He was a little guy with the spunk of a bantam rooster, less education than my dog Poodreau, and mulish insubordination that had already put him in the brig three times.

—————»((•))«—————

"Shannon, get your black ass back here!"* bellowed Slewfoot. "Take Watkins's shovel and Watkins, get over to supply and pick youse'f up another shovel, and I mean right now!" Shovels in hand, the two fractious privates clowned around, tossing mud every which way, jabbering noisily between themselves. Shannon jabbed his shovel in the wet ground, shouting "Long thrust!" Watkins picked up the bayonet theme, crowing "Butt stroke," as he waved his muddy implement menacingly at Slewfoot.

Slewfoot ordered the duo to stand at attention before him on the edge of the ditch. Without warning, he lifted his size fourteen triple-A shoe and deftly kicked first Shannon and then Watkins off the road and into the watery trench. Knocked breathless, they

---

* "Black ass" was a common slang term, especially among the old prewar regulars. Many of us were referred to in this fashion by irate NCOs.

huddled in the mud. Slewfoot was sobering up. Glaring balefully, he threatened the two insubordinates with a month of company duty, and with a wave dismissed us from ranks. We all promptly went back to bed.

"Hey, Shannon," someone queried. "You okay?"

"Fuck."

Someone else: "Hey, Watkins, buddy, what you say?"

"Fuck."

The two revolutionaries shared a smattering of celebrity the next morning; Shannon took credit for the back porch singing. In the shower he was limited to "Who Broke the Handle on the Shithouse Door?" delivered in full voice, so he had broken new ground as an entertainer.

The next night Slewfoot, who still appeared only at reveille and retreat during duty hours, made off early for the noncom club. He returned late to find his bed, footlocker, clothes press, and all his belongings in a muddy pile outside his window. His extra shoes were gone. The entire darkened barrack echoed from their bunks, in unison, a chorus of "Pistol Packin' Mama" as Slewfoot sullenly recovered his chattels.

The insurrection ended in a standoff. Slewfoot couldn't take his out-of-line cause to the authorities. The two screw-ups managed to stay off the boat for overseas, which was their sole objective. Watkins missed shipping out by flushing his full set of false teeth down the toilet (until then, no one even knew he wore them). The chompers were his ticket to trigger an early discharge, and he timed it well. His pal Shannon went over the hill (AWOL) just before we shipped out, and hadn't been caught when we finally sailed for the old country.

——————————⋙«◇»⋘——————————

The final postscript was Slewfoot's masterful stroke in ducking the shipping order himself. He applied for and was awarded a last-minute transfer to Officer Candidate School (OCS). I hoped they'd kill him at Fort Benning, but I never did find out what happened to him.

A GI Word That Says It All

—————————— ❖ ——————————

Fuck.

During WWII, and during every war before or after, the word *fuck* was, and still is, the most frequently used crutch-word in the military. There's little doubt that, based on sheer frequency, it had special tenancy in the infantry. So dissociated has the word become from its originally accepted application to gratuitous or forced sex that it is no longer a "dirty" word. It certainly was not inventive invective.

"Fuck" in my Army was the choice whether or not your vocabulary offered a more appropriate option. Sometimes you said it while you tried to think of another, more appropriate word. More often it was a pure expletive that automatically insinuated itself into dogface talk.

Few are the WWII soldiers visiting home on furlough or weekend pass who did not slip up at the dinner table and ask a younger sister or sweet old grandmother to "pass the fucking butter."

The word was embraced generally in the shorthand of military lexicon to describe futility, failure, and in particular, inefficiency: SNAFU stood for Situation Normal, All Fucked Up. Anyone who holds that the *F* in SNAFU stands for "fouled" instead of "fucked" is simply not with the fucking program. Many soldiers didn't really know what the letters stood for, just that SNAFU described a screwed-up event as in: "Was that field exercise yesterday a SNAFU?" "Shit, it was worse than that. It was fucked up."

Small and gross catastrophes took on variations. FUBAR: Fucked Up Beyond All Recognition. TARFU: Things Are Really Fucked Up. FUBB: Fucked Up Beyond Belief. To goof off in a major way was doggin' it: fucking the dog. But the word was seldom printed as *fuck*, except on latrine walls and in phone booths where an accompanying phone number invoked its earlier definition. To have been fucked yourself meant merely that you had been wronged, victimized, usually by the orderly room, which was Slewfoot's kennel.

Ranting and railing in fuck-ese was a boring turnoff, the last refuge of the inarticulate. "I'm fucking tired of this man's fucking Army, and I'm fucking well goin' to fuck off every fucking chance I get, and you can fucking tell any fucking officer you fucking see that this is fucking where I fucking come from. And if you don't fucking like it, fuck you!"

Overseas, during serious weapons instruction, I discovered that men paid closer attention to the message if I avoided the fuck-word and swearing in general. They took me more seriously, knowing instinctively that empty expletives lack substance and credibility. And they damned well better had, or I would have fucking killed the assholes!

From Home Front to The Front

$$=\!\!\!\!\!\!\!\!\!\!\!\!\!\!\ll\!\!\bullet\!\!\gg\!\!\!\!=$$

After sixteen months in uniform, I felt like I had the record for longest time in grade as a lowly private in military history. Finally the Army decided it should confer on me the distinguished rank of private first class, in recognition of my acquired professional status as mortar gunner. I wrote my mother that fifteen thousand divisional troops, in full dress splendor, passed in review to commemorate my prestigious new adornment. Truth was, Slewfoot, our hideous first sergeant, threw two pitiful little scraps of cloth on my bunk and ordered that the chevrons be properly sewed on in time for Saturday inspection.

My pay was raised from $50 a month to $54. What in the world to do with all that extra cash? I squandered the $4 buying extra chevrons, a sewing kit, and a necktie more suitable for weekend passes than the rough-textured GI rag that had been tossed to me by an old-timer supply sergeant.

There's no Army rank lower than private, unless it be supernumerary private, reserved for the rawest rookies awaiting assignment to a squad, or a body to fill out a casual work-detail short a man. I was on my way up the ranks.

How far was I from the pinnacle of enlisted rank? Private, private first class, corporal, buck sergeant, staff sergeant, technical sergeant, and the ultimate: three stripes up, three down, with a diamond in the middle: first sergeant. Without the center diamond, six stripers were master sergeants. It's appropriate for a PFC to be humble, but no need to overdo it. In addition to my single stripe, I had my expert rifle medal, earned back in my first basic, using a WWI model 1911 .30-caliber Enfield bolt-action rifle. Now, in a division headed for overseas, other arms skills were required: Proficiency with a brand new semi-automatic Garand Rifle M-I, followed by the .30 semi-automatic carbine, Browning Automatic Rifle (BAR), .45 pistol, and the light machine gun. I liked that little carbine with its stubby .30-caliber cartridges. It was meant for in-close fighting and personal defense; it was light, handy, and accurate up to two hundred yards.

I was pretty good with all the basic infantry tools, and so hot with a BAR that I turned in a score far lower than I actually shot. No use risking being assigned to carry that twenty-one-pound magnet for enemy fire. Scuttlebutt was that BAR men had less chance of survival than machine gunners. I specialized in carbines and mortars. In a weapons platoon, proficiency was required in both light mortars and air-cooled machine guns.

Wartime scarcity required that our machine-gun proficiency tests be carried out with modified barrels that fired little .22 cartridges. The exercise didn't seem real and was far from satisfying. I tripped off a few bursts of real, GI .30-caliber bullets just before we shipped out. Red-tipped tracers were mixed in the 300-round ammo belt. The deafening noise and fiery stream of real bullets made me a real believer. When that gun is spitting out lead a handful of bullets per second, you feel a rush of invincibility. A man behind a machine gun is a man in charge!

Mortars go back as far as gunpowder itself. You set off a propelling force under a projectile in a tube that gives it direction, and lob a missile high in the air, usually over a wall or rampart. Whether it is a stone, cast-iron ball, or high explosive shell, the missile drops almost vertically on its quarry. Explosive mortar projectiles usually vault over a hill or defensive barrier. Their almost silent arrival is a lethal surprise to the enemy. Defenders don't care much for death dropping silently from straight above.

Artillery, on the other hand, is like a rifle bullet, seemingly straight at you, actually in a low arc. Functionally, mortars and artillery are both able to shoot at an angle forty-five degrees above horizontal. That is exactly midway between level and straight up in the air, producing the maximum range for both weapons. For that matter, anything propelled forward—be it an arrow, a spear, a baseball, the catapult that preceded the mortar, or David's rock at Goliath—achieves maximum range at a forty-five degree elevation.

The artillery piece decreases reach as the barrel is lowered toward horizontal. Pictures seen by the public usually depict the artillery gun barrel at a high angle, thirty degrees or more. That's because most pictures are taken when the artillery outfit is shooting a good way to the rear, far from the enemy, safe for the observers.

Mortars decrease their range as the barrel is raised from forty-five degrees toward vertical. Theoretically, at ninety degrees, the projectile would go straight up, and then fall right back down the tube from which it was fired. Come to think of it, maybe that's why the firing range table topped out at eighty-three degrees and displayed the minimum range as two hundred yards. For sure, none of us ever tried to drop one in any closer.

Another distinguishing difference between artillery and mortars is that artillery pieces are rifled—lands and grooves inside the barrel rotate the projectile before it emerges so that the speeding bullet or shell is spinning to produce more precise accuracy. Mortar barrels are smooth, perhaps conceding that accuracy by spinning would be wasted in the long journey up, then down, subject to wind aloft, temperature variances, and imprecise aiming.

There's no such thing as a smooth-bore artillery gun, but there is a rifled mortar: the 4.2-inch chemical mortar, designed to deliver poison gas, but actually employed in WWII to deliver high explosive shells and chemical phosphorus. The 4.2 was a superior weapon, and while its operators never came far enough forward to be seen, they were called into play occasionally when we requested artillery support. The burning phosphorus they delivered on request may not have been poison to breathe, but I can still hear the screams of an enemy exposed to showers of a white smoke and burning chunks that could not be extinguished and that, indeed, fried bare flesh with ever-increasing intensity.

The smallest mortar, which was hand-carried in a rifle company, was the 60mm Mortar M2. Like many of the weapons GIs used in WWII, this one dated back to WWI, virtually unchanged over the decades. After all, you can't do much to redesign a smooth piece of pipe less than a yard long.

That the mortar was not a new, state-of-the-art weapon bothered me not at all. After all, my ROTC artillery training had been with WWI French 75s; and the model designation 1911 for my Enfield dated it years before WWI even started. The '03 Springfield was that much more ancient.

The critical factor in training is how fast the crew can prepare for firing a mortar, which makes sense for a weapon employed in ground infantry tactics. We got pretty good at it, winding up training with a range exercise where we could see the explosions and have the satisfaction of adjusting range and direction until we hit the target, in this case, buildings in a simulated community about a half-mile away.

After the firing exercise, our three-gun mortar section was marched down-range a thousand yards to witness the effect of our onslaught. Some temporary shacks had been erected purely for target practice, and two or three abandoned junk-cars lent realism to the target scene. We examined the battered shacks, the splintered wood, and one car that had a mortar shell explode right next to it. The craters dug by 60mm shells were not very big, but the carnage wrought by the spray of shrapnel was an eye-opener.

The shiny, thick metal containers had exploded into thousands of chunks and shards of flying steel. We were convinced that nothing and no one could survive within twenty-five or thirty yards of a strike. The front fender of the old car was nowhere to be seen, the hood was punched full of holes, the crankcase busted open, and the rest of the body attached to the chewed-up front displayed ragged holes and deep scratches from flying shrapnel.

That this degree of damage could be caused by one small three-pound projectile from one little smoothbore tube rendered us sober and silent; no wisecracks were offered. We felt like we had in our one mortar section the firepower to destroy any and every thing we were likely to encounter!

My squad leader came back from pass the following Monday and was busted to private, his penalty for having contracted a dose of clap. So I was now squad leader, Third Mortar Squad. It wasn't the last time my promotion would take place because the man above me went away. I was now qualified to be a three-stripe buck sergeant, skipping the rank of corporal along the way.

The Army was to wait until we were ready to get on the boat at POE (port of embarkation) to pass out my stripes and increased pay. Rank recognized when you shipped out was a "saltwater" promotion. When the boat left for overseas, I would be a "salt-water buck." Meantime, Uncle Sam saved a buck by deferring the rank that went with the job.

The knowledge that I was now fully in charge of four other men, and could conceivably one day give them an order that might cause them to die, was weighty. I was no longer a rookie or the new kid on the block. I was a soldier, trained, like the general said, to kill enemy soldiers . . . lots of them.

———————=»«◊»«=———————

There and then loomed the weightiest consideration of my young life. I knew what there was to know about the infantry. I knew nothing about being part of a war where the other guys tried to shoot or blow you up. I was scared for my own skin, terribly worried that I would fail before my peers.

CHAPTER **2** | # BATTLE OF THE BULGE

Moving Up

F inal field maneuvers ended, and it was time to leave training camp and Slewfoot behind. Furloughs were passed out. My own bed felt good, Mom's meals were great, but it wasn't exactly like a comfortable vacation at home from school. Asked about my training and experiences, I was uncharacteristically taciturn. None of my pals were around town. I got drunk with some strangers a couple of times, and when I reported back to the company, I felt, strangely, more at home. It was time to get on with it. I might have reveled a bit more during my final visit home had I received my sergeant's stripes. In any event, sometime during the past few months I had completed the transformation from civilian to soldier. I was trained to kill the enemy.

At the port of embarkation in New Jersey we drew brand-new gear, though many items in our possession were in fine condition. I guessed that they wanted everything to wear out at the same time. Orders for my new rating came down, and I sewed on my three saltwater buck sergeant stripes.

The nine-day troopship (we soldiers persisted in calling it a boat) voyage was not measured by days and nights, sequestered as we were way below on D deck, just above the sloshing bilge. No use worrying about being sunk by submarine; there was not the slightest prayer of reaching an open deck up the series of steep single-file ladders and steel stairs. Twice a day, according to the color of your meal ticket, you went through a chow line and ate a flavorless, boiled meal on a metal tray, while standing at a high metal counter. Actually, you could eat at any hour. There were so many seasick that meal cards could be had for the asking. We smelled diesel fuel, urine, salt water, ship's paint, and each other. Nested in hammocks four deep, unfortunately the sick were not always in the lower tiers; the ship's hold smelled always of vomit.

Finally on land again in Plymouth, England, we staggered in our first march formation, unable at first to adjust from rolling sea to terra firma. Sea legs seem to work both ways. Still far from a battlefront, we did nonetheless see our first bombed-out buildings, whole neighborhoods destroyed by German bombs. The Battle of Britain may have been fought in the skies—for the poor bastards on the ground, however, the battle was evidently hardest on innocent civilians and their snug village homesteads.

The division had to wait for some late-arriving equipment and men before heading to France. My company bivouacked for three weeks, ten men per room, in partly damaged houses of a neighboring English village that had largely escaped enemy bombing. Despite conditioning marches and constant weapons practice, we had a swell time. "Arf-and-arf" warm beer, tea laced with milk, friendly villagers. We wondered if the folks back home could have lived through such carnage and remained as laid-back and seemingly warm and casual as these good folk.

Overseas, the conduct of our young soldiers changed. First, the men took weapons training seriously, convinced they might really have to use the tools of infantry. Second, there was widespread promiscuity among some of the younger members; for the first time they were far away from home and family accountability. They lived out their parental defiance.

In late November, a Limey troop ship took our battalion across the English Channel from Plymouth, England, to Le Havre, France. We scrambled down landing nets and ladders to American vessels called LSTs (landing ship tanks). These ungainly, ugly steel boxes were designed to disgorge mechanized vehicles and cargo on alien shores. Crowded like cattle in a gathering shed, we troops finally stumbled into shallow, cold water at the bottom of the huge ramp when it was lowered near shore. We splashed uncertainly through the briny surf, up the beach into France, not one of us feeling like, nor pretending to be, a conquering hero.

Our first view of mainland Europe was the incredible detritus on the beach that had accumulated over the five months since D-Day: burned-out tanks, abandoned artillery and antiaircraft guns, huge piles of discarded wooden crates, stacks of construction materials, and everywhere the trash and garbage of the thousands who had preceded us up that shore. Not one complete building remained standing in the village. From the dirty harbor water protruded hulks of sunken ships of every imaginable size and shape.

"Guess they don't have time before morning chow call to police up the area," suggested one wag. And true, neatness was not the rule; getting people and usable weaponry to the front was the order of the day. All about the harbor area were servicemen, construction battalions, and hired natives. Whatever priorities propelled essentials to the front, we soon wised up that we ranked right up there with gasoline and bullets; wet shoes and all, we marched straight through town and off on a dirt road into the countryside.

Our first night in Europe was endured in pup tents in a rain-pelted, muddy farm field. A few of the guys bellyached about their wet belongings and cold feet. Instead of sympathy, they got advice to ditch around their pup tents to divert ground water next time, just like they'd been taught in training. We overlooked that quite a few of the late joiners had not been taught this technique in the first place.

A short march with our incredibly heavy, wet gear, and we boarded our first European railroad car. On the narrow-gauge European rail system, we mounted the same 40 & 8's that greeted our forbears in WWI. Stenciled in faded black paint was the phrase: *"40 Hommes, 8 Chevaux."* The markings were left over from that ancient war when each car supposedly carried forty men and eight horses. Twenty-five of us with our equipment and weapons in each car were so crowded that we had to lie down in shifts. (Where the hell did they put the horses?)

The seemingly square iron wheels on our train bumped start-and-stop for two days to Belgium, pausing often enough to allow for the foot soldier's favorite pastime: lighting up a bonfire with any materials at hand. We often had time to bargain with the welcoming natives for wine and food. We became accustomed to a countryside touched by war: destroyed buildings, huge bomb craters, no civilian vehicles, threadbare people, and delay after delay. The ubiquitous kids peddling wine and cheese were runty, attesting to a hard life and short rations during their interminable war.

The cooks passed out salami (mule dick) and cheese sandwiches, which went pretty well with the *vin ordinaire* red wine we bought along the way. Dogface soldier boys are more interested in alcohol than in vintage. As usual, there was plenty of coffee, which we reheated at our railside fires.

Buzz bombs, or as some called them, doodlebugs, were a real reminder that a shooting war lay ahead. The German V-1 was a compact, jet-propelled, short-winged airplane with a ton of high explosives as its payload. There was no pilot. The lethal little crafts were launched day and night toward troop movements like ours. The V-1 couldn't actually be aimed at a specific target, only at general areas.* Each was apparently provided with a different amount of fuel, so that when the engine quit, the craft stopped flying. Down it went, in Belgium, Holland, or France. The resulting explosion and crater were stupefying. As it flew over, a buzz bomb sounded, even at aircraft altitudes, like a very noisy and badly tuned motorcycle. When the nasty engine-blat quit, the silence was heart stopping. The bomb glided briefly, then tumbled haphazardly to explode in an empty field, on a residential street, or in a crowded neighborhood, with all the selectivity of a dart thrown at a map.

None struck within a mile of our train, but the first seeds of the uncertainty of war were sown. It was clear that if a raucous buzz bomb did have your name on it, you'd be the last to know. Those huge craters served the intended purpose of creating fear and trepidation. The impersonal, pilotless bombs also provided unintended seasoning for us green troops that helped to prepare us for a later accumulation of even more fearsome events.

---

* Most V-1s fired during the war were aimed at England and intended to be Hitler's "vengeance weapon." However, in the fall of 1944, these primitive missiles were aimed at Antwerp in an attempt to disrupt Allied reinforcement and resupply.

The noisy motors propelling the buzz bombs gave us a sense we were getting nearer to a fighting war, and a growing suspicion that we were to be an active part of it. The thought that pending battle might be any sort of romantic adventure had by now pretty well dissipated.

The war sort of crept up on us, as our train crept toward it. We green troops ended up just across the Belgian border in Germany, weary, cold, and scared. We pitched tents a second time in Europe in a heavy, dark pine forest near the German border. We heeded advice to scatter our two-man tents widely, taking the precaution of locating on the lee side of terrain between us and the unseen enemy. There was no shelling of our bivouac, but distant rumblings of heavy artillery could be heard in pitch dark, and the far-away horizon lit up with flashes of a battle we could only imagine. Now fairly close to the front, fearsome thoughts ran rampant. Sleep-robbing anxiety seeped into our tents and sleeping bags.

Deep snow in the Hürtgen Forest muffled sound and produced an eerie, shadowy vista. Pulling guard in the super-quiet was nerve-racking. To test our defensive preparedness, officers and noncoms tromped about the woods, approaching sentries to test our mettle. We were posted on guard without ammunition. That provided some assurance that we were under no immediate enemy threat. It also probably saved some American lives from trigger-happy, nervous rookies who might have shot and asked for the password later. It was very, very cold.

"Who goes there?" we guards would challenge in a hoarse whisper.

Silence.

"Let me hear the password." Growing tension.

"Brooklyn."

The nervous reply: "Dodgers. Step forward to be identified." Profound relief as a uniformed GI materialized out of the pitch darkness.

Of the millions in Army uniform during WWII, most received field training of some kind. Many who were never to be tested in battle completed at least a short infantry basic—and bragged about surviving its rigors. Few, including me in the early going, ever thought they'd be called on to exercise the field skills they supposedly had mastered: creeping, crawling, bayonet fighting, riflery, hand and arm signals, long marches with full field packs, digging holes, and so on. Now all of us had experienced living outdoors in tents during extreme winter weather, struggling to stay dry and reasonably warm as the snow piled up. We had plenty of clothes, blankets, and cover. More, we learned, than we could ever carry along in a fast-moving war.

Tension clung to us like the hoary frost that accumulated each night. Rumor was that one rifleman in Baker Company had shot himself in the foot to escape the unknown trial of battle. Whether true or not, the story focused our thoughts on the possibility that we might get hurt (we still rejected "get killed") in a real war.

Ignorant about what we might face, it was more convenient to imagine that this might be just one more training-type exercise. Surely they wouldn't let a bunch of us be hurt and killed right off the bat. We'd ease into it. Yet, the rumbling explosions conjured up for me a foreboding mud-and-ice battlefield, the image of which remained in my imagination from *All Quiet on the Western Front,* that epic of WWI infantry warfare.

On December 12, 1944, the order came to move up. We rolled slowly through the snow in trucks and off-loaded in late afternoon so the trucks could safely withdraw. Now the moan or whine of artillery shells was distinct, obviously passing over us from both directions. We were in the middle, protected by a steep hill for the moment from incoming mail, as we would later describe enemy artillery.

These explosions were for keeps, not drill exercises. The general who told us we were being trained to kill Germans told only half the story. There were obviously a bunch of really tough guys on the other side who had been trained, and had been practicing, the same thing: killing enemy soldiers. And we were they!

It was dead-of-winter frigid. That didn't help a cold sweat. I was hungry, but at the same time nauseated. I watched one of my ammo bearers vomit, and just in time took a leak before I pissed my pants. Others weren't so lucky. The moment we had all felt would never really arrive was at hand. There was only one thing left to say: "Fuck!"

Soldier's Soldier

Canvas-covered GI six-by-six trucks delivered Able Company late in the afternoon to the bottom of a steep, heavily wooded hill just inside the German border from Belgium. Out of sight beyond the top of the hill lay a thousand-yard stretch of snow-covered pasture sloping gently down toward the farm village that our green company was to attack at dawn the next morning. We felt no little uneasiness when the trucks took off quickly, leaving us standing there with our gear. The resulting silence, punctuated occasionally with a high-passing artillery shell, left no room for grumbling, just the queasy feeling that we had been sold out, left on our own.

It was not reassuring to be told that a livestock fence just over the crest was our LD (line of departure), an arbitrary dividing line between opposing forces. Would the Krauts be right on the other side of the fence? Or was there unclaimed middle ground to traverse? What does an enemy look like? Who'd shoot first? Hell, maybe the bad guys wouldn't even show up. Yeah, sure. Misery and dejection settled over us along with a cold, winter mist that quickly froze, coating everything with a veneer of ice.

Sensing an unprecedented, critical climax in my life, my breathing grew thin and rapid, like when you're a little kid and some big guy says he's going to beat the living shit out of you. I found little reassurance looking into the anxious eyes of my comrades. The day that I had not believed ever would arrive for me was here: I was at the front line of war.

We learned that a massive concrete structure at the top of the hill had been assigned as our CP and OP (command and observation post). Like a giant igloo with six-foot-thick concrete walls, the combination troop shelter and pillbox had served as an anchor in the formidable Siegfried line of defense the Germans had erected to protect the fatherland. It appeared so impregnable, so formidable, that we could not imagine how anyone could possibly have conquered its defenders. Beyond it lay rows of antitank dragons' teeth and countless similar pillboxes yet to be overcome. How many lives had it cost to make this single fortification ours? And toward those pillboxes was where we were going?

A briefing of Able Company officers and platoon sergeants was called at the pillbox just before dark. Toting just his carbine and no pack, the hike up the snowy woodlot hill was no problem for the Fourth Platoon's Technical Sergeant Oaks, six feet tall, two hundred pounds, and well conditioned from years of field training. The prominent ball of his jaw muscle, which intimidated trainees, projected the intended image of soldierly determination and grit. We had to admit that he, among all our noncoms and officers, exemplified what a seasoned, combat-ready leader should look like.

I was relieved that we had Oaks's experience to lean on to assimilate and explain the attack order. While he was on his briefing mission, I reflected on what had brought Oaks to this point in his military career. Unlike the rest of us, he was not forced into the service. He was a career infantryman. We were lucky to have him.

From conversations during field exercises and long marches, I had learned from George, and others who knew him better, that the Oakses had been poor before the Great Depression, and survived as little more than white trash as the South worked its way out of the economic doldrums of the 1930s. George had known a couple of fellows not much older than himself who had pulled a hitch with the Civilian Conservation Corps (CCC). Hard work, they said, but three squares a day, pretty decent-looking work clothes or uniforms, and a good bunch of guys.

George concluded in 1938 that a uniform might allow him to blend into the world around him and make its own statement as to who he was. Posters at the small town recruiting office looked promising, inviting—as did the authoritative, ribbon-bedecked enlistment personnel. He didn't have to get drunk or be goaded by a buddy to sign up. He did it dispassionately one Thursday morning without so much as telling his family, acquaintances, or the two or three guys that might have been classified as friends.

That he was part of an Army destined one day to wage war apparently never occurred to him—even as news events heralded the emergence of Nazi Germany as a war power way over there in Europe. Even farther away, those little Jap guys with their odd, red-ball flag were raising hell. He seldom read a newspaper, preferring to get his news from the Pathe newsreel before the feature movie at the base theater.

After four years, Private First Class Oaks won promotion to corporal, a rarity in peacetime. He learned perfectly how to tuck his blue-piped cunt-cap exactly so under his web belt for indoor decorum. A well-laundered khaki shirt with sharp pleats splitting the pockets vertically, and fresh-creased pants above spit-shined shoes completed the picture. With his marksmanship medals and regimental ID pin on his cap, Corporal Oaks cut quite a figure. He had become the soldier on the recruiting poster.

Once a noncom, Oaks took up serious reading for the first time. His commanding officer handed him a manila-covered booklet, dated December 11, 1940, titled *Soldier's Handbook*, the basic field manual of the U.S. War Department. You had to believe that Oaks read it slowly, laboriously, not really comprehending as he struggled with the words and syntax. Then he read it repeatedly, understanding more of the text each time.

Oaks became a letter-perfect product of the military manual. From the eleven General Orders to a perfectly laid-out field inspection, he could and would quote at length from his military bible. It taught him everything but character. As the war heated up, the book helped him rise to the top rank for a line infantry noncom: five-stripe technical sergeant, three inverted "V" stripes up, two rockers down.

We listened up well when Oaks trotted down the hill to report to us that the briefing had been familiar, routine, like the maneuvers he was used to Stateside. The battalion commander reviewed an acetate-covered map of the area, described objectives, estimated scattered enemy strength in the village, identified possible defense strong points, and ordered the company to move up the hill under darkness with full equipment.

As he passed along the attack plan to us, huddled in the snow and ice on the "friendly" side of the hill, Oaks smugly concluded that the orders were pretty cut-and-dried SOP (standard operating procedure). He seemed almost bored relaying orders to us. Nothing he hadn't heard in hundreds of such meetings during training. His confidence that the exercise was to be by the book was temporarily reassuring to all of us. Instead of facing gross and manifold hazards, we were apparently about to engage in a standard field operation.

However the unknown battle might shape up, we had a tough job facing us before any such engagement. No one had calculated the difficulty of moving the company up some three hundred yards of mountainous, icy, snowy, pinewoods at night. Following on each other's heels in the Hürtgen Forest dark, the paths were churned into mud as slippery as the snow and ice. Each of us toted a field pack (containing a rolled-up sleeping bag), a long wool overcoat, a gas mask, and all sorts of items hanging from our apparel. There wasn't a spot left around the web cartridge belt to hook on or loop anything else. Of course we all carried individual weapons: rifle, carbine, or, for officers and gunners, a .45 pistol. Then came mortar shells, radios, boxes of machine-gun ammo, extra hand grenades, and rifle ammo bandoleers. We in the Fourth Platoon also had to deliver to the hilltop three forty-two-pound mortars and two thirty-five-pound machine guns, and be prepared to carry them into battle.

Sixty-millimeter mortar and light machine-gun units had to make several trips. The twelve-round canvas mortar shell carrier was designed to hang bib-like, front and rear, impossible to accommodate that way with all our other baggage. The option of looping the carrier on one shoulder imposed a burden hard enough to balance on level ground, much less for the required climb. Boxed belts of machine-gun ammo also required extra trips up the hill, as did the guns themselves. Even the toughest GIs were left winded, sweaty, legs trembling from strain. Those who didn't make two trips or more took to their trench shovels to gouge a troop shelter out of shale under the thin topsoil. No hot rations could be delivered, no fires could be lit. It was a miserable supper of D bars—chocolate laced with a kind of fat meant to generate energy, but not to melt in mouth or throat. It was well after midnight when we settled down. Then, near morning, the shelling.

Our company commander, Capt. Benjamin Goodspeed, had ordered us to excavate large troop shelters on the backside of the hill instead of digging individual foxholes. Covered with branches and dirt, the dugouts offered some protection from incoming artillery. The captain correctly assessed that his untried recruits needed to spend their first night at war together, not scattered in lonely foxholes. The imminent danger was 88mm artillery bursts touched off as the detonator noses of the shells ticked high branches in the tall pine trees topping the ridge. Shrapnel plunging down from above is particularly lethal.

The first nighttime salvo of enemy shells whined and whooshed over the treetops to explode far enough away in the valley to the rear that they did not seem too threatening. Still, each speeding shell left behind a lingering trail of fear and foreboding, even when it did not explode nearby. Once heard, no soldier ever took the scream and whistle of an artillery shell—ours or theirs—for granted.

The fast rising pitch of a shell as it went directly overhead was heart stopping, followed by brief relief when the Doppler sound pitched down and away as the projectile sped on by. Then it happened. Blam! With no warning, a tree-burst above us rained pine branches and debris around our shelter. It was the loudest sound I had ever heard.

The explosion decapitated a tree about twenty yards to the right of our troop shelter. A veteran of observing artillery range explosions hundreds of yards down range, and an old hand at infiltration courses with their planted nitro-starch explosions, Oaks was not prepared for the intensity and incredible energy of the real thing, a scant few feet above his head. It was too close, too real, too deafening. We were all stunned. Oaks groaned and curled up fetus-like, rolling to face the damp wall of our little cave.

Adding to our confusion and fear was the lack of bright flash we expected from having seen movie versions of exploding shells. Instead, the explosion was a dark, crunching, punishing, downward thrust, the reverberating thunder pressing us flat on the earthen floor of the shelter. The unreal report echoed in our heads long after the actual sound waves had dissipated into the distance. A faint voice from another hilltop dugout finally made itself heard: "Medic . . . medic . . . medic."

In the acrid silence that followed, Oaks lay still as death, arms wrapped around his knees. His rasping breath sounded as if someone had kicked him violently in the balls. The rest of us were stunned speechless. Machine-gun squad leader Imo, of the Fourth Platoon, was the only one who remained calm. He had been cleaning mud and water from his treasure—the M1919 A6 air-cooled .30-caliber machine gun that was his charge. With faint rays from a carefully hooded flashlight, he continued to wipe and stroke the gray metal stock with mechanical precision, no expression on his face. Panic threatened to overtake the rest of our group.

"Jeesus Kee-rist! What the hell was that?"

"Hey, turn out that fuckin' light."

"Where's my helmet? . . . Let's scram outa here."

"Hey, Oaks. What the fuck we s'posed to do now?"

Then a cold flat command: "Shut up, men, and stay put. Keep your helmets on and wait for orders. It's almost morning. Prepare to move out."

Although Buck Sergeant Imo was assigned command only of his four-man machine-gun squad, his voice took full charge of all the men in the shelter. Order, laced heavily with foreboding, returned to the badly shaken group of young soldiers. I caught my breath, stilled my shaking hands, and thanked my lucky stars for Imo's timely intervention. If he had not provided that instant stability, I realized that I might have panicked with the rest. I gruffly repeated his admonition for the men to stay put.

The exploding artillery round had been an 88 for sure,* the universal German calling card, hurled from the other side of the village designated for our attack. It was the first artillery served up directly to our freshly committed company, the first "shot in anger." There were to be hundreds, thousands of "incomers" to be endured before the end of our combat tour, but none would have the memorable impact of this first one. It confirmed that the people we were to attack played for keeps.

No one now paid any attention to the five-striper officially in charge. Technical Sergeant Oaks lay huddled under his wet overcoat by the shelter entrance. He exhibited no response, nor did he challenge Sgt. Imo's take-charge command. Our model noncom had been reduced to an empty husk by his first taste of lethal enemy fire. The 88 missed his body, but destroyed his fragile will.

The explosion left me shit-scared and temporarily disoriented, but the shocking behavior of my hero, Sergeant Oaks, had an impact that all but disabled me. Oaks had appeared to me to be the most proficient and mentally prepared fighting man among us. He was a tough taskmaster, a thorough and competent teacher, a model military leader. I crawled under the low ceiling to his side, sure that he had suffered some grievous wound to so completely neutralize him. Unable to engage him in conversation, I satisfied myself that there was no blood; despite my entreaty, he refused even to open his eyes.

I drew a deep breath and looked around me. I caught Imo's eye and gave him a mild thumbs up that I was okay. Realizing that I had abandoned my carbine to hasten to Oaks's side, I sheepishly recovered it, adjusted my helmet strap, and joined Imo in readying the men to form up for the attack.

However similar, or, in Oaks's case, dominating, a man ap-

---

* Most German artillery fire during World War II was in fact 105mm, but it was not unusual for new troops to assume they were under fire by 88mm, due to that weapon's fearsome reputation.

peared to be in uniform, it was impossible to gauge that individual's adaptability to kill-or-be-killed combat. Oaks had folded like a paper sack; Imo had emerged instantly as a reliable leader. Anticipating how a man would behave under the stress of combat was all but impossible. Some pussycats became tigers; some roaring lions became mewling kittens.

Combat leadership springs from the most unexpected places. Imo had it from day one. Others would shrink from it. Still others would grow into it. I went into my first battle more concerned with disgracing myself than with suffering injury or death. I would have forty days in the Battle of the Bulge to find out.

My Longest Day

I was outpost guard in a foxhole that was the nearest thing to a home I had experienced since we had been committed to our first infantry attack a few days earlier. The Germans must have thought our untested infantry division was crazy. We launched our attack three days before December 16, 1944, when they threw their entire might against the Allies in World War II's last great German counteroffensive. A scant few miles from us, Nazi armor and infantrymen were pouring into Belgium. At this point, all we knew about the Battle of the Bulge was that we had express orders to hold our one corner of the big pocket, forbidden to surrender our now strategically vital village under any circumstance.

Our bedraggled little town had long ago been vacated by its residents. Most, if not all, of the livestock from the rural village had been killed in earlier battles. The rest had simply starved and frozen in their stalls and stanchions. Our battle booty was a few streets of ruins—an occasional room intact, but mostly homes reduced by explosives to a few walls, fewer roofs, and cellars that offered protection for attacker or defender.

Grim as were orders to hold at all costs, the prospect of attacking up the long, open slope to the next village in front of us was even more dismal—suicidal, we all agreed, based on the pasting we had taken coming down through the opposite open fields to

33

our objective. To the rear lay that earlier attack route, sloping back up toward the woods and our LD. Visible from both hilltops, at the base of the two slopes, was our snow-clad fish bowl of beat-up houses. The enemy picked at us relentlessly with 88s, mortars, and sniper fire. Since the field to our rear was heavily salted with hostile mines, and under enemy surveillance, securing food, ammunition, clothing, and replacements for our casualties was difficult and often lethal.

Maybe we'd been there a week. Time had lost its measure in terms of days. Whatever the exact day-count, I could not believe my fate nor really comprehend what had happened. Illogical or unfair as were many circumstances thrust on me by Army life, I had usually been able to unravel some sort of rationale for what had happened. But this was crazy! No one had prepared us to be part of a mass slaughter. I felt used, violated by the Army that had fed, clothed, and cared for me thus far. Where the hell was relief, or maybe a little sympathy? There was to be neither for well over a month. And even then, no sympathy.

Gradually, the events of the first day under fire came back to me. If I had attempted to describe what happened right after that terrible day, or really, any earlier than several days later, I would have simply shaken my head, unable to put in words what had befallen us. More violence and death had been unexpectedly compressed into a few moments and hours than any of us had imagined could occur in a lifetime.

I had been terrified that first morning, starting down the forbidding slope from the high ground now to our rear. We had not even reached the farm fence a few yards from the crest when the first heavy dose of enemy shelling and machine-gun fire caused us to drop flat and shed onto the snowy crust bulky overcoats, field packs, gas masks, most personal possessions, blankets, everything. Stripped down to our field jackets in the bitter cold, most of us kept our woolen gloves, and thanks to a training reflex, our weapons and ammo. We did not need to be told to hold onto and wear our steel helmets. We had "hit the ground" during training; we now learned and yearned to hug it.

Like everyone but our gunners, we mortarmen each carried

into battle a dozen three-pound 60mm mortar shells in a canvas bib. As enemy shells struck, the bibs simply wouldn't let us lie flat enough when we hit the ground. So we twisted the two canvas carrying loops into a single supporting strand, and carried the load with one hand, or over one shoulder, just as we had coming up the hill into position the night before. That way, the ammo could be shed quickly when we dove for cover, and quickly scooped up when we moved forward again.

When we got the nerve to rise and resume the attack, we encountered tough going. Two feet of accumulated snow had melted down to half that, covered with a thick, brittle crust of ice. Every few steps, the frozen surface gave way. We staggered along, propelled by fear, anxious not to lose contact with each other. To find yourself alone was unthinkable, the ultimate nightmare.

As we climbed over the strands of barbed wire livestock fence that marked the LD, I looked down the line of fence posts and spotted T. Sgt. Fred Coleman, Third Platoon, leaning over the top strand, apparently cutting wire. Anxious to perform an immediate, useful task, I went over to help him. He was not leaning over the fence. He was draped over it, blood from his head splattering the white ice.

I reclaimed his field glasses from the scarlet-flecked sncw, compelled by conditioned deference to hand them back to the senior noncom. This closer look revealed that he was as stone-dead as the lambs I had helped butcher back on the farm, their stiffening bodies hung by the heels from a rusty steel hook. If unfamiliarity with violent human death required dramatic confirmation, the pinkish-white crater above his left eye convinced and sickened me. A chunk of his forehead had been shot away. I was looking at our first KIA (killed in action): Sergeant Coleman, whose professionalism convinced me he was possibly the most invulnerable soldier in the company. In training, I rated him even above Oaks, and had wished I could serve under him.

Other than a little boy's glimpse, at parental insistence, of my grandmother's body laid out in our "company" parlor, I had never seen a dead person, had never attended a funeral. I had never had occasion to steel myself for bloody death right before my eyes;

certainly not the death of a person I knew well, whose vitality had been so assertive. Sergeant Coleman couldn't really be dead. But he was dead, dead as a mackerel. This death was no accident. He had been killed, murdered. And we were sanctioned by our nation to murder in return; in a nutshell, we were really at war. I wanted to pay back for Coleman someday.

Sergeant Imo said it well when the first bursts of bullets bored into our ranks: "Watch your ass. This ain't no fucking infiltration course." He was referring to a Stateside training exercise where troops were taught to creep and crawl under noisy-but-safe overhead machine-gun fire.

War movies I had seen depicted battle casualties as impersonal enemy bodies being tossed about by pyrotechnic, billowing explosions, falling like flies all over the battle scene. The faceless hostiles threw their arms askew as they tumbled to the ground. The good guys, if they died, crumpled gracefully, often in the arms of a comrade, bearing no discernible wounds. In all cases, they were pretty noble in their demise. Some even managed to gasp a few heroic last words.

I stared at Coleman, even started to speak to him, but no. He was disheveled, bloody, and still very dead. Unfeeling fingers grasping his wire cutters, he struck no image of nobility as in a John Wayne movie. He'd had no chance to commit any final, defiant act of bravery to leave as a legacy. He'd simply been snuffed out by a burst of machine-gun bullets he never saw coming from a Kraut soldier who probably didn't know his bullets were striking a human target. I was catching on fast that there was to be no discrimination in how killing takes place or who gets killed in war. And there was only one way to escape Coleman's fate: be lucky.

So here I was, days and many deaths later, pulling guard duty right in the very first combat foxhole I had ever dug. I had chosen the location for this particular hole as darkness fell at the end of our first day of a battle that had continued well into the night. Daylight proved the spot too exposed to the enemy up the hill to be a tenable mortar position. It now served as a forward observation post (FOP). We were connected to the company and my hidden mortar through a skinny sound-power phone wire, which was repeatedly spliced back together after enemy shellings.

When we dug in that first night, no field manual had provided "how to" instructions on foxhole preparation under the conditions we encountered. Our inventive and imaginative battalion commander had come up with the means to dig in frozen ground, even before the need arose. We each had a quarter-pound block of nitro-starch explosive adhesive-taped to the trench shovel handle hanging from our belts. I tore off the tape and stuck a detonating cap in the little round recess provided in the yellow block of explosive. A twenty-second fuse protruded from the cap. My foxhole buddy Jimmy and I used our trench knives to ice-pick a six-inch-deep hole in the frozen earth. I packed the nitro in the hole, topped by a pyramid of loose dirt and snow, the end of the fuse just showing. The conical shape was to focus the explosive energy down into the ground.

The next move was to light up. When we heard the fuse sizzle, we scuttled a few yards down the hedgerow and covered our ears. The explosion was muffled because of the thorough burial of the charge, and in any event, the noise was lost in a fusillade of other bangs and explosions still echoing through the village.

We waited until we were sure that our little eruption had escaped enemy notice (no incoming 88s) and started digging our hole, easy going until we removed the earth and ice loosened by our energy-efficient charge. From there on down, the earth was not frozen, but it was hard-packed and stony.

My partner Jimmy was Pvt. James Lount, the most innocent and the youngest GI in our platoon. I buddied with him because he looked like he needed someone to keep him steady. He turned out to be a good worker. Partly concealed by a hedgerow ridge on the enemy side, we toiled without pause to hollow out a safe place for ourselves and our weapons. I locked my trench shovel blade at right angles to serve as a pick to shape the sides and increase the depth of the den. Lount doggedly pitched all the loose dirt out and over the top toward the hedgerow.

We received added incentive to dig deep in the dark. Platoon leader First Lt. James A. Jewell made the rounds of his two machine guns and three mortars to pass along a report from Battalion S-2 (intelligence) that a column of enemy armor was headed our way in counterattack. We recalled a Stateside exercise where old training tanks carefully straddled our foxholes to demonstrate to the occupant that a soldier could remain safe below the ground in an armored attack. That had been scary enough, but these were huge Tiger tanks with blazing cannons; they would not be careful not to squash us or blow us up.

This, our first combat foxhole, had its share of stones and roots to be chopped off. The hard work in cramped quarters produced sore muscles and blisters. But the enemy tank rumor fueled energies beyond what we believed possible. Lount and I went so deep we had to fashion a firing step at one end to climb up on so we could observe from the hole. We hollowed out a shelf at the other end to stow grenades, ammo, canteen, and bitter chocolate D bars.

In the dark we found enough branches severed by artillery (ours or theirs?) to cover the position and support several inches of dirt removed earlier. We then filled our helmets with snow from a few yards away and carried enough back to spread around for reasonable concealment. The site did not have to be pristine white; the entire village and our environs were pocked with dark shell holes and blackened in streaks with burned powder. The temperature was too low to allow water accumulation, so the finished cave was grave-cold, but reasonably dry.

The earthen cover was constructed short enough to provide for an entrance above the firing step. The entry could be sealed off with a poncho, or after we scraped one up in a ruined house, by a white spread of cloth. We guessed that the hedgerow might deflect passing Tiger tanks; anyway, that fear evaporated when the report came down that the enemy column had veered off to follow the main German column into Belgium. That nailed down our company mission to hold onto one shoulder of the penetrating German blitzkrieg that was to be memorialized as the Battle of the Bulge.

The nearest village building across seventy-five yards of pasture behind our den was a partially destroyed barn. Attached to the barn was the typical German companion two-story house, or what was left of it. The two buildings shared a livestock courtyard, as did many rural village farmsteads. It turned out that one first-floor room on the far, or friendly, side of the house, was pretty much intact. That room was adjacent to the front door, where a set of steps inside led to a cramped dirt basement. The underground space with its coal bin and root cellar became sleeping quarters for survivors of the Fourth Platoon not on guard or gun duty. It was cold, dirty, and damp, but in candlelight it basked in the warmth of comparative safety.

The room above was designated as our Fourth Platoon command post. In time it became known as our "day room," a euphemism derived from training base recreation rooms provided for the enlisted men. That's where we spent our time when we were not pulling duty or sleeping in shifts in the cellar.

On our first night of occupation, I checked in with my boss, mortar section leader Sgt. Leo Foote. Staff Sergeant Foote was the rock-solid head of my and two other mortar squads of the Fourth Platoon. We showed him where we had dug in, ran a phone wire to our hole, located the other two mortar squads, and learned that our machine guns were providing support for house-to-house forays still in progress. Redundant contact was provided by short-range, hand-carried radios. Communications facilities were all part of routine learned in field training.

———⟫«⟨◉⟩»⟪———

From our CP doorway, we looked up a cobblestone street of destroyed homes to a looming, unpainted barn that had deliberately been bypassed by our riflemen during the attack. The weathered boards turned out to conceal a concrete pillbox with extra-thick walls that contained well-engineered embrasures covering the approach route we had just taken into town. From these slits in the wall, the Krauts had a field of fire clear back to our original LD. They had used the advantage with devastating effect in the early dawn. When we American troops finally overran the position, they simply buttoned up and waited for a chance to sneak back to their MLR (main line of resistance) under cover of darkness in the next town.

An effort had been made by our engineers to blow the pillbox. One brave GI had dashed up to the concrete wall and leaned against it a pack of high explosives on the end of a pole. This "satchel charge" was to be activated by lighting a fuse, but it proved to be too wet to ignite. Under persistent, unfriendly fire from such an impregnable enemy position, attackers are well advised to move on to where they can inflict damage and cut off the occupants' escape by isolating the fortification. Maybe those who were thwarted by the pillbox became casualties. Maybe they just plain forgot it in the heat of subsequent battle. At any rate the pillbox and its inhabitants were totally ignored.

Late at night, five defending Kraut soldiers ventured out of the fort in pitch dark and surprised and captured two GI riflemen who had unluckily chosen a spot on the enemy route of withdrawal to catch their breath and a little rest. The German squad, not knowing we had taken the whole town, started up the street with their two prisoners toward the one road that ran out of our village to their refuge in the town atop the long slope opposite the one we had traversed in our attack. They were anxious to reach safety and security, and had in tow a real prize for their commanding officers.

Their route took them past the damaged house appropriated by our Fourth Platoon. A few exhausted members had been granted permission to sack out in the cellar. Though no sleeping bags were available, to a man they fell into the troubled, deep sleep of pure exhaustion. Most did not even loosen their cold, wet shoes. Sergeant Foote did not have the heart to wake a man to stand guard. He stood in the doorway himself, fighting sleep and an almost irresistible urge to lie down.

Sentry Foote took his carbine from its slung position over his shoulder when he heard muffled voices and movement. He did not speak up to identify himself or to ask for a password. Something told him to see what was up first. He could hardly believe his eyes when five gray-clad soldiers emerged from the murky night following the single ray of a hooded flashlight that placed in relief ahead of them two American GIs, fingers laced behind their heads.

Hands starting to shake, Foote slowly and quietly leveled his carbine at the formation, using the doorjamb as a much-needed steadying rest. The two GIs saw him first, but signaled no recognition. Then, in unison, they dove to the ground, and as the lead escort exclaimed and pointed his burp gun (a small submachine gun carried by many enemy soldiers) at them, Foote shot him in the face. He'd been pretty calm until the enemy soldier dropped. Buck fever set in. Crouching and firing at the same time, he shot two more of the escort squad as he hurriedly emptied the clip in his carbine. The remaining two Krauts had not soldiered these many years to be taken for patsies. They leaped to the side of the street and were lost in the darkness. They'd have their tale to tell when they found their own lines again.

The two American privates lying in the street, almost in the doorway, got slowly to their feet, brushing off snow and dirt.

"Thanks, Sarge. Owe you one. Any idea where the Third Platoon might be?" Sergeant Foote replied laconically: "Police up these bodies and I'll check around. These dumb assholes broke curfew. Serves 'em right."

When he and the two rescued riflemen policed up the enemy casualties, the first man Foote had shot was dead. Foote had no place to put him, so they left him lying in the street. The other two Germans were alive, but wounded so severely that they had to be dragged into the hallway, moaning woefully. It was apparent that they didn't need to be tied up.

Private First Class Beales emerged from the cellar to investigate the noise, and to relieve Foote at guard duty. When he saw the carnage, he volunteered to fetch a medic. Foote told Rube to forget it. He explained that our own heavy losses left plenty for the medics to do. Our wounded had to be carried or led through open country and minefields to the aid station well back in the rear. Maybe they'd get to the banged-up prisoners the next day, he said.

While hard-frozen bodies of farm animals or people do not give off noxious odors, that wasn't true of the two wounded soldiers lying in the small hallway. Like all German field soldiers, they possessed that sour rye bread and grease smell generated by carrying their black bread, cheese, and sausage rations. You never found a German infantryman who didn't have at least a few black crusts on him for emergency sustenance. The younger of the two enemy casualties, hardly old enough to shave, died quietly, adding to the odor the involuntary voiding that comes with death. A pool of blood and urine around him attested that he had been badly torn up by Foote's frantic firing.

The surviving prisoner started to whimper, eyes darting about in abject fear. He muttered a few unintelligible words, but when no one acknowledged his pleas with even a glance, he fell silent, suppressing the sounds of pain. No one bothered even to open his long coat and underlying uniform to explore the extent of his injuries or apply rudimentary first aid.

"I'd kinda like to help the bastard," said one gunner. "But I keep seeing our company medic, Tanner, back this morning. He was trying to patch up a GI who was hit out in front of that there pillbox and took a couple of hits hisself. When he stood up grabbing his stomach, one of the Huns in the pillbox shot him right through the big, red cross on his back. So what the fuck we owe these people, this guy?" he said, indicating the fallen man. The enemy soldier didn't understand a word, but with deepened foreboding, he turned his face to the wall. There was no mistaking the hate and hostility in those foreign voices.

I don't know whether that wounded Kraut ever did get first aid, or whether he was evacuated. When I was relieved at our OP foxhole the next night and reported to the platoon CP, the shot-up German was gone. Someone had dumped the guy who died in the hallway into a manger out in the barnyard, after he had been relieved of his watch, cigarette lighter, and anything else that might be useful.

Days later, the squarehead (common name for Germans) first shot by Foote still lay on the stone walk along the street, rigor mortis extended indefinitely by subfreezing temperatures. At first our men passed him by with averted eyes. But gradually he became part of the scene, like the dead cows in the barn. Cold kept the animals from bloating as well as smelling. And it preserved the dark, gray-blue cast of our dead host's face, with the neat, round hole bored beside his nose, just below the left eye.

The dead Kraut beside our Fourth Platoon headquarters developed into a local personality and landmark. "Just come up the street to the guy with the hole in his head, turn right, and there we are."

As was customary with enemy KIAs, his watch had been lifted before he was cold. I had his little blackout flashlight. After a few days, someone looted his wedding ring by neatly snipping off his ring finger. At least one set of company wire cutters apparently made it through the attack and into town. If a trench knife or bayonet had been used, more fingers would have been hacked off the stiff hand. Our unknown enemy soldier had not been turned back over, face down. Even those callous enough to rob his corpse chose not to stare at the gaping hole the exiting bullet had left in the back of his head.

Someone had gone through the dead soldier's pockets. Krauts wore identity discs and relied on ID papers. There were also the usual family photos scattered about the corpse.

"What was his name, Sarge?"

"Hard to read. Looks like Steiner."

"Shit, man, I know a Steiner. BAR [Browning automatic rifle] man in Charlie Company. From Buffalo or someplace. Now ain't that somethin'!"

Imo in Action

Rube Beales admitted being bent out of shape as badly as I was during our unbelievable introduction to carnage. We farm boys found out in a hurry that confronting a real, live enemy was a long call from an overnight deer-hunting jaunt. It wasn't just that the quarry shot back at you with rifles and machine guns; it was their awesome artillery, "them eighty-fucking-eights" as GIs eloquently described Germany's most feared ground weapon.

Avery sheepishly admitted screaming in terror louder than he'd ever yelled at bayonet drill when the 88s first struck among our advancing ranks. Probably no one heard him, or if they did, his call of raw fear was drowned out by explosions, other shouts of alarm, and strident pleas for medics. As dawn broke, and we staggered through the icy crust toward the enemy village, Rube and I regained enough presence of mind to shoot back. If their bullets and shells caused that much fright among us, it stood to reason that the squareheads might feel some of the same if we poured it on them.

The belligerent statement of outgoing bullets is what made pros like Imo so attached to their M1919 A6 machine guns. The Fourth Platoon machine-gun squad sergeant felt a sense of invulnerability as he put his gun into action. He grinned happily and poured forth burst after burst of .30-caliber bullets, the canvas belt of cartridges fed smoothly left-to-right by the assistant gunner. Imo was supposed to be observing and directing the fire of his regularly assigned gunner; but in extreme circumstances like our first attack, he had decided in advance to do the shooting himself.

The barrel of the A6 is wrapped in a steel jacket with holes cut in it to serve as a cooling radiator. The jacket dissipates enough heat to keep the barrel reasonably cool. The Heavy Weapons Company sported a machine gun that shot the same ammo, but which had its rifled barrel surrounded by a water-filled jacket designed to keep it cool during sustained fire. Much heavier than the A6, the water-cooled version required an extra man to carry its heavy tripod. After the heavy piece was mounted on its base, it was a formidable weapon in defensive or static modes where protracted fire was called for.

A modern, lightweight stamped-metal stock for the gunner's shoulder extended back from the rounded pistol grip on Imo's A6. In action, the automatic weapon was almost as mobile as, and maneuvered in a manner similar to, the Browning automatic rifle (BAR). Both were equipped with a bipod at the end of the barrel. The difference was that the BAR fired its ammo from a replaceable magazine of twenty cartridges and weighed fourteen pounds less. The larger machine gun had much greater firepower with its belt of three hundred rounds.

All the tactical skills in the world went for naught in machine gunning if the weapon didn't work. That meant fastidious cleanliness. As the hot barrel cooled, moisture and resulting rust were drawn into every nook and cranny. Burnt primers and powder fouled the action, stopping it or leaving it gummy and sluggish. The front barrel bearing and booster, a cup-shaped device at the muzzle, loaded up with carbon and had to be removed frequently and painstakingly scraped clean. A clean booster used escaping gas from fired cartridges to assist strong, reliable recoil operation and rapid rate of fire.

In Imo's first combat fire mission, measured bites of six to ten rounds, each burst taking less than one second, went on their way from the three hundred-round belt that spilled out of the green metal ammo box and through his assistant's fingers. Imo tripped the trigger at irregular intervals every few seconds, choosing a new target each time. Nearby, his two ammo bearers had four more full belts, each folded in its protective box.

If a stream of outgoing fire made him feel supreme, Imo guessed the German machine gunners also felt like tough guys when they were shooting at us. Their MGs chattered at a faster and fiercer tempo than ours, as did their little hand-carried automatic Tommy guns, which we called burp guns. If they were meant to scare the opposition, their characteristic staccato rip sure did the job.

For personal automatic weapons, our infantry guys had to settle for "grease guns," .45-caliber fully automatics that were cheap metal-stamped knockoffs of the heavier and more expensive wooden-stocked Thompson submachine guns carried by the tankers and featured in Hollywood action movies. Jimmy Cagney would have tossed aside our GI grease gun in gangster disgust.

Uneasy over the partially exposed position picked for his first mission, Sergeant Imo abruptly ceased fire after a couple of minutes and flipped open the lid on top of the gun. His assistant gunner jerked away the belt. Then the whole five-man squad scuttled quickly thirty yards to the left, the two gunners squirming into a hollow behind a rotted stump. The rest of the squad scattered themselves in nearby cover so as not to afford a group target. Imo's regular gunner, standing in for Imo as observer, found a niche that overlooked the next target, a row of battered houses. The maneuver was right out of the tactician's handbook. The chief advantage a light machine-gun squad has over the water-cooled heavies is mobility. Fire and move, fire and move. That's how rifle company machine gunners stay alive.

When the enemy spotted a hostile machine gun or mortar, or established map coordinates for it, it became a priority target for counterfire from their own automatic weapons, an objective for a flanking move by riflemen, or an instant assignment for one of their tanks, artillery guns, or mortars. Best not to be there when any of those alternatives were exercised. At his new location, Imo carefully grounded the bipod hanging from the end of the barrel, steadied the shoulder stock, and called for ammo. He slapped the cover down over the offered belt, pounded down on it once for luck to be sure it was secure, jerked back the operating handle, and resumed firing short bursts into the village.

Actually, Imo's air-cooled machine gun, although basically a World War I era weapon, had been modified for this war's required troop mobility. Trench warfare a generation earlier had seen the same machine gun mounted on a substantial, sixteen-pound tripod that served as a base and fulcrum for firing. The foxhole style fighting of World War II mandated that the old fixed tripod be replaced by two light support legs that swung down from the muzzle, and a shoulder stock. An assistant usually fed the belt, but the A6 could be fired effectively by one man.

It seemed to Beales and me that Pete Imo spent every waking moment fussing with his machine gun. In addition to preempting certain firing assignments for himself, he also jealously saw to the nitty-gritty of maintenance.

As an artist himself with the standard M1 infantry rifle, Beales greatly admired the deft, instinctive way Imo handled the MG. His moves were as natural as those of a fly fisherman working a back cast to lay his lure in a particular spot with no apparent effort. Tapping the cover and gently tugging the empty belt feeding out the right side, he would grasp the stubby operating handle with his right hand and work it back ever so gently, sensing that the critical head space was absolutely right. Imo did this repeatedly when not firing, usually ending his rote by hitting the rear of the bolt with the heel of his right hand to confirm that it was tightly closed. Then he'd hunker down, left hand pressing the stock down tight on his right shoulder, confirming with the sights exactly where the gun was pointed. He was always prepared to fire at a moment's notice.

Although he had excelled at target practice in the States, Sergeant Imo had determined that the MG was not a precision instrument. It was to be used like a hose, spraying as many locations and troops as possible. To increase the dispersion of his "hose," just before combat, he had deliberately held down the trigger to burn up a full belt. This was against all manual instructions, which ordained short bursts at spaced intervals to keep the barrel and

steel jacket reasonably cool. Imo's full-belt barrage left the barrel
so hot that cartridges were set off from barrel heat alone, without
being struck by the firing pin.

Pete Imo's objective was to "burn out," or wear away, the shoulders of the rifling grooves that provided accuracy. At two hundred
to three hundred yards, instead of pumping six shots into one
enemy soldier, the bullets scattered from the sloppy barrel randomly over several feet, increasing chances of bringing down
more than one and adding to the fear and distress of more enemy
soldiers.

My mortarmen kept an eye on Imo's gun, and when his crew
picked up from its second firing site and displaced forward to seek
a new position nearer the village, I ordered Beales and the other
three men in the squad to move to the shelter of the first few
houses in the village outskirts.

Two battered houses offered concealment if not complete cover
from enemy fire. As squad sergeant, I ordered Rube into action.
He deftly readied the forty-two-pound mortar for firing. I handed
him the sight, which he popped into the slot next to the tube.
Beales moved the elevating crank upward a few turns. The gun
was ready for action.

I designated an upright timber remaining at the left corner of
one of the shattered buildings to serve as an aiming point. Rube
moved the legs until the sight was pointed roughly at the upright,
and peered through the aperture to refine his aim to the left edge
of the improvised aiming reference. He quickly centered the leveling bubble in the sight by adjusting the height of the left leg with
the threaded leveling screw. His assistant had a round in hand,
ready to drop in the smooth bore.

I felt satisfaction in having come this far with my men and my
weapon, and I was proud that it was ready to fire. The problem
was, I didn't have the slightest notion where the enemy was, how
far away they were, or whether we had friendly forces between
us and them. So I ordered "out of action," and we made our uncertain way into town with the riflemen.

Reviewing that very first day of our war, the weapons platoon
was functioning, by gum! We found refuge in performing the oft-

practiced exercises of gunnery. The repetition of training was paying off. We carried out our tasks with practiced precision. To an observer, ours looked like a simple Stateside camp maneuver. Imo had done himself proud, and we mortarmen would get in plenty of our own shooting later.

Living with Death

A ble Company sector was still chaos. Frozen corpses lay all about, some of them our guys. One of the reasons so many more enemy dead still lay in our zone was the difficulty in getting help into town to haul them out. The field we had put to use for our attack was in sight of the enemy and salted with snow-covered land mines. The only access road was still under surveillance by a bunch of mean pricks who ruthlessly applied punishment with their limitless artillery and mortars. The only good news was that the barrels of the 88s trained on us often shot wide of their targets, the consequence of hard use and worn rifling. The road was nonetheless used sparingly, at night, by jeeps equipped with barely visible blackout lights.

Insulated Mermite cans made it possible for the cooks to handcarry hot stew and coffee from where the vehicles had to stop. So far, we hadn't lost any kitchen people, but this was one infantry mess crew that at least had a taste, as it were, of real war. On some chow runs, Jerry would lob a few 88s in their general direction. Fortunately, the path marked by phosphorescent stakes for the cooks through the minefields was beyond enemy light mortar range. To a cook whose job sheltered him from enemy action most of the time, a near miss by an 88 was a particularly traumatic moment. But harassing shells never stopped them from delivering the groceries. Our cooks had concern and they had guts. Later a more direct route for their jeeps was marked, making the task faster if not safer.

Hot chow was often mutton, or veal, or something, sort of stewed up with onions and poured over reconstituted, powdered potatoes that turned cold instantly on contact with an aluminum mess kit. Nonetheless, we wolfed down the tasty, fresh food as welcome relief from icebox-cold C, K, and D rations. Whoever ordained that mess kits be made of aluminum may have had a clue about ease of cleaning, but must have known that the bright metal took away heat as surely as a block of ice. Everything quickly became the same temperature as the canned fruit mix that was ladled in for dessert to keep our bowels loose, as though that was needed!

A few more details of the first morning of our attack seeped back into my memory. Among other escapes, I recalled and marveled at the dumb luck brought me by the crusty snow. I had paused to catch my breath, fast and shallow from effort and panic (it's hard to hyperventilate in subfreezing air, but I was as near doing it then as I ever had been). As the morning light improved, I discovered that the snowy hump I had chosen to lay my rifle on was actually a huge German land mine. The trip-ring had providentially gathered enough ice beneath it to prevent triggering. It was meant to blow off a tank tread, so maybe it took a lot of pressure to set it off anyway. I sure didn't want to find out. I carefully picked up my belongings, and with renewed energy from a fresh flood of adrenaline, started off again toward the machine gun and rifle fire still directed at us.

Adrenaline was the tonic that got us going, but sometimes disaster struck unexpectedly, before such defense mechanisms could be ignited. Things being quiet around our forward hole, my ammo bearer, Private Lount, climbed out and stood erect in the snow to let some rare rays of sunlight bathe his face. It was welcome relief from several days of scudding clouds and snow. I warned Jimmy not to hang around too long out there, but he was enjoying the welcome sunshine so much that I was tempted to join him.

The peaceful moment ended with a bang. A small enemy mortar shell (I think it might have been a 50mm vs. our 60mm) landed almost on top of our hole. It came with no warning, no sound except the flick-of-a-whip swish that precedes the almost simultaneous sharp explosion of a light mortar. I recoiled farther into our foxhole, like a woodchuck that drops in its burrow to seek shelter from a hunter's fire. The chocolate drink I had just heated with a waxed remnant of K-ration box was still in my hand, miraculously unspilled, but scummed over with burnt powder. Staring at it, I set the cup down deliberately and carefully on the firing step without spilling a drop and stuck my head out cautiously, not really aware at the moment just what I was doing. The direct hit along with the rest of the salvo (uncounted) that fell with it, had left me lightheaded and disoriented.

Private Lount lay at the hole entrance, his face even with mine as I poked my head out for my first look around outside the shelter. At that very moment, nothing but a blank look indicated the catastrophe that had befallen him. His eyes were sort of glazed over, but I had never been eye-to-eye with a badly injured person. I did not recognize then, as I would after more practice, the first stages of shock. It was too early for pain to have set in.

I was slow to emerge from the deep den, mindful that Jerry had us in range, and that more death might be on the way. Then I saw the huge blotch of red snow. I scrambled out of the hole shouting "Medic, medic!"

Lount's left leg was blown apart, not very tidily, at the knee. Stretcher bearers came from their station in the village, dashing to the position like broken-field quarterbacks. They exchanged looks, shook their heads negatively, applied a quick tourniquet, and loaded Lount and his severed lower leg on a canvas stretcher. Then they hauled ass to safety.

I picked up the boy's helmet and rifle, crouched, and ran to the medics' shelter. Lount was speechless, but appeared conscious. His eyes grew increasingly cloudy as pain finally set in. The aid men busied themselves cutting away the upper leg of his pants and long johns. They sprinkled sulfa powder over the chewed-up stump, tightened the tourniquet above it to stem the bleeding, and swaddled the ragged thigh in surgical gauze. They gave Lount a hurried shot of morphine.

The kid was writhing, near delirium by now. With unusual strength, he pushed us away and sat bolt upright on the litter, staring at where his lower leg had been. The grisly sight triggered deep panic. His breathing grew fast and rasping. He broke into a cold sweat. Rapid, thin puffs were interspersed with frantic, squeaky pleas to his mother for help. We tried to comfort and reassure him, but he paid us no heed. Not knowing what more to do, we helplessly watched him slowly go into shock before he had a chance to be taken back to the battalion aid station. Death would soon follow. I stumbled aimlessly away from where Lount lay, heading in the general direction of our outpost. Someone grabbed me and led me to the platoon shelter basement, where I curled up on my accustomed sleeping spot atop a stored kitchen stove, chosen earlier because the metal legs discouraged climbing rats. I immediately fell deeply asleep.

Hunger woke me from the unconsciousness I had found refuge in after Lount's slaughter. A vision of the chocolate drink left on the foxhole firing step, coated with acrid powder, squelched my appetite. It would be a long time before I could drink hot chocolate again. I lay there trying to find some meaning or way to rationalize the deaths that were occurring, my chief concern being how to keep my own wits about me and stay alive.

Lount's life ended five months after his eighteenth birthday. Sergeant Coleman still lingered in my memory, but Lount's beseeching cries long remained with me because I had been so powerless to help him, and because the fragment that killed him had missed me by a whisker. Coleman's death had been instant. Lount's unstoppable and accelerating slide to death was a sobering example of what happens when shock ranges unchecked.

From day one, I had desperately wanted to find a way to describe war to my family and other folks back home. But at this juncture, I wrestled to formulate an explanation, a rationalization, just for myself. While my own acceptance and conception was still taking shape, I did form a perception of combat's effect on our organization, Able Company.

To arrive at my new insight or perspective, I pictured a group of two hundred young men picked at random from as many towns and cities, arbitrarily thrown together in a "club" called Company A. Other than their uniforms they had no commonalty, such as interest in baseball, music, hiking, religion, scholarship, whatever. They had little enthusiasm for their assigned duties or training, not having chosen to join the club in the first place. Reluctantly, the gang learned to march in lockstep, shoot weapons, and respond to commands. But they were still a disparate assemblage of individuals, little altered in their reactions to each other by forced companionship.

The relationships changed dramatically the moment they were thrown together into combat. A new element was introduced that had been no part of any other fraternal, sports, or cultural club: unplanned, random, shared death and rampant physical injury throughout the club.

Despite recruiting posters to the contrary, I realized that our bunch of GIs was not fighting for mother, country, and apple pie. Bullshit. We wanted to live. Our ties were to those unfortunates fighting next to us, sharing the same fate, and beating the same odds. These were relationships of greater importance than any we would have with fellow men for the rest of our lives.

A lot of combat reports indicate that our fine soldiers didn't really hate the enemy, nor really take personally the grim battles between our forces. Not so with what was left of A Company. We had grown to hate the Krauts with a vengeance. Each slaughtered comrade added to our venom. No way you can foster a warm, fuzzy feeling for a bunch of badass guys who spend all their time trying to kill you, and who succeed at it so well.

Home in the Bulge

———⟫‹‹◉››‹———

Every detail of the key village we held in the midst of the Siegfried defense line had been plotted in detail on German military grid maps: pillboxes, antitank pits and dragon's teeth, mine fields, supply roads, every building, tree, even the slightest depression or knoll.

Unlike troop shelters with a single wall of thick concrete, many critical pillboxes had double walls. They were designed so that if a shot or shell came through an outer wall doorway, the next entry was offset a few feet so the interior concrete wall took the hit, leaving the people inside perfectly safe. There were hundreds of these pillboxes nestled among the border defenses.

The concrete fortifications we controlled in our sector had been reduced to rubble by demolition teams from the Army Engineers on the theory that if we did get kicked out in a counterattack, the pillbox embrasures and their preset fields of fire could not be brought back into play by the enemy. In any event, they faced the wrong way to be of any benefit to us. Our line of attack lay in the opposite direction.

The squareheads were using every bit of their charted information to intimidate us and cause our withdrawal. Our possession of even a small part of their permanent defense mechanism was unsettling and very offensive to the home team. A vengeful counterattack to retake our position was not out of the question, even though the main German forces were flowing into Belgium through a large breach in Allied lines not far away.

We wised up quickly as to which were their favorite targets. With no warning, salvos of 88s and mortars would rain down on access roads, foot trails, street and road intersections, and former defensive strongholds. The Krauts rightly guessed which locations we had chosen for our own defense. A regular target was our house, from which Sergeant Foote had rescued by carbine our two captured GIs.

Trial and error established a fairly safe path for the chow jeep from the kitchen truck someplace in the rear to a ravine at the edge of town. There we were treated to chow call. A hanging Lister bag of chemically treated water was provided to replenish canteens. Next to it over a fire of broken boards was a drum of boiling, soapy water and one of hot rinse for use at mealtime. As important as food itself was keeping mess kits, spoons, and drinking cups clean and sterilized. The trots (dysentery, the "GIs") was not only debilitating and damned messy; the condition badly undermined fragile nerves and allowed panic to sneak in as liquid bowels moved out.

Despite resorting to a slightly different path each day, our individual dashes from foxholes to secure food attracted shelling, consistent enough that the daily chow run was called "88 Alley."

We got our first letters from home, relayed through our cooks by a mail clerk reluctant to visit from the rear echelon in person. Runners from the Company CP delivered it to the platoons. Our surplus clothing, shelter halves, packs, gas masks, and equipment cast aside during the panic of our initial attack had been carted off from the original LD to a rear-area supply dump. Our supply sergeant even tried to save abandoned personal items for us. New-issue ponchos replaced our raincoats. A few full overcoats were made available for cold, long shifts in outpost foxholes. Over time, everyone was provided a blanket roll or fartsack (wool-lined sleeping bag).

Battlefield Company headquarters lacked the comforts of our Fourth Platoon base with its cellar and remaining one room. Captain Goodspeed had shrewdly located in an open field with no distinguishing terrain features or buildings. An abandoned stonewall barn foundation had been further hollowed out, and provided with a timber roof topped with a thick layer of earth covered by snow. There was insufficient clearance to stand erect inside. Otherwise, it provided safe cover for the command group including the CO, his executive officer (our Fourth Platoon leader), the first sergeant, message runners, radio operators, wiremen, and our body-count scorekeeper, the company clerk. The CP had so far escaped the notice of enemy artillery spotters.

Casual visits to the CP were forbidden to avoid establishing any recognizable traffic patterns for enemy observers. In-and-out traffic was limited to nighttime. For further security, trip wires to flares had been strategically installed and paths between them to the CP deliberately obscured in the snow by avoiding the footsteps of anyone who had preceded. One of our Fourth Platoon machine guns was dug in with a commanding field of fire over the CP for additional protection from possible enemy forays. It was manned day and night.

Time hung heavy between shifts on outpost and on guard duty. There were long lulls between shellings, affording time for us to prepare for a dreaded counterattack. My personal world came slowly back together, like an out-of-focus picture that gradually adjusts itself to regain definition and form. Back in high school, I'd taken a dare to dive into a high waterfall that plunged into a deep swimming hole. The swirling water grabbed me, sent me rolling and tumbling, and stripped me of all sense of direction or scale. As I frantically clawed to right myself, the torrent finally coughed me up in calmer, manageable water. That's how infantry combat had left me: afloat, thanks to no noteworthy accomplishment of my own, disoriented, bruised, and feeling not a little betrayed.

Had we not been completely green troops, I reflected bitterly, we might have hesitated to rush headlong into the withering enemy fire that first morning. We were so dumb that we kept right on advancing, each man wondering how and why he was alive when so many were dropping all about him.

Beyond the physical devastation that had befallen our infantry company, I sensed that our awesome exposure to intense combat had transformed our standard military unit into a profoundly different societal entity. Formal military hierarchy had been reordered by the natural tendency of men under strain to gravitate toward demonstrated leadership, regardless of rank. Individuals who had never aspired to "take charge" were suddenly looked to for guidance, direction, assurance. In short order, many were awarded rank to match their natural gift of leadership.

There were dead and wounded in apparently equal measure among officers, eighteen-year-old draftees, rawhide-tough ruffians, out-of-shape rookies, Regular Army sergeants, college kids, even the brash soldier-of-fortune types. Of nearly two hundred men who had shipped out together from the States, over half already had become casualties, most of them victims during the first few days. The losers seemed to be plucked by fate like Ping-Pong balls catapulted by air jet out of a glass bingo game bowl. As for the old distinction between the quick and the dead, a lot of the quick lay among the dead.

On the first day, it was Kraut rifle and automatic weapons and mines that took their toll. Then it was artillery shells and mortars that maimed with shrapnel and killed by concussion with nary a visible scratch. A few men stepped on Schu mines. A couple of GIs were evacuated, unable to speak or respond to instructions after the nearby blast of a random, giant German howitzer shell that sounded as it approached like a railroad freight car tumbling end over end. An alarming number of evacuations were due to frozen or rotting feet.

I had learned a little late—the third day—that care of one's feet in cold weather topped the list of all tasks. An order came down from Army headquarters that anyone not removing his boots and changing socks at least once a day would be subject to immediate court martial. We Americans were losing more to frostbite, frozen feet, and trench foot than to the combined might of the German Army. The end result was fully as bad as a serious wound. A foot amputated for gangrene is as gone as one ripped off by enemy shrapnel.

Experience taught us how to avoid damage to our feet, and even to remedy frostbite and the scary white, wrinkled flesh that warned of trench foot. Arctic temperature foot care was an acquired skill. Pertinent instruction had had no place at our tepid, muggy, southeastern U.S. training camps.

In a shared foxhole, men learned to sit facing each other so as to hold and massage each other's bare feet while heavy, leather combat boots aired out. That rubbing someone else's stinking feet might be distasteful was overridden by sheer necessity, and the hard fact that you desperately needed the same personal care for your own feet. Extra dry socks were as coveted as a choice snack. Frostbite had left my toes an alarming white. Both feet were too swollen and tender for regular footwear.

A frantic message to our faithful supply sergeant located some big overshoes which I slipped over dry stockinged feet. Stuffed with fine, dry grass, the galoshes allowed the sort of peeling and healing one experiences after a sunburn, and, finally, restoration of pinkish color to my toes. The key to improvement was replacing the soft, absorbent grass twice a day. Hay or straw wouldn't do. I needed that fine fuzz with which mice build their nests, painstakingly harvested from frozen grass clumps under the snow.

That's one I had learned by observing a captured Kraut stubblehopper. He was scarcely able to walk, and had swaddled his feet in scraps of cloth wrapped around fine, dry grass. I was able to do better than he with grass-lined, sturdy overshoes. I figured later that the German soldier had probably learned the technique from the Russians on that far-off and bitterly cold eastern front.

Fortunately, our defensive assignment meant minimal walking. After a week or so, I could tolerate loosely laced shoes again. You can bet they were removed to accommodate dry socks at least twice a day. Had our situation not been static, I would doubtless have been evacuated. I could not have endured even a short march. My ingenuity in self-healing may have been commendable, but in the final analysis, it could well have saved me for a far worse fate.

Sweat-damp socks were dried in two natural body incubators. When lying down, I held mine between the thighs, well up in the crotch. When up and about, socks were safety-pinned under the arms. Both places signaled "dry" when the dampness no longer brought discomfort to these sensitive but warm body areas. Harder to come by than extra socks were the attaching pins. I would have given my last dime for a regular, old-fashioned safety pin, and still can't stand throwing one away.

In one of many command blunders during the Bulge, when we originally moved through Belgium toward the German front, our Regular Army "work" shoes and leggings were replaced with newly designed combat boots. The quick-buckle straps on the high-tops were a welcome replacement for leggings. But then, black, greasy waterproofing "dubbin" was distributed. Warned that we would encounter rain, snow, and mud, we were ordered to treat our new boots liberally with the evil, medicinal-smelling stuff. That sealed the boots from moisture coming in—or going out—sealing also the fate of many a soldier. Dubbin was no better than a sinister poison.

If the killing, maiming, and freezing to date had seemed random, those lucky enough to have escaped bodily harm were subtly imbued with a tiny spark that would grow with time and practice: the will for and knack of survival. Luck and fate be damned. If there was even the slightest chance to improve the odds, take it. If a bullet missed by inches, maybe it was because you chose cover a little more carefully; if shrapnel chewed up a bush nearby, maybe it was because experience had pointed you to a safer place.

Hardly a devotee of superstition, I nonetheless came to terms with a solid belief in hunches. Stuck in any particular location chosen for protection, tactical advantage, or just convenience, I would suddenly be afflicted with an irresistible urge to move, to get out. I would imagine unseen eyes seeking out my hiding place and preparing to prowl up or direct hostile fire at me. The only way to assuage my apprehension was to get the hell out. I acted impulsively, giving no tactical reason for my action. I was simply convinced in my own heart that great harm would visit that particular spot if I stayed there another minute.

More often than not, I felt foolish when my brusque move produced no reward. On a couple of occasions the place I had just left was visited with enemy fire, vindicating my hunch. I had to admit my decision was based more on luck than on reasoned military judgment. Those successful occasions, however, encouraged me to continue to have and act on hunches that really had no supporting rationale. I tried to forget a wrong guess that took me by whim from a safe spot to one visited with a flurry of mortar fire. I dismissed the error in choice by concluding simply that I zigged when I should have zagged.

Along with hunches, an inevitable fatalism replaced or diluted permeating fear. We survivors recovered a little of the esoteric and consistently crude humor universally shared by men in uniform. We didn't exactly laugh at death, but by treating it more casually, the grim reaper might be held at bay just a little longer.

Letters Home

"Talk about tense. You couldn't drive a needle up my ass with a post maul. Sons 'a bitches. When we finally feel a little like we can relax, they're on us again. It's like they know just how much we sweat between rounds." My buddy Rube succinctly described our feelings of suspense and sick anticipation between enemy artillery barrages. I said nothing.

Silence in our Bulge foxhole hung like persistent fog for the better part of an hour as we awaited new incoming shells. My headache intensified. The end of a barrage is a nonevent because there is no prompt for some subsequent action, or any reassuring confirmation that it's really over. For the moment, nothing was happening.

"Rube," I said. "I got to tell you. I am not becoming any fonder of being shot at day after day. I can't get used to it. I never will get used to it. It gets worse every time. The anxiety hangs on, builds, eats me up. It's like when we walk up a street in an enemy-held town. I keep my stomach muscles tense, as though that would stop a shot in the gut. Even now, every muscle is tense, waiting for that old 88; even my eyebrows."

"Them near-hits lift you right up off the ground and shake you like you was on the straw rack of a threshing machine." Rube was on a roll with his patented country descriptions.

"What I thought this war would be is all turned around," I admitted. "My impression came from books and movies. When we were sent up to the 'front' to launch our first attack, I had in mind a beat-up field, peppered with shell holes, and guarded on both sides by big, old trenches. I had some hazy idea we'd skootch down in one row of them until Captain Goodspeed blew the whistle. We'd all take a deep breath, look at each other, and then pile out. 'Over the top,' it was called in World War I. When the real thing came, I thought we were still just jockeying around that morning when we started through the snow at our LD. I couldn't believe that this was the real front until we started to get pasted by MGs and artillery."

"I don't know how we got dealt this hand," replied Rube. "I hang on here day after day thinking of all those guys we saw in the rear on our way up. The service clubs were full of guys with steady jobs in offices, warehouses, whatever. All the niggers were high-balling traffic, working motor pools, handling crates, doing heavy work; you name it. I don't expect they asked for them jobs any more'n we asked for ours.

"Then there's tons of guys in the service way back home. Not many of them will ever get overseas. The ones I know have cushy jobs, or at least safe jobs. Tell me, just what percentage of soldiers actually end up being shot at like us? And why us? It's not simply being shot at that gets me; it's getting shot at and hit gives me trouble," Rube concluded with a deep sigh.

Again with nothing to say in return, I decided to seek solace by writing home, the one refuge of security and warmth I could still conjure up from a dimming memory of pre-combat, stateside life. I tried consciously to relax my stomach and shoulders. My nerves slowly settling down, I put pencil stub to paper:

Dear Mom and Dad:

There are lots of lulls in the fighting, and while I can't tell you where I am or what we are doing, it is a wonderfully crisp and sunny day—much like you'd see this time of year up in the Adirondacks. Plenty of snow.

I just finished a cup of coffee after a filling meal, and have some time on my hands. I want to thank you for the socks and the scarf. No one ever has too many dry, warm socks.

I have a GI scarf, so your woolly one is wrapped and pinned around my chest and down around my kidneys, the places I am most likely to feel cold first. It's made of nice, soft yarn.

The assistant gunner in my four-man mortar squad is a buck sergeant just like me. He's a friendly Polack named Martin. Until recently, he was handling rations in some Supply Depot. My Gunner is a 250-pound Boston Irishman, a PFC. The two ammo bearers are Southern teenagers. No education, but strong and as good workers as ever we had on the farm. Best thing is, the two privates are always cheerful.

For now, just know that I am OK, safe, and unharmed. I will be coming home one day same way!

Love, Your son Johnny

PS. Please send candy and peanuts. Especially peanuts in cans. Also, I lost my Zippo lighter. Can you send one?

Since I had earlier described the men in my squad, the folks might conclude from this message that all had been replaced by new faces. The original members? One KIA, one battle fatigue, two out with trench foot. But no use going into all that and worrying everyone. Anyway, the company officer censoring outgoing mail would probably cut it out, the holes in the paper causing even more questions and worry at home.

The significance in saying that my assistant gunner was also a buck sergeant carried the message that personnel being transferred to the infantry were assigned any job they might perform, regardless of rank attained in some other branch of the service. For instance, a staff sergeant fresh from quartermaster duty came to us far short in qualifications and training required to lead a rifle squad, or head up a light weapons section. But stripes and all, he could lug a flame thrower or pitch grenades, or drop mortar rounds in a tube as well as the next man; so that's the kind of job he got.

The word "replacement" was in such common usage that few

paused to appreciate its dark connotation. Replacement simply meant someone taking the place of someone who been removed from the ranks. There were two ways to get out: in a body bag or on a litter. A replacement could only contemplate a similar fate.

It did develop that there was another way out of our infantry company: a transfer to a fighting unit that had even fewer men than we had. During the Bulge, six men were sent from Company A to a rifle company in another battalion that had suffered even deeper losses. Since we were at less than half strength, I shuddered to think of what had happened to that outfit. And I was horrified to think of being transferred myself to a different part of our infantry division. However few there were of us, good old Company A was still "home."

I wrote often, avoiding censorable items, just to let the folks know I was still alive. In the pile of letters saved by my mother during the entire war, those from the fighting front had least to say.

I folded the V-Mail form for the cooks to take back so an officer could read it before it was sent to the States. Then, Rube and I continued our vigil, listening for the next sign of "incoming mail" from those bastards on the other side.

Getting Tough

———————><«O»><———————

As sure as a soaring hawk scatters a barnyard flock of chickens, the overshadowing threat of enemy artillery decreed that combat GIs not seek comfort in groups. "Spread out, men. One shell could get you all," was oft repeated and universally obeyed in the infantry. The whine of incoming mail broke up crowds of as few as two people.

Except for brief exchanges with an occasional foxhole buddy, we were confined to our own individual resources under fire. During a pitched battle, there is no opportunity to pause as a close-knit crew, talk about the contest, exchange experiences, seek guidance. We were flat denied the consolation of comforting intercourse that miserable, shocked people seek and need. We had to synthesize our own solace, erect our own unique mental defenses.

Personal conduct rules that had governed our young lives until then were dashed the moment we crossed that first farm fence into enemy territory. Back home, we had lived under civilized rules that carried no significant penalties for occasional infraction as we played our roles in life's little contests.

Abruptly, a new code of competitive behavior was thrust on us. It demanded one stunning, inescapable response to our adversary: Kill. No half measures. Eliminate the enemy in any way possible. Shoot, blow up, bludgeon, stab; show no mercy. Just one mission: Kill. Or suffer the harshest penalty—your own life.

They (the enemy) have their sworn task: to kill you. So, no choice but to kill them first. No free foul shots, no penalty box, no time-outs. There is only one way to win, one resolution to the contest: Kill. Kill 'em all. Now. Such was our civilian "live and let live," "turn the other cheek" code invalidated by the exigencies of mortal combat.

The brutal shock of what we endured on the opening day of our incredible, grisly adventure gradually merged with even more barbaric experiences, piled up week after week. Exposure to violence produced its own narcotic, dulling recall, minimizing and miniaturizing events that at the time were monumental. Not that intensity and strife were incessant. We had plenty of time between violent episodes to contemplate our lot. Idle time had no measure. Frontline soldiers are unable to predict the next threat to life—in a minute? An hour? Tomorrow? Where? By what lethal weapon?

To explain the impact on a young mind of that terrible first day of battle, it was as though all the painful calamities of a lifetime were compressed into a few minutes of adversities never before imagined or measured. Armed conflict is a once-in-a-lifetime experience, unique because it stands such a good chance of being the final experience of a lifetime. Flashing, bright snapshots of violence piled one on the other to form a kaleidoscope of nightmare-class memories.

The Battle of the Bulge was a vast, sweeping undertaking involving whole armies. From the German breakthrough to its grinding halt deep in Belgium, tens of thousands of Allied and enemy soldiers were killed and wounded. It was the lot of Able Company to be at one shoulder of the huge pocket, ordered to prevent the loss of that critical pivot point. No more than we knew when the next 88 would strike did we know how long we would be required to occupy the shattered village that had cost us so dearly. Time hung heavy some days. By then, however, I was no stranger to coping with idle time.

Boredom rose like tar bubbles on a sun-baked asphalt country road during school vacations back when I was growing up on the farm. To relieve the monotony, a couple of us kids would take our .22 single-shot rifles and hitchhike to the city dump. More often than not, we ended up walking the distance; drivers aren't inclined to pick up gun-toting youngsters. We would sneak up to the board fence surrounding the evil-smelling garbage heap, ease our rifles to the fence-top for a good, steadying rest, and each carefully pick out a primary target from the seething, squeaking swarm of rats.

We'd squeeze off our shots as near simultaneously as possible. Except for an occasional bloody gray carcass resulting from a lucky hit, all of the rats disappeared instantly, as though connected from underground by a network of strings all jerked at the same time. Remaining motionless as possible, we'd scan the piles of tin cans, citrus rinds, boxes, grocer paper, and discarded vegetables until an adventurous denizen made a brief appearance. We'd cut loose, both at the one target, usually a split second after the quarry had again disappeared. Then we'd hold still until the next opportunity . . . always after a much longer interval than the last.

After maybe three volleys, we'd tire of the increasingly long waits between rat appearances and wander back home, plinking road signs and glass telephone pole insulators as we went.

Now it was the equally bored Krauts trying to pick us off in a community that had been reduced by explosives to a garbage heap. There had been about sixty houses in the town we held. Every one had been heavily damaged or obliterated. I never did visit all the ruins myself. The count was courtesy of Farmboy Beales, who, in a typical Rube-ism, allowed that he came up with the total by counting the cellar walls and dividing by four. We hunkered down in those cellars, or in excavated foxholes, rarely venturing abroad farther than duty called, and never showing ourselves during or right after a barrage by German artillery or mortars.

Rube served part time as platoon messenger, making rounds of our entire company position, feeding the thin sound-power communication wire that connected our units through gloved hands as he went along. When a break was discovered, he'd make a quick splice, his pause undertaken at risk of enemy discovery. We were all subject to pot-shots from the enemy at any time. It was prudent to stay on our own turf, close to familiar cover. When enemy observers saw one or more GIs, they often took a crack at us. We ducked, usually before the rounds struck, but they shot at us anyway, maybe out of plain old boredom, like us kid rat-hunters.

Staying alive in heaps of rubble took rodent-like ingenuity. We developed heightened awareness to the slightest whisper of an incoming projectile (light mortars), eyes in the backs of our heads for a patrolling enemy sniper, improved skills at using or improvising concealment in moving from one place to another, split-second reaction in diving for cover at the slightest alarm, or sometimes just on a hunch. So familiar were we with our surroundings that we could negotiate our way in the dark almost as well as in daylight.

By mid-January 1945 our month of defensive action had taught us survival. Only able, resolute men could fight effectively. By pounding away at us in the ruins of our village, Jerry unwittingly helped us hone individual techniques for surviving in Arctic fighting conditions; at the same time we were acquiring the mental toughness to become an effective combat unit.

Most of us who had jumped off that first day were experienced combat soldiers by the end of the Bulge. In total, we were not an effective, battle-hardened company, our ranks too diluted by untried replacements, and a few survivors rendered permanently ineffective by the ferocity of that first attack. I wondered if any of those new men, or for that matter my old pals, knew how shit-scared I was? Probably they were so wrapped up in their own anxiety that they really didn't care.

Shooting Back

The stubborn Huns whomped us unexpectedly and often in our ruined cellars and foxholes. We yearned to get back at them. With plenty of time and some good binoculars (Coleman's, actually), I spent a lot of idle hours examining the hill ascending to the enemy fortress. Twice we caught white-clad daytime patrols working their way toward our lines. Our mortars chased them back once, and on the second occasion we called in the battalion 105s (also known as the "cannon company"). The big guns didn't come close, but out of the failed fire mission, we learned to mark up on our own aerial map-grids specific artillery and mortar targets that could be called up in short order.

Fourth Platoon was still using my old foxhole as an observation post. We maintained phone contact back to the company CP, and manned the position twenty-four hours a day. The two-man daytime duty guard came to the hole just before dawn, and was relieved shortly after dark by two fresh men. Guard duty made for a long and boring day (or night), except for the diversion of calling up our own mortar fire missions, relayed through the CP to a well-camouflaged gun position. The main communications catch was that you couldn't "ring up" the other party on our crude sound-power system; someone on the other end had to keep the receiver close enough to his ear to hear the hiss when we blew sharply into the speaking end to signal that a message would be voiced. It was tedious duty.

Ever since Lount had been killed by mortar fire because he ventured out of the hole in broad daylight, we were careful to conceal any movement around the position. Even at that, the Krauts randomly fired a few rounds on us every so often; they managed to hurt a few people, and to keep the rest of us honest.

One diabolic German mortar tactic was to drop three successive rounds in the tube. Thump, thump, thump. Due to the high, long trajectory of a mortar shell, the sound of its being fired arrived several seconds before the armed projectile, giving us, the quarry, time to take cover. Then, as the shells exploded around us, the German gunners would drop in one more, its warning thump lost in the explosions of the arriving trio. Anyone in the open, or even sticking his head up out of a foxhole, was fair game for the single round that sneaked in with no warning, almost half a minute after the first salvo. So it was prudent to stay under cover awhile after any arriving mortar salvo. The squareheads must have learned the same lesson, for we copied their technique in an effort to sandbag them.

Because there is practically no advance warning from a mortar round, the chances of ducking one are goose egg, none. But then, they say the artillery shell that is destined to strike you directly telegraphs no warning either. Problem is, there is not a very large sample base of surviving respondents to argue that theory. Anyway, artillery whines, mortars swish, and German rockets called "screaming meemies" scream.

We wore scrounged-up white sheets and pillowcases draped or tied over our helmets to obscure observation when not in our hole. While we tried to avoid wearing a visible footpath through the snow to the OP, it really didn't matter. The field was badly torn up by 88s and mortars, making the dark journey difficult when changing guard, and downright ridiculous when enemy shelling or machine-gun fire prompted flat-out speed. Our positions were distant enough from Jerry that bullets from small arms were not effective, except from snipers who occasionally crept unseen down the hedgerows to take a crack at us.

Half the time on OP duty was spent observing; the rest sitting, dozing, eating, haranguing a foxhole buddy, or writing letters. Taking an empty K-ration box, I learned to fold and shape it so that the wax-impregnated cardboard could be lit to emit a steady, almost smokeless flame. Holding it at a precise distance of flame to cup allowed heating a partial canteen cup of water to somewhere between tepid and warm. Stirring in coffee, lemonade powder, or shavings of bar-chocolate, as I had when Lount was killed, made a passable drink companion to the hardtack biscuits (which we called "cookies"), canned eggs, cheese, or spam.* Dessert was a dried fruit bar. The box of four Chesterfield or Chelsea cigarettes (never Camels or Luckies, damn it) went in a pocket. The little pack of toilet paper was tucked inside helmet-liner support straps. If the sugar packet did not go into the drink at hand, it was wolfed down like candy.

The enemy harassed our cooks with 88s during their daily chow delivery, so we developed our own agenda to get back at their cuisine. Toward morning on cold, crisp nights, we could hear clanking in the enemy-held town that battalion intelligence (S-2) told us was a horse-drawn provision cart with big, steel-rimmed wheels rolling down cobblestone streets to fetch chow for the Krauts. The Kraut stubblehoppers called the cart a "goulash cannon," according to the translation of one prisoner's description. The standard offering was "fart soup," made of peas obviously close kin to our Navy beans.

Without real hope that we would cause serious damage or casualties (although we would have liked that), we spent long daylight hours with aerial maps trying to figure the route and stopping points of the chow cart. We'd sneak a mortar crew out in daytime to lay the gun for azimuth and distance based on our best-guess map coordinates. A gunner and assistant manned the piece at night. We'd use the sound-power phone to order up rounds fired when we thought we heard their chow cart near one of our se-

---

* Here the author is not referring to the popular spiced ham food product known commercially as Spam, but rather to Army K-ration "Meal 2—special biscuit, ham preparation, dextrose tablets, lemon powder, and sugar." The GI commonly referred to it as *spam*.

lected impact areas. I don't think we ever got the ration wagon or its horse; somehow, their cooks delivered every night, as did our own kitchen crew.

On cold, sunny days, the Krauts all had their field glasses out and, probably as bored as we were, they called on their seemingly inexhaustible hoard of large-bore ammunition to pick on targets of opportunity. Our well-known OP was a popular target. It was battered, the dirt and log cover scarred by near hits; anyone on duty had to worry that one day a lucky round would enter the hole and wipe out the position. It had already happened to one Fourth Platoon foxhole, our Second Squad machine-gun nest. When the 88 struck, we were changing detail, and no one was in the hole. Scratch one bent and battered machine gun. We hoped odds were that lightning wouldn't strike twice in the same manner, praying that our reclaimed den would lead a charmed life.

Almost every night, battalion intelligence ordered our company to send a patrol out to ascertain enemy movement and strength and, if really lucky, to pick up a prisoner. Patrols were the job of the riflemen, and we in weapons were glad to leave it up to them. Playing nighttime hide-and-seek with heavily armed adversaries wasn't high on my list of new hobbies.

But this one time, I agreed to go along in hopes of capturing a Kraut prisoner, one I had observed at his OP for several days. He had turned into my special chum, relieving himself in plain sight at regular intervals, but always ducking back inside his hole before we could get him with our mortar. He was too far away to shoot with a sniper rifle. Hours of studying aerial and topographical maps indicated a safe and devious flanking maneuver through the hedgerows that might allow us to surprise and take this enemy observer prisoner.

Draped in white sheets, we slogged our way in pitch dark through deep snow, along a guiding hedgerow. When we had moved out maybe three hundred yards, aerial flares went off, and in their brilliant light we froze in position or dropped to the ground. Almost in our faces, burp guns popped off. We all went flat. The fire rate of the little sub machine guns is so fast that they sounded like the ripping of a sheet of canvas, a thousand times amplified. Our guys fired grease guns and carbines wildly in return. We had met an enemy patrol out doing the same thing we were. Both units moved helter-skelter back to their respective lines. We made it safely, as I am sure they did.

We had no prisoner.

They had one, though, our lead scout, nineteen-year-old Pvt. D. K. Onderdonk, First Squad, Third Platoon. He had overrun the Kraut patrol before we discovered each other. The rest of us returned sweaty, bone-weary, scared, deflated, humiliated. The debriefing by Captain Goodspeed was uncharacteristically scathing. Just before daybreak, we slunk back to our regular positions.

My nerves were shaky. Anxiety and patrol tension had produced a case of the GIs (the trots), headache, sour stomach, and low, low spirits. Sparring with the enemy through patrol action was a game all right, but the price of losing was too high. I rationalized that I was exposed to enough danger by hanging around machine guns and mortars, always favorite enemy targets. Late that afternoon, such dreary thoughts were interrupted by a loud voice from the enemy position.

It was our first exposure to propaganda as a combat device. The Krauts had fired up a giant loudspeaker that could be heard all the way into our town. We peered warily from various cover to listen up, curious, and just a little uncomfortable that the enemy would be so brazen. Their "announcer" spoke English without discernible accent to tell us the mighty troops of the Third Reich were already deep into France and that the Americans were defeated. He invited us to surrender and not suffer sure and inevitable annihilation.

That was a big laugh until he got personal. He accurately called off the names of our battalion officers, plus Captain Goodspeed and our platoon leaders, and asked them by name to give up. Spooky, really.

But then, bully for our guys, they rolled up our own loudspeaker and blasted a loud invitation for the Krauts to give up, featuring actual prisoners testifying to their complete satisfaction with their treatment by their American captors. During the exchange, there seemed to be an unspoken rule allowing the two sides to take turns talking, like part of a giant stage production.

Right back at us, an American soldier on their loudspeaker reported that he was doing fine in their care. We were trying to guess who was behind the voice, distorted by the giant loudspeaker, when he revealed that he was our own Private Onderdonk, captured during our ill-fated night patrol. He spoke haltingly about being nicely treated and well fed, and described a meal provided by his captors of his favorite, stewed meat and gravy on bread. That broke us up, and set Onderdonk on a pedestal of admiration that would long endure. Many of our hot meals at the front were creamed dried beef or creamed hamburger bits slopped over sliced bread. Onderdonk in particular hated with a passion S.O.S. (shit on a shingle). His was a real stroke to tell us on a German loudspeaker just how good it was over on their side. A pretty ballsy stunt!

The Kraut announcer came back on to reiterate that they knew everything there was to know about us, reciting casualty figures that most of us didn't know. It was like someone had given him a copy of our Morning Report. He warned that we were in for some very rough treatment if we didn't surrender and return all their prisoners.

With all that time listening, our forward observers had figured map coordinates for the Kraut loudspeaker location, and we heard our own 105s pass overhead. They plastered the area we suspected was occupied by the German loudspeaker, and within a minute, the 88s roared over our heads to retaliate against our loudspeaker, hidden somewhere back in town.

We had expected counter-battery fire, and hence remained under cover. Jerry doubtless did the same thing. It was a new level of name-calling, though. The war of words was a nice respite from shooting each other, but it didn't make us like the Krauts a bit better. We bitterly wanted to get even. And boy! The things we thought of that our guys should have told them when our loudspeaker was on! Inventive repartee dreamed up for several days was wasted on our comrades.

War Games

Idle time with no measure had to be coped with during the Bulge, right along with lingering dread of the next hostile shell or enemy counterattack.

Our Fourth Platoon had it pretty good when it came to a haven during those long days. The barn that was part of our village farmstead was between us and the enemy, concealing most of the house itself from direct observation. Occupied by a dozen frozen-stiff cows (and for a while the dead Kraut we threw in there), the livestock shed intercepted artillery fire intended for the house. Its hayloft, which earlier had been a vantage point for nighttime observation of the front lines, was weakened by shellfire and had crumpled into the yard.

The room farthest from the enemy, our first-floor "dayroom," was a happy gathering place, home to us. We scrounged up chairs from our own and other houses. A small stove with a tiny oven was set up, fired with coal briquettes. Smoke to alert the enemy? No way.

It was a tough hardware item to come by, but the platoon found enough pieces of stovepipe in the ruins of flattened houses to run flues over the width of a vacant lot into a house that still had a chimney. The smoke piped through the system did not point a finger at our haven for the benefit of Kraut observers, and pretty much dissipated before ever escaping up the chimney. On and in the stove wondrous culinary experiments were conducted to enhance the palatability of K rations, or to reheat food from the kitchen chow run.

Winning the inventive food popularity contest was a two-layer patty made up of half cheese and half spam, sliced in equal parts while still cold. The odd mating, possibly forerunner to the cheeseburger, was then baked in the tiny oven or fried on the stove top until the cheese melted and the red hash browned. The inch-high mess was squashed with a trench knife onto K-ration hardtack (aka cookie), and topped with another biscuit. A memorable snack was born.

The stove was also host to a pot of hot water (melted snow, so as to save canteen water hauled in from the chemically treated Lister bag) for instant tea, coffee, or lemonade powder that came in boxed rations. Extra envelopes of powder were readily available from guys not up to preparing regular hot drinks in their foxholes.

Canned scrambled eggs failed as a gourmet candidate, defying the most imaginative combinations. Taste improved with limited warming, but too much heat rendered the unpalatable inedible. And any experiments in melting or mixing those evil chocolate D bars were soon dropped from the short list of potential gourmet recipes.

While the dayroom was reasonably shielded from artillery, nothing was safe from the insidious little Kraut mortar shells that plunged down almost vertically to threaten the backside of our house. One tore holes in our streetside wall, fortunately when the dayroom was empty. This prompted a work project to build a sandbag barrier on the inside of the dayroom for future protection, as well as to restore our ability to black out the room for nighttime candles. One catch was that there was no sand available for the empty bags we had called up from the rear.

So our appointed construction engineer, Pvt. Joe Magid, called on his days as a highway construction worker to organize a dirtbag brigade. Concealed from enemy observers by the house, Guinea Joe's crew blew holes in the frozen ground next to the house with nitro starch, and during the many hours of idle time, filled the bags with fresh-dug earth. Soon he had three six-foot-deep holes hollowed out far wider than the frozen-crust entry circles. The crew filled bags down in the holes, and passed them up to helpers who piled them ceiling-high inside the dayroom. Reasoning ran that swimming pools can be built above ground. Why not a giant foxhole?

Two weeks after our big attack, we received replacements by the score. Like all "new boys," they were the butt of many a cruel prank. Our mortar shells were delivered from the rear in cluster packages secured by long metal rods between end plates that held the projectile cartons together during transport. One of our platoon pranksters planted a cluster end plate in the bottom of each sandbag pit, the long steel rods pointing upward toward the entry. The peculiar holes with their guard-spears naturally elicited "what" and "why?" from the newcomers. The delighted and tongue-in-cheek response was that they were hog traps.

It was soberly explained to the rookies that the village had long ago been deserted by the farmers, who left the pigs they had kept in their barnyards untended. The pigs had turned wild and vicious, the story went, so we improvised protection from them with traps. We explained that you could escape a pursuing hog by cutting sharply around the corner of the house. The ungainly, pursuing hog would slip and fall prey to the deep trap and sharp iron rods.

"You've heard say," one grizzled teenage veteran told his even younger, gullible audience, "that a soldier went to shit and the hogs ate him? Well, that's more'n a country saying up front here, and we built these here traps to see it don't happen." Juvenile humor? Hell yes. Behind grimy faces and bristling weapons, we were still just a bunch of kids.

One of our untested replacements, anxious to win recognition and acceptance, pulled a stunt that he thought would be funny. It was dumb, dumber than spit.

A half dozen of us were sitting around the dayroom after a shift change in outpost guard when our towering, six-foot-four Irish rookie, Mike the Mick, lumbered into the room, nonchalantly tossing a hand grenade from hand to hand. This drew no particular notice, but interest did perk up when he put his pinkie through the ring attached to the arming pin, and started whirling the grenade around his finger.

At the time, I was sitting in a chair tilted back against the inner wall of the dayroom, relaxed, just starting to feel the welcome warmth of the fire after pulling guard. I looked up to see the grenade spin away from Mike the Mick's circling hand. The little bomb bounced on to the floor.

Even the casual movie fan knows that a hand grenade is harmless as long as the little handle is secured by the safety pin. After the pin is pulled, it's still safe as long as the handle is held tight against the grenade with the fingers. It takes little strength to hold the handle secure, but there is a natural tendency to grip it very firmly, just in case. When chucked stiff-armed toward the intended target, the handle flies off with a characteristic clang. Four to five seconds later: Boom!

When the grenade Mike the Mick was playing with hit the floor, the handle clanked off, and in the completely still room, the sputter of the burning fuse was as menacing as an amplified rattlesnake's alarm.

A couple of men attempted a ridiculous Laurel and Hardy exit. They hit the door together and jammed it in their struggle to get out. A couple of others hit the floor away from the direction of the device, which was rocking gently on the floor after its fall. The rest of us had no place to go, no time to get there. We shielded our faces, hunkered down, and turned away from the pending blast.

There was a muted Chinese-firecracker "pop!" and the grenade broke into two pieces, emitting a white, acrid fume. My chair was still tilted back, and if I appeared composed, it may have been because I sensed that the perpetrator himself took no extreme measures to get away or protect himself. I had accepted the futility of a flight path that would have taken me closer to the grenade, with no chance to reach comparative safety beyond it. My heart, nonetheless, was well up in my throat, way before the fuse burned down.

Mike the Mick had unscrewed the top of the grenade and poured out the powder to play his little trick. The powder granules inside a grenade can only do their work, like the explosives in most missiles, when set off by a detonator charge. Clad in copper, and resembling a pencil eraser, the detonator alone could blow a finger off or blind you, or in this case, provide enough explosive power to crack the cast-iron grenade body.

"Hey, Sarge, you're some cool head," chortled Mike. I could not summon a response.

"Look at them guys. Man, did they ever move!" Mike continued his inanity. "Was that ever a wake-up call? . . . or I'll kiss your ass."

Sergeant Imo slowly uncoiled and rose from his balled-up defensive posture. He unsheathed his trench knife, the one he honed razor-sharp when he wasn't cleaning his machine gun. Before anyone else had the presence of mind even to move, he jammed his left elbow into Mike's solar plexus, and when the hulking Irishman sought to double up from the blow, Imo held the knife point at his Adam's apple, a tiny trickle of blood indicating how close. Imo's mouth worked as if he wanted to speak, but words wouldn't come. He spoke volumes anyway by holding the knife point on its target for several seconds.

"Hey, guys, I didn't mean no harm," mumbled a chastened Mike the Mick. "It was just a little joke, you know," he trailed off, eyes downcast, shaken by the ferocity that radiated from the furious MG sergeant.

"You ever come near me or any one of my machine gunners, you're dead meat," Imo was finally able to spit out.

He turned to the rest of us, shrugged in helplessness, and sheathed his knife. None of us added a word. Mike the Mick meekly retreated to the dark basement sleeping area.

That incident was ancient history a day or so later when five Fourth Platoon men were seated in a semicircle in the dayroom. They were glum and moody. There had been an 88 barrage concentrated a few houses up the street, and a First Platoon rifleman had stuck his head in to accuse our gang of drawing enemy fire to them with smoke from the fire we stovepiped down their way from our precious coal stove. Our guys released some tension of their own by telling him to piss off, but it failed to restore spirits.

Common Senses

$$\longrightarrow\!\!\!\!\!\rangle\!\langle\!\langle\bullet\rangle\!\rangle\!\langle\!\!\longleftarrow$$

In every one of my letters that piled up at home, tumultuous emotion and trauma had thwarted my ability to describe fully, on a one-page mailing form, just what war was to me. The words I came up with had the stale flatness of a snapshot taken of a skidding, roaring race car passing on the track at high speed. The print, returned a week later, conveys no snarl, no roar, no smell of exhaust, oil, and rubber, no sense of blinding speed. When you display the blurred picture, you can only mumble to the unimpressed viewer: "Hey, you had to be there!" Such was the task of describing battle.

The swishing 50mm mortars, moaning heavy mortars, snarling 88s, shrieking screaming meemies, and whip-snap, high-velocity antitank missiles created distinctive sounds before they exploded that could be partially captured in the language of "sounds like." But when they struck? I couldn't come up with a satisfactory word-picture of a cataclysmic explosion.

Part of my frustration was dealing with concussion, waves of explosive-propelled air so physically disordered that they were almost visible, like cartoon-style, speeded-up roiling thunderheads pierced by brilliant thunderbolt claps. But the flashes and stars we saw came from in back of the eyes, not through their lenses. The physical consequences were bleeding ears, bloodshot eyes, and sometimes instant death. Concussion signaled that the projectile had been blown into flying steel shards. If concussion didn't get you, shrapnel surely would.

So many lethal weapons: Schu mines that blew away a foot; Bouncing Betty mines that sprang from the ground and exploded at waist height; Potato Masher grenades; Panzer-Faust rockets operated by soldiers and civilians alike; hysterical burp guns; heavy MGs; and MP 44 rifles. Their sounds and smells were mixed with rumblings of Panzer tanks, or the deep-throated roar of sixty-eight-ton King Tiger* behemoths. Strafing from low-flying planes came closest to resembling what we perceived of that action as it was portrayed in the movies. Whoosh! And they were gone before you could even hit the ground, leaving telltale holes chomped in a long line along the ground and missing you only by luck.

I was anxious to sit down with family and friends and straighten out for them the unreality portrayed in newsreels and movies of what battle was really like.

On a home television set, the boundless intensity of war is miniaturized, limited by the mechanical devices recording and playing back the noise of battle. The fiercest explosion is at a level no more ear splitting than a shout, a snare drum rim shot, or a puffing locomotive. Tumultuous sounds are conveniently downsized to fit the living room. We listen to the sounds of D-Day, the salvos of cruiser guns, rocket launchers, aerial bombs, machine-gun and artillery fire from all quarters—a huge panorama of the largest and noisiest battle concentration ever assembled. The home version is no louder than the recorded strains of a symphony orchestra. Those who were in battle squirm in discomfort and frustration to observe grand-scale pandemonium compressed into such a tidy, civilized package.

The cacophony and compounded decibels of battle noise defy description. When I finally returned home, I tried to explain by recalling for my folks the earth-shaking boom when we hired that guy to dynamite stumps in a woodlot we were clearing. I asked them to combine that noise with the clap and rumble of a big

---

* Also known as the PzKpfw VI Tiger II

summer thunderstorm, and then throw in the din that awed our family when we took the "Maid of the Mist" boat ride at the foot of Niagara Falls. I asked them to imagine that while all that was going on, someone was simultaneously boxing their ears with ham-sized, meaty palms. I had more elements to add, but by then I felt foolish enough, and ended with a less than satisfying "never mind."

The smells of war. The cascade of odor in battle, of course, is missing in any type of picture. Only by being there can one experience the acrid, nose-twitching odor of burnt primers and powder that accompanies the boom and tremor. You must be cold, miserable, and wet to have etched in your memory the unique clinging, leathery, sweaty stink of GI wool socks. Even death has its own distinctive smell, from an extremely subtle perfume, to a cloying stench that sticks in the back of your throat and gags you as corpses grow old. Rotting farm animals have a less penetrating odor, but still enough to make you catch your breath.

The smell of death penetrates with a deeper sensing than smell alone. Shortly after my return to the States after the war, I was waiting to board a train at Pennsylvania Station in New York City. War was not part of my musing, when suddenly, like a dark cloud descending over the cavernous station loading area, the confusing and sickening feeling that goes with being in the presence of combat death swept over me. The hair on the back of my neck rose. I was more disturbed at feeling the sensation in these peaceful surroundings than with by phenomenon itself. Then, on the adjoining platform, I spied a somber group of GIs unloading caskets from a mail car, piling dead soldiers on dollies for transport elsewhere.

These were sealed boxes, not body bags. I cannot imagine even the slightest whiff of decay escaping any of the airtight containers. So why, why just then, did the presence of battle death return so vividly, so powerfully? Perhaps there are pervading sensations clinging to death that range beyond its actual smell. Some people may feel it when visiting crypts in ancient churches. But it is nothing like the atavistic revisiting of battle death that soldiers have experienced through the ages.

There were other military-life smells. Back in the field kitchen, GI yellow soap and the flour-grease fumes from cooking pancakes that transported me to winter breakfasts at home. Coffee. Even heating the powdered version caused an olfactory twinge evoking brighter times and cherished interludes. No infantryman who served in the European theater of operations (ETO) will forget the smell of sticky Cosmoline gun-metal preservative, of oil used to clean weapons, chlorine in the drinking water, flea powder, pine pitch from freshly severed branches, fresh-dug earth, or tank, truck, and jeep exhaust fumes.

The battleground had its own unique smells, mainly things that burn: greased metal, motor oil, tires, paint, houses, coal briquettes, waxed cartons, candles, bonfires, flesh. There were uniquely German smells: cabbage, sour-rye bread, cheese, and sausage carried by soldiers, stale-sweat wool, harsh tobacco, sugar beets (fresh and rotten), turnips, cherry preserves, and yes, even sauerkraut. Household walls and plaster blown to bits and exposed to weather had their own forlorn, unique odor, as did manure piles left before the animals were killed.

Winter war lacked color and cheerful light. Our battlegrounds were like a World War I movie scene: a black and white background overlaid with blobs of gray for the enemy, dull olive drab for us. Man-made illumination was so lacking that it took the lighted Statue of Liberty and downtown Manhattan to make us dogfaces realize that we had existed in a virtual blackout. The only bright lights in Europe were in the operating theaters of hospitals. Even after combat, with electric service partially restored, fuel shortages left lighting spare and dim in Europe's desolate towns and cities.

Beyond common physical senses were unexplainable feelings, almost all about death. Even in a circle of close family members and best friends, it was too wrenching to describe a battle death, too close to describing what might well have been your own demise. Families of our enemy and most Europeans had seen, and had often themselves been participants, in death by war. Americans, sheltered for generations from conflict on their own turf, had been insulated from the realities of sweeping, violent death. How to tell them?

To try to describe a fellow running around like a chicken with its head cut off is one thing. It is something else to describe a young American beheaded, jerking, kicking, fingers flexing spasmodically for what seems an interminable period while blood spurts with final heartbeats from severed neck arteries. Men do not fall instantly and remain perfectly still like the guys in black hats shot by Buck Jones in the Westerns, or like uniformed soldiers, both friend and foe, mowed down in war movies. In real war, they twitch, they flop, they tremble, they void themselves, they whimper, swear, cry, yell.

Battle wounds are grisly, messy, painful. Severe and fatal injuries are so overpowering that they demand the only relief nature provides: moans and screams and entreaties. Only men whose deaths occurred instantly were denied those final utterances.

One forlorn fatality in our platoon was Willy Anderson, a machine-gun ammo bearer who had survived at his craft for several weeks. When the squad hit the ground for incoming artillery, little Willy would drop to one knee, bow his head as far as he could, and remain in that compact posture until the all-clear. Repeated warnings and direct orders to fall flat did not alter Willie's behavior, and we gave up in frustration, admonishing him to keep his helmet over his ass if he wouldn't lie flat. Arguably, however, he made a pretty small target, all balled-up like that, a more difficult target certainly for plunging tree bursts. The rest of us preferred flatter profiles. Hugging the ground gave us a feeling of security, even if it did make us a larger target for tree bursts.

After heavy enemy shelling during a major winter attack in the black Hürtgen forest, Willy was discovered along a wooded trail in his characteristic kneeling position, stone dead. He did not fall over on his side. In fact, he appeared not to have stirred at all when he was hit. We did not know what caused his fatal wound or where it was on his body. No one had heard him cry out, if indeed he made any sound when hit. The confusion and haste of conflict required bypassing his silent, almost praying, form. Our losses were so severe in that attack that both our dead and those of the

enemy lay where they fell, some for several days. It was wrenching to hurry by Willy's statue-still, helmeted form. We didn't even
have a spare camouflage cloth or blanket to throw over him, and
no place to take him if we had been able to move his body.

Willy was one of dozens wounded or killed in that desperate
action. All units were so short of manpower that our platoon was
forced to contribute a volunteer for an afternoon to help Graves
Registration police up the many American bodies in the kill zone.
I felt that the work detail could prove permanently unsettling to
any line soldier assigned. By then I was a four-stripe staff sergeant
in charge of the entire section of the three mortar squads of the
Fourth Platoon. It occurred briefly to me that I ought to take on
the unpleasant assignment myself. No way. Army-wise, I passed
the buck. I could tolerate viewing a dead body, but found very
unnerving the sight of parts—a hand, arm, headless torso, entrails,
genitals, exposed bones, or the worst, an unidentifiable chunk of
human flesh that resembled some kind of roast in a meat market
display case.

Unable to face sending an old friend or proved trooper to do
something I wouldn't undertake myself, I pointed to a replacement private so recently arrived that I could only call out the first
name that came to mind.

"Dogface! Yeah, you there! Go with that T-4 from Headquarters
Company and he'll detail you the rest of the afternoon." "Dogface"
trudged off in unknowing innocence. He never came back, nor
did I ever see the Headquarters sergeant again. Nor did I want to
see either of them ever again. Perhaps the first time poor Doughboy picked up a dead GI by his feet and the rest of the body stayed
where it was, the horror destroyed his ability to cope.

I never did spell out how men died, or what they looked like in
death, when I got back home. Not to my family, not even when
reminiscing with old service buddies.

Winter Bath

Friendly Belgian natives had outfitted a homey, warm dining room next to the U.S. Army rear-area shower point and rest camp. The chow was a welcome relief from boxed rations and field kitchen fare: fried veal cutlets, boiled potatoes (real, not dehydrated), canned string beans, freshly baked bread with loads of butter and tasty local jam, real milk, and hot apple pie. Maybe the apples were canned or dehydrated, but with a piece of warm cheese, dessert was a lip-smacker. The entire meal was served on china plates, a wondrous change from the usual quick-to-cool aluminum mess kit, and with silverware in place of the big spoon I packed for use with all foods set before me.

I had been rotated in mid-January 1945 from our defended village to a rear-area supply depot with a truckload of frontline troops to take our turn at cleaning up. A few minutes before eating, I had taken a hot shower, the first since—when? Let's see. We had been on the front lines for a month. And before that, it had taken three weeks to get from England to the front just inside the German border. No showers in that stretch. So it must have been two months since I had removed my clothing, much less washed all over.

A well-stocked supply room issued new OD long johns, wool outer pants, a prickly wool shirt, and thick socks that felt good inside my combat boots. I turned down the BVD-type underwear that provided no warmth. Living as we did outdoors, too many underclothes had proved to be just one more obstacle to digging out your pecker when you needed to go, and go fast. I turned down a new green field jacket in favor of keeping my faded tan, extra-long combat coat, which came down over my hips. That extra length, plus the heavy sweater and blanket strips or scarf I wrapped around my kidney area, provided me adequate, if not complete, protection from the cold.

Despite the warm room, I was strangely uncomfortable and a little bit shivery. The new clothing was scratchy and did not snuggle to my body like the smelly rags I had just discarded. No one back home (on the front lines) had complained about my odor. When you live outside fulltime, B.O. (as in the Lifebuoy Soap ads) just isn't a problem. The only smell I associated with my body over those unwashed weeks was the pungent flea powder we shook down the front of our shirts and pants when we experienced an itch that might herald an invasion of "crotch crickets."

Actually, the clothing I turned in had served me well over those many weeks. First, there was the cold, windy, wet boat ride across the English Channel and in the LST which dumped us on the beach in France; then, drafty freight cars to Liège, Belgium; canvas-covered trucks to the front lines; the attack; and roughing it outside for weeks during one of Germany's coldest, snowiest winters.

Rarely were any of us really warm and comfortable. For us dog-faces, there was no relief, no warm home and soft blankets to drain away the dregs of cold. It was like standing on a cold street corner all night, then all the next day, then for a week, never being invited inside. We simply had to endure. Oddly enough, we got somewhat used to being perennially cold. We looked beyond discomfort to the practicalities of avoiding frostbitten toes, fingers, and ears. Only rookies or self-destructs contracted trench foot any longer. We did get to sleep in our bombed-out basement, but save a little body heat, that root cellar was cold as all outdoors.

With cold there is an accompanying shroud of misery. Spirits sag. Eskimos are said to be always happy and serene; it must take countless generations of exposure to cold to leave anyone happy about being frozen half to death all the time. No wonder those simple bastards live in snow huts and eat whale blubber, I figured. I hated being cold. It made me grumpy and frosted over the sense of humor we so needed to endure frontline life.

Maybe I was uncomfortable and uneasy in my newly issued clothes because I knew that this temporary complete warmth and comfort would have to give way eventually to relentless cold and suffering. I dreaded going back out in that cold, no matter how well dressed. I wanted more than a shower and a hot meal. I wanted out.

If anyone could have granted my wish to get out of the situation in which we all found ourselves, he sure wasn't at the shower point. A loudspeaker in the dining room dinned that we would be boarding trucks to return to the front in ten minutes. One last swig of coffee, and I busied myself locating my new wool cap, fresh wool mittens, and recovering my rifle. Someone had taken my piece during our brief stay and cleaned it inside and out. Pretty classy joint!

The bumpy ride back to the front left no room for reverie or regret. On one straight stretch of dirt road, we encountered what for us was a first: strafing by enemy fighter planes.

We truck passengers knew something ominous was up when the six-by-six jerked violently sideways and lurched into a ditch that left it tilted, perilously close to tipping over. Tossed on top of each other, we scrambled as best we could out the rear and scattered into the snowy fields on either side if the road. No one had warned us about the possibility of being strafed; a rare bright day had apparently emboldened the Luftwaffe. Our wake-up call to scatter was cannon fire and wing machine-gun bullets striking at intervals behind, then passing over our truck. The flurry of automatic weapons flashed by in an instant blur. The planes came and went so fast at low altitude that by the time any of us got out of the canvas-topped carrier it was far too late to get even a glimpse. We could not be sure whether there were two or three planes.

They were gone as fast as they had come, and did not return. "Jeezus Kee-rist!" sounded a voice from ground level in the field.

"Here we are, first time we had clean clothes in two months, and already I pissed my pants. Shit!"

I sat up, wiped snow and mud from the rifle that a few minutes before had been dry and sparkling clean, and felt the familiar cold return as moisture seeped from the wet snow into my clothing and enveloped my body. I hadn't wet my pants, but maybe I should have. It might have been the one warm spot in a returning siege of relentless chill.

Back in the truck, relief at our narrow escape loosened the tongue of a rifleman I had known since Stateside. He told me he wished Sergeant Shepherd had been pinned down with the rest of us during the strafing attack. It would serve him right. I hadn't thought about the First Platoon squad sergeant since we entered combat. So, he was gone. So what?

"What ever happened to that prick?" I asked my friend, choosing the description to fit Shepherd's wide reputation as one mean bastard.

"Got what was coming to him" was his terse answer. Then, responding to my awakened curiosity, he elaborated in hushed tones how Squad Leader Shepherd got an early ticket back home.

Staff Sergeant Shepherd had worse enemies than the Germans he never encountered. He suffered a shattered thigh several yards before even reaching the LD on our first day. My informant said his expression resembled one he had seen on the face of a lady badly injured in an automobile accident in front of his house one time: a puzzled, goofy look, eyes glazed with disbelief, then a temporary demeanor of serenity. He was quickly left behind as his squad joined the attack.

But good old Shep was no auto accident victim. His injury came about because he was the most unfair and vindictive sergeant in the battalion, much less our company. The Second Rifle Squad he supervised included five disillusioned ex-air corps cadets and former ASTP (college Army Specialized Training Program) students. They formed a conspiracy and drew straws to see who got to carry out the promise they had made their leader one night toward the end of Stateside training.

While chickenshit is as common to infantry privates as it is to a chicken roost, Sergeant Shepherd made petty harassment an obsession above all other passions. It consumed his every waking moment. So, back in camp, a committee from his rifle squad caught up with their despised squad sergeant on a deserted training field that also served as a shortcut to the base noncom club. Careful that there was no one within earshot, the committee told Shepherd plainly that if he didn't cut out the chickenshit, he would be properly dealt with if and when the company was ever thrown into combat. His men flat-out told him he'd be shot. Shep paid no attention to the warning, devising, instead, even more sadistic tortures for his charges, and in particular, for the "sissy airplane drivers and schoolboys."

He may have thought the youngsters' threats were empty; after all, they were always fooling around, and their sophisticated chatter often went right over his head, Shep's own sense of humor being limited to a faint smile when he ran over a cat, pulled wings off a fly, or poured out a trooper's canteen during a twenty-five-mile march.

No Second Squad member ever confessed to the shooting, nor told how the deed was done. Under cover of the noise of the incoming machine-gun bursts that killed Coleman, someone put an M1 round through Shepherd's thigh as he climbed the hill to the LD. The wish that he be a victim of the airplane strafing suggested they had done him a favor, sparing him being killed or badly wounded in combat. But he would live with a game leg and the haunting memory that he was so despised that his own men did him in.

The harsh revenge served on Shepherd was devised and executed by the better educated, and supposedly most civilized, members of his squad. While infantry training sought to foster unit conformity, it took combat to engender a cohesive fraternal bond. The five college kids in Shep's squad were bound together by their civilian background and collegiality. Bitter and disillusioned at having their privileged wartime careers rudely terminated, they possessed the imagination to assess better than most of their fellow squad members that they were being turned into cannon fodder with a high likelihood of being killed. This demeaning downgrade was wrought by the same government that had earlier declared them among the Chosen. Once combat-hardened, they would have ignored Sergeant Shepard. Trained to kill, their first combative act was to eliminate the homeland practitioner of base humiliation.

Even though I kept my ears open after the confessional in the shower truck, I failed to identify Shep's assailant. Finally, one of his college boys, a five-stripe platoon sergeant by the end of combat, let slip that Sergeant Shepherd was supposed to be shot in the ass, but that the man executing the sentence was such a lousy marksman that he hit him down in the thigh. I guess my informant had been trying to tell me something when he admitted being unlucky as hell when it came to drawing straws. I already knew he was a crummy shot.

CHAPTER **3** | # HARD ROAD TO REMAGEN

Dreaded Second Round

———————◅《◉》▻———————

We hiked in the dark to the rear from the ruins of our familiar Bulge village on well-worn but frequently shelled supply routes, through the cleared mine fields, to our initial line of departure and the village a mile behind it that now served as regimental headquarters. The tattered core of our original group that had launched our first attack was convinced we were on the way to a long, well-earned rest in a far-rear area. Our heavy losses and privation would be rewarded. We were still well under TO (table of organization) strength, despite the large influx of replacements—further reason to expect a pause in the fighting.

So long to my good old foxhole in the hedgerow. So long to our sandbagged "dayroom." So long to the pricks who'd been shooting at us with such impunity. Gotta believe, we're headed for good times!

The American First and Ninth Armies were on the move again. The enemy-held town that had looked down on our defensive position for over a month would be the attack objective of a force approaching its flank and better positioned to make a move from level or higher ground. Our option would have been straight up the hill, head-on into the embrasures of the pillboxes covering our position. Anyway, we'd had enough for the last few weeks. Let someone else take on those bastards. We were headed for safety, security, and a good long rest.

Our company arrived on foot, tired, and sweaty despite the cold, at the motor pool behind regimental headquarters. It took the typical four hours of nighttime confusion to organize and load our guys and the rest of the downsized battalion into a convoy of six-by-six trucks. As it grew light, K rations were passed out to eat in transit. The trucks took off finally for points unknown. We old-timers were sure our destination was rest camp. We passed time on the drafty, frigid ride describing to each other the cozy rewards that would greet us at the recreation area: beer, beds, hot food, showers, new clothes, maybe even skirts! We invented visions of being delivered by truck to the lobby steps of a luxury hotel in Liège, Brussels, maybe even Paris!

After intermittent stops and starts, some for piss call, it was near dusk on a short, dour day when our part of the convoy crammed into a cobblestone-paved square in an unnamed town. Chilled to the bone, we stiffly off-loaded. Like the village we had left, there were no civilians, no live animals, no undamaged houses or barns. Consistent was the general, desolate, unkempt look of a battle-ground, rather than of a community once home to regular people. Discarded equipment and wrecked vehicles, U.S. and German, said the town had done plenty of hard time as contested territory.

So this was the fucking rest camp! Screwed again! I'd never, ever again believe an upbeat rumor.

The advance party had spent the day ferreting out acceptable quarters and passed out billet assignments. My mortar squad and Imo's machine gunners lucked out by drawing a small, weathered barn that still had some of its roof and enough siding to afford protection from the cruel north wind. Luckily, it contained a large stack of fodder. In short order we tore into the pile, fashioning hay-lined nests for a little protection from the bitter, windy night. We spread out fart sacks that had been brought up with our trucks, and answered chow call.

A kitchen truck had preceded us. Hot S.O.S., plenty of bread, and gallons of coffee restored strength, but induced a desperate call for much-needed sleep. Our two squads worked into their hay like dogs turning repeatedly to make just right a chosen spot to bed down. We were asleep quickly, drowning the bitter disap-pointment that we were to have no vacation.

I had barely drifted off when the captain's runner summoned me and other squad leaders to report immediately for a briefing at the company CP. I hurriedly put on my socks and boots, the only clothing I had removed, slung the M1 rifle strap over my shoulder and stumbled down to the former pub that now was Captain Goodspeed's domain. The Old Man (GI-talk for commanding officer, but literally true in Goodspeed's case) looked worn and disheartened. He made a deliberate attempt to perk up as we filed into the CP, frost covering clothing exposed to our breath.

"Boys, we fall out at 4 a.m., head for new positions, and form up for an attack," the CO announced. "We will be the lead element in a new offensive to secure a bridgehead over the Roer River, and thereby access to the Cologne Plains and the Rhine River. Make no mistake about it . . . this is a major operation. And they've picked us to be the point," he ended lamely.

The captain spread out an aerial photo and a German road map. We gathered around, still unwilling to comprehend this alternative to the wishful thinking that had prepared us for warmth, luxury, and most important, safety. I couldn't wait for the briefing to end so that I could return with shredded hopes to the solitude of my haystack in the barn.

I knew I needed a good rest to endure what promised now to be a most trying day. Sleep usually settled in on me like a protective cloak when I was overtired, scared, and threatened. But the crushing news that we were to skip R&R (rest and recreation) and indeed go into new and unknown trials of combat pierced my mind like an irritating, tiny, hot wire. I was agitated, writhing with the agony of pending doom, unable to believe fully, or accept, the bad fortune that had befallen us.

Until now my existence in the military had been endured much as I had coped with other temporary disruptions in my life. YMCA camp, the summer I lived with an unsympathetic family while my parents were away, my first stay away from home at school, even the first seventeen-week course of basic training. All those experiences had a definite, predictable term. They were mere interruptions in life that could be tolerated and ticked off on the calendar as the days passed. I was as sure my pleasant life at home would resume as I had been sure that Dad would send money if I ever really needed it.

I expected combat to be the same. I had confidence that after a period, the end of the Bulge for instance, I would be able to see my way clear to normalcy for a while. Assignments so far in the military had had a predictable life, an end point. They just could not keep us in action forever. It was supposed to end, like field maneuvers always did. For Christ's sake, even the flyboys stood down after so many flights. How many patrols, shellings, and firefights did we have to endure before respite?

There was no talk of an end or even a pause in our commitment to action. What had heretofore been annoying glitches in life had been swapped for the worst, permanent sentence imaginable. Without even a chance to be sick, I was terminal!

Lying in the hay, I harshly revised, too, my personal criteria for survival. I considered my body and soul simply "on loan" to the government. Like others jerked from an easy civilian and civil life, I measured my personal tolerance for what I had to endure by how much my comrades were able to take. If they didn't break, neither would I. Now the choice was which of us died first, no our matter individual endurance, strength, or battle skill. I'd seen enough battered bodies to conclude that I was living on borrowed time, running away from the law of averages.

In my heart I did not feel like I was really a soldier, despite harsh exposure to combat. I was a guy from a nice American home, with a predictable selection of future prospects in life. The most soldierly thing my folks had to remember me by was an over-exposed photo of myself in uniform, taken in a curtained booth at the railroad station. Good old John Boy wearing a funny hat and an ill-fitting uniform. That's all they would have to remember me by. Except for my letters. I should have written more.

Fast evaporating was any conviction that, after a purely lucky start, I had become experienced enough to keep myself alive beyond ordinary odds. I prided myself on being something of a survivor. I'd even reviewed casualties in our company and concluded that privates were far more likely to be casualties than soldiers with rank. Of course there were a lot more privates, but I didn't factor ratios; I just took comfort in the more likely survival of an experienced sergeant. Now I wondered.

I resorted briefly to my private drill of planning personal moves that seemed most likely to preserve my life on the battlefield. There didn't seem to be any attractive choices. I curled up tight in the hay and, for the first time in the service, I gave way to tears.

Big, tough infantry sergeant, lying in the hay with his loaded thirty-aught-six rifle and a bandoleer of bullets. Clutching the hand grenade hung on his lapel. Lethal trench knife digging into his thigh. Nitro-starch explosive taped to his trench shovel. A defenseless, broken child, dissolved in tears. I grimly remembered an old sing-song saying: "Ain't got no Ma, Ain't got no Pa. I'm a Son-of-a-bitch." That was me: one lonely, cold, scared SOB.

Before I could catch any shut-eye, the company messenger arrived like a scythe-bearing symbol of death and rousted me out to assemble my cannon fodder and turn to the killing fields.

I stumbled to my feet, caught my balance, and took a deep breath. Time had been so short that I hadn't bothered to remove my boots a second time. I felt for the nests my men had burrowed in, and shook them hard to bring them out of their deep stupors.

"All right, men. Get with it. Fall out of them sacks. Fall in outside. Uniform of the day: fatigues and leggin's. Let's go. Do it! Do it now! Saddle up. Get these men out of the hot sun. Let's go!" All by-rote mouthings of a real basic-training sergeant.

I ran into Imo in the dark, busy awakening his gun crew.

"Let's go get them heinies, Sergeant," I challenged, with forced good cheer.

"Bet your ass, Sarge. Let's have at 'em!" I heard the familiar clank as he picked up the machine gun he had slept with.

We two coaches were the first out on the playing field. The men straggled out one after the other.

"Third Mortar Squad present and accounted for," I sounded off to Lieutenant Jewell and the first sergeant.

Mortar section leader Staff Sergeant Foote ordered my squad to climb onto the cold metal floor of the truck and accepted a hand to hoist himself up to the hard wooden bench.

We were ready to face the cold, the wind, and our next disaster.

Fight in the Open

Soldiers of Able Company waited uneasily in the dark, cobblestone square of an obscure German farm village,* stomping on one foot and then the other to encourage circulation in the subzero cold. Raw fear supplanted the vague dread that had preceded our first taste of battle. Underlying worry about the unknown had been overlaid by searing, recent experiences of reality. The broken instruments of war scattered around us served as silent, grim reminders of the violence that lay ahead. The darkest dark just before dawn was chilling, depressing. Those lucky enough to have woolen facemasks produced white, clown mustaches as their exhalations instantly turned to frost on the fabric. Even the metal of our guns seemed to draw warmth away from our bodies.

The temporary flush of victory and puffed-up self-confidence from our survival in the Bulge were rudely destroyed by the new attack order. We were embarking without pause on an even more frightening adventure, a new type of ground warfare. We were not to attack, conquer, and hold. We were to attack and attack and attack, in open country, a desperate, back-against-the-wall quarry

---

* It was not uncommon for the troops at the time to have no idea where they were on the large-scale theater map of operations, or "The Big Picture."

that would use his familiarity with home turf to exact from us a huge price in dead and wounded as long as we pursued him.

My own sense of foreboding was so profound as almost to compel that I faint, be paralyzed, unable to march forward. The bravado with which Imo and I had rousted out our men was fast fading as I contemplated my own sad fate. If only I wasn't a sergeant, I lamented. I'd hide back in the barn, plead insanity, wail and roll on the ground, or maybe clam up and never again in my life utter a single word. My squad was dumb enough to heed orders and climb into the back of a truck. A hand reached down to give me a lift, and I reluctantly assumed my drafty position by the tailgate.

The battalion moved before gray dawn broke that cold, cold morning, to establish a new front line. A short truck ride and we off-loaded in wind and snow under vague orders to hike to and occupy a field and woods above the unseen town that was our next objective. Judgment was that we were too exposed to risk further transportation in vehicles, though it was to be quite a hike to the new line of departure.

On the long march, I carried a regular thirty-six-pound load of mortar rounds, a light carbine in place of my usual M1, grenades, ammo clips, rations, and poncho. As we slogged along the icy road, my eyes got heavier and heavier. I knew what to do. I asked Second Mortar Squad ammo bearer, Pvt. A. J. Potter, to guide me, as he had on occasion during forced marches in Stateside training.

A. J. knew the drill. All I needed was a hand at my elbow to keep me from straying right or left. Somehow I managed uneven ridges, even holes in the path. My balance worked even as I slept. My feet kept moving forward. Direction was my only problem and A. J. took care of that. How long did I march and sleepwalk at the same time? Maybe ten minutes, maybe longer. Whatever the length of time, they were minutes away from the reality of war.

I awoke on that cold, blizzardy march as a spoken warning was passed back down the line: "Eyes left, up at the crossroads."

The admonition was to spare us the sight on the right of three men from an American machine-gun crew, sprawled dead at the intersection. I might have missed the scene completely had not the warning come down the line. As it was, I couldn't resist looking, nor could others. I allowed my eyes to dwell on a dreadful, surrealistic scene.

Whatever had destroyed the three men would never be known. Since it was an intersection, maybe artillery had hit in their midst. Or, being an MG crew, maybe they had been wiped out by counterfire. Or it could have been a land mine, but no vehicle was around to support that scenario. The steel-jacketed gun was scarcely distinguishable, ground deeply into the earth by truck wheels and tank tracks. Whatever the reason, their deaths had probably occurred the day before when the route was a virtual no-man's-land.

The task of reconstructing what had happened to these American soldiers was made impossible by their present condition. Streams of American tanks and other heavy vehicles passing the intersection with dim blackout lights during the night had flattened the unseen bodies like raccoons run down on a busy highway. The forms were ironed flat by the ponderous machinery that had rolled over them. Even their helmets were crushed like tin cans. Buck sergeant's stripes could still be made out on one trampled sleeve. One man's lower legs and feet appeared not to have been in the line of traffic. It was as though some macabre artist had imposed a three-dimensional element onto a grisly two-dimensional tableau. New boots, too. Replacement troops? We'd never know.

Scarcely awake, I took in the grisly scene, dropped my head again, and lapsed back into semiconsciousness. If sleep to that point had been fatigue induced, what followed was 100 percent escape.

A long time after my walking nap, we finally stopped marching and scattered around in a large pasture, starting fresh foxholes tactically dispersed to the satisfaction of Company Commander Goodspeed. We were cold and desperately tired, and it made me ache even more to see his thirty-eight-year-old, bent-over figure continually moving here and there to adjust our positions and check on our welfare. Any thoughts I had of giving in to weariness and suffering and fear were shaken off by the example the Old Man set. It had become obvious that the attack would not be until the next day. The short day was about done. The outfit was stopped for the night.

We faced new living conditions with sickening dread. In this next phase of fighting, no longer would we have a familiar "home" base. No more smelly but safe cellar, dayroom, or reusable outpost foxhole. As the cheerless, bone-chilling day grew pitch dark, we had no place to return to, no refuge, no familiar spot to stop and rest, no comfort. Hopes evaporated that there would be a hot meal. Homeless, we had to make do with boxed K rations or chocolate D bars in the new foxholes we blasted with nitro starch and dug as deep as waning energy permitted.

We were henceforth destined to fashion some sort of burrow each night with blistered hands, sore muscles, diminishing strength, and growing despair. The nightly hole, shallow or deep, was needed as much for protection from the raw wind and sub-zero temperatures as from enemy fire. After dark, cold formed around us like wet concrete poured over our sweat-drenched bodies.

While the absence of a home base was the most unsettling difference between static and mobile warfare, there was also desolate loneliness for GIs in a wide-open battlefield. We were too far apart to receive comfort from any companionship, save occasionally a foxhole buddy when we had time to dig deep and wide enough for two. Mostly we had to settle for hasty, individual, shallow slit trenches. We enlisted men had only a general sense of the whereabouts of the company as a whole, and no idea of where we, our battalion or regiment, were in relation to the "front."

In my shrunken world the first night of our new attack, I was painfully mindful of my own lonely plight, and just vaguely aware that there were one or two shallow foxholes nearby. For the most part, I was abandoned to my own fears, doubts, and thoughts. Where to turn for support, sympathy, understanding, confession? No place. No one to talk to.

I bitterly regretted my own decision to dig in alone. As the company scattered over the many acres of open field we were to occupy, my four-man Third Mortar Squad was ordered to dig in with the Third Rifle Platoon. Not an unusual assignment. Third Platoon was to lead the company attack the next morning, and we were to attack with them and provide support. But for now we were lost in holes scattered over a twenty-acre field that was more like Arctic tundra than an erstwhile grazing area.

I had been a good guy and paired up my two gunners in one hole, the two ammo carriers in another. That left me as squad leader to make out alone. Because we'd be moving out by dawn, I decided to settle for a shallow trench, just deep enough for concealment and shelter from artillery shrapnel. Digging was slowed by frozen clay and large rocks. There were no materials at hand for a log and dirt cover. Once I got the hole long and deep enough for concealment and minimal cover, I lay down to try it on for size, and marked locations in the bottom where I then scooped out depressions to accommodate my hip, elbow, and shoulder. That allowed me to lie on my side with less discomfort.

We had only the clothes on our backs for warmth and protection. Cooling sweat drained off body warmth like an open spigot. My ever-handy rain poncho either had to serve as a liner to separate me from the cold, wet earth, or as a cover to protect from wind and snow turned into fine dust by the extreme cold. I was so buffeted by that wind that I had no choice but to use the poncho as a windbreak and outer wrapper.

Hoarse whispers and muted calls a long time after dark proclaimed that bedrolls were being distributed. I had no idea who dropped one in my hole along with a box of K rations, but I was almost tearfully grateful. Trouble was, I was so cold that I could scarcely manage to line my hole with the poncho, and struggle into the fart sack. I was too cold to feel warmed and comforted, but I hoped the wool-lined bag would protect me from frostbite or terminal freezing. Somehow I struggled out of my boots, squirmed into the bag, and took up as much of a curled position on my side as the narrow confines would allow. The elbow, shoulder, and hip depressions I had fashioned were not ideally located, but I was too beat to care. I succumbed to exhaustion.

As I sank deep into unconsciousness and ethereal dreams, we

were discovered by the enemy and subjected to a fierce artillery bombardment. The Germans had called on their gridded contour maps for battery fire to respond to the very circumstances we had brought about. They raked our field up one side and down the other with 88s and mortars. I was numb, neither alarmed nor frightened. Fatigue drove me far under the threshold of awareness that otherwise would have sparked survival mechanisms.

I slept on, even after awakening briefly when one 88 hit so close as to shake my den violently, crumbling one dirt side onto and partly over my cocoon sleeping bag. I screwed my eyes closed even tighter to shut out the flash of the 88 shell explosions. I dreamed on, knitting up the raveled sleeve of care. I was not aware when the barrage finally lifted.

After unmeasured time, I surfaced slowly to consciousness as hands under my shoulders lifted me to a sitting position, freeing me from the earth that had all but entombed me. It was Rube and a new replacement I did not yet know. It was daylight.

"Sarge. Hey, Sarge! You hurt? You okay? We thought you were a goner for sure from that direct hit. When you didn't come out after the shelling, we waited a while and figured you were a goner. Didn't even call the medics. Well, Jesus! You're moving. Must be okay. It's a miracle. Man, you look like shit. Here, lemme brush you off."

Still grumpy from interruption of my "nap," I struggled out from under the rocks and frozen chunks of dirt, the sleeping bag holding me virtual prisoner as I tried to stand up. The boys helped me out of the dirty sack, assisted me with my boots, and stood back in awe.

"You're a fucking mess, buddy. You sure you don't need to go to the aid station? You okay?"

"Yeah, I'm right as rain, guys. Just catching a little shut-eye," I said dully. I licked my dry lips, tasting the burnt powder that had sifted over me. I had no sensation of relief at being alive, no sense of narrow escape, nothing. Certainly no glimmer of hope.

From the shape I was in, I could scarcely be termed ready and fit to face what would prove to be rougher conditions than most of us could ever have imagined.

No-Man's-Land

========= «‹O›» =========

As a stingy dawn slowly shed light, the one-time pasture we occupied looked like a farm field freshly plowed by a reckless, idiot farmer. Snow cover was visible in only a few patches that were not random shell craters or impact areas covered by earth blown out of the craters. That only three of our company had been killed during the nighttime barrage was an amazing testimonial to the efficacy of the celebrated foxhole. That no one was wounded proved that it took a direct hit to produce a casualty when foxholes were properly prepared. And, by now, we knew how to dig them fast and right.

We had been delivered a clear message that the Krauts were not going to welcome our attempt to capture the key town they held. The squareheads were doubtless chowing down this early a.m., congratulating each other on wiping out the advancing Amis (German counterpart to our "Krauts"). It had been an impressive and unprecedented concentration of German artillery.

As they chewed their greasy sausages, the opposition must also have been smugly satisfied that the invading forces had gotten taste enough of the strength and vitality the defenders of the fatherland were still able to muster. They also had a track record of repulsing three American divisions in their attempts to take this particular objective or kicking them out if they were successful.

The one outfit that had actually occupied the village was driven out with horrendous losses in a bloody counterattack.

Well, the Germans indeed were leading from strength, and prospects of being the fourth unit chewed up at the site were not very cheering. We knew we were in for it soon after a company of Sherman M4 tanks lumbered up from the rear. We foot troops huddled behind them for protection and a little warmth from the engine exhausts. We were poised just back of the crest of the hill overlooking the town. The tanks were set to charge down the road, S-2 (battalion intelligence) having told them there were no mines. The infantry was to scurry along through the woods on each side of the advancing armor and invade and mop up defenders in the town. At least that's what they told us at the briefing. Each of us was mindful of the proven ability of the Germans to plaster us with artillery. "We're standing here with our bare asses hanging out," grumbled a Third Platoon rifleman.

It was plain that no one from high command had ever personally observed the terrain we were expected to traverse or, if he had, he was a fucking pervert under the spell of the enemy. The road for the tanks was probably mined, no matter reports to the contrary. The tanks had no option but to maneuver parallel to the road, not through mature trees, many reduced to stumps. If unable to traverse the road, they were left the horrible choice of lining up on the crest of the hill to deliver fire into the village. There, they would be sitting ducks for armor-piercing 88s.

The Sherman M4 tank weighed in at an impressive thirty-three tons. However, the German Panther D had ten tons more heft, and a 75mm gun of much higher velocity than our 75s. If we were unlucky enough to have Tiger tanks opposing us, they were made up of fifty-five tons of armed fury. If we faced King Tigers, forget it! They were indeed kings of the battlefield, with over twice the weight and firepower of our Shermans.

To a novice, or a remote strategist armed with map pins, the route for our attack through heavy woods looked like prudent concealment, a safe course to pursue. But we had already learned in the Hürtgen Forest what artillery tree bursts do to troops. The heavy nighttime barrages had largely denuded and mangled the woods, making them even more impassable to tanks. Our road maps failed to show the plunging deep ravines that hemmed in our approach. Why anyone had chosen this impassable, impossible ground for fighting was beyond us. But it was the only choice we had. To run away cross-country from this fight would require mountain-climbing gear and lots of luck.

I remained desperately tired after the explosion-induced slumber in my muddy foxhole the night before. My head was still ringing, and it ached behind my eyes. We were all shivering, stomping our feet, clasping gloved hands under arms to induce a little warmth. A couple of men had even dragged along their fart sacks from the assembly area. They stood in them, and wrapped or draped themselves for added warmth, ready to shed the bags when the order came to move out. We weapons platoon men had our heavy ammo loads and guns to carry into battle. Forty pounds seemed like a hundred. Artillery incomers resumed. The kitchen was unable to reach us with a hot drink or even boxed rations.

Section Sergeant Foote placed my four-man mortar squad behind one of the tanks. We were a sorry lot. Humor, even our usual gallows variety, was submerged in misery and foreboding. The unfamiliar throb of the tank engines added to our general disorientation, and threatened to loosen our bowels.

"Move out," echoed down the line. Tank engines went from idle to full-bore. Off they clanked to the brow of the hill, while we dogfaces scattered to both sides, turning to parallel their general direction. We could see no village, no enemy, just mangled pine trees.

Our Shermans had barely reached the ridge when all hell broke loose. One after the other they stopped abruptly as treads were hit, or they went up in spectacular bursts of flame. The vicious crack of high-velocity antitank projectiles was interspersed with whining HE (high explosive). Surviving crewmen crawled from the under-tank escape hatches, running, arms flying, in jerky cartoon-like haste for the woods. There was an occasional report from one of our Sherman cannons, but their fire was fruitless. The high-velocity big rifles on the German tanks could smash one of our tanks from a mile-and-a-half away. The Sherman's 75s could reply effectively from only about a half-mile, and then cause damage only to the side or rear of any of the enemy tanks. Armor-piercing projectiles striking elsewhere on their tanks left only scrub marks.

A look inside a Sherman that had taken a direct hit was stunning. The tank's interior was painted a bright, glossy, hospital white to enhance the dim lighting for the crew. The armor-piercing projectile entered the tank by driving ahead of it a column of molten steel, rendered liquid by the force of the speeding round. The melted metal made up of the tank's armored hide turned into thousands of tiny, red-hot steel bits that caromed off every interior surface they struck. Gray pockmarks were everywhere. It was plain that no one in their path was likely to survive that hornet-swarm of shards.

All too often, when the chassis of the M4 Sherman took a direct hit, it burst into flame. Small wonder its crews called their track-laying fortresses "Ronson lighters." Those not escaping immediately were roasted or pulverized when their magazines of ninety-some 75mm shells went up. It was better to have a tread destroyed and at least stand a chance of escape.

Tanks were not friends of the dogface. Their noisy engines and clanky tracks drowned out the sound of incoming enemy shells and small arms fire. Their mere presence was a magnet for enemy retaliation. At first we felt cheated to be outside, unprotected by their thick armor. That feeling soon gave way to relief at not being locked up in a burning steel death trap. Given a choice of our biggest, toughest armored tank and a foxhole . . . well, hand me a shovel.

"That takes care of following the tanks," said our poet of understatement, Sergeant Imo. "Feel sorry for them bastards." Imo nodded at a dead GI tank officer draped over his turret. "What a way to go. Like fish shot in a barrel. Guess we'd better get on with it." He shouldered his precious machine gun and trudged into the shattered woodlot.

Hunched over to distribute my load of ammo and gear, I scarcely had strength to maneuver a step at a time. Plodding alongside, PFC Oscar Fay plopped down with a grunt, his ammo bag tossed aside. Fartsack Fay had been a mortar man for two or three weeks, with potential to be promoted to gunner. A big, overgrown Irish kid, he must have played guard or center on his high school football team. Right now he was a whiny youngster, wet behind the ears.

"Can't go no further, Sarge. I had it. Gotta lie down. Gotta rest. I'm pooped, I'm through. Blisters killing me," Fay puffed disconsolately. For a moment I didn't know how to react. My first and fervent wish was simply to sit down and join the exhausted lad. I eased my burden to the ground to take pressure off the painful, broken blister on my own right foot. What to do? Oscar's usually ruddy, schoolboy face looked out of focus, as gray and unattractive as a handsome older woman stripped of her party makeup and exposed to unkind morning light. Private First Class Fay had surrendered all personal defenses and pride; no remaining facade of dignity, resentment, or anger; he was a cowering coward.

The Army taught us limits and had proved to us that conditioning and training extended our capabilities. Bayonet drill, forced speed marches (rat races), twenty-five-mile hikes, night exercises. All were designed to push us to our physical limits, each one higher than the last. We learned to assess our own personal stopping points. I had skinny arms. Those long levers limited the chinups I could do. On the plus side, my wiry build was blessed with strong stomach muscles; I had once done one thousand sit-ups without stopping, far more than the required minimum, more than anyone else in the company. But there are finite limits to strength and endurance. Or so I thought.

Fay's physical surrender stirred understandable sympathy, but at the same time threatened serious implications for the cohesion required to maintain us as a unit. I was weary and mind-numbed myself, but recognized that I had to stick with the survivors, not with the quitters. I told Section Sergeant Foote that I had to leave Fay behind and that he was sitting in a very exposed spot for enemy shelling. I picked up my ammo bag and stumbled along to catch up with the rest of my squad. Any idea of tank support was long gone.

Staring down at my shuffling feet, I indulged in a game I played when fatigue grew overwhelming. I counted my steps, vowing that after a hundred, I might stop or quit altogether, or maybe start another hundred. Close behind me neared a groaning, puffing companion. I glanced briefly. It was Private First Class Fay!

Shocked fully alert by the unexpected sight, I looked around. Following close behind us was my section leader, S. Sgt. Leo Foote. I slowed to let him catch up and asked what in the world had happened to get Fay back in the line of march.

"Simple," said Foote, his eyes, too, riveted to the ground just ahead of him. "I just loosened the flap on my .45 holster, took out the old Ithaca, and told Fay to get moving or I'd blow his fucking head off. When I worked the slide and loaded a round, he got the idea and moved on out. Strong kid like him? Shit, no reason he should dog it," Foote ended breathlessly. We plodded on together. I had learned one more secret of how to extend a man's physical limits, and had Foote to thank for it.

Well down the enemy side of the crest, the heavy pine growth was even more devastated. My God! How many shells had it taken to scrub a heavily wooded hillside practically bare? No need to worry about mines. They'd all been blown up by the Krauts' own shelling. We still had not seen the enemy, but they apparently knew where we were. With banshee shrieks, more 88s poured into, mostly over, our position, exploding back in the fields we had occupied the night before. The intense scream was attributable to their barely clearing our knoll, passing just over our heads. How far over our heads became an absolute measurement when an occasional shell caught a remaining treetop or trunk as it sped over. The detonation from overhead sprayed hot fragments far and wide. Random, flying shrapnel caught Sergeant Foote. He fell, clutching a bloody knee and shin.

"Well, buddy, you just made staff sergeant," the mortar section leader grimaced. "Take care of all these squads, buddy. They're all yours now." A quick glance confirmed he was bleeding badly. The platoon was double-timing toward the village, more intent on escaping the barrage area than closing in on any objective. Voices urged me on.

Foote struggled to his feet, and half hopping, half limping, started for the rear-area aid station before pain and shock could immobilize him. Odds of being hit again over that long stretch of enemy artillery coverage were at least as bad as for us moving onward in attack.

I tossed Foote a peremptory salute, and joined the scattering of men limping and staggering down the desolate slope. Private First Class Fay was still humping along with us. At least Foote had left me with a warm, if not very trustworthy, legacy.

I might have stumbled on forever, but Captain Goodspeed materialized, magically it seemed to me, and told us to hold up, seek cover, and await further orders. I made sure my boys got the word, and wondered briefly about the welfare and whereabouts of the two additional mortar squads that were my charge now that Sergeant Foote was gone. I saw a huge crater, the kind made by a big aerial bomb, and tossed into it my ammo bag and the carbine I had swapped for my heavier M1. An 88 struck nearby, propelling me in behind them.

I hugged the greasy, cold dirt on the inner wall of the crater. Behind us was a killing ground, thoroughly chewed up by tanks and shell holes. For all we could see ahead of us, it was the same desolation: muddy craters, splintered wood, broken pine boughs, stumps, tanks and vehicles destroyed in earlier battles, corpses old and new. The objective village was not yet in sight.

Then I realized where I was. This was no-man's-land.

Second Survival

$$\text{====}\ \text{«○»}\ \text{====}$$

The no-man's-land bomb crater in which I sought protection was certainly deep enough, but so big around as to risk being invaded by an incoming artillery round. I clung to the slope of the crater nearest the enemy, apprehensive that an explosion against the far wall would probably be fatal. There was no choice. There was no other place to hide. And I had no energy to seek a new hiding place, if indeed one existed.

My labored wheezing from the forced march through the ruined forest subsided. I dozed fitfully until awakened by a chill that clutched the sweat of recent toil. I had not quite reached that stage of exposure where cold is unfeeling, persuading one to give in to false comfort and drift away, as I had read of happening to people as they froze to death in the wilderness. Cold was still very painful for me, so deep rooted at the moment that pulling up my coat collar and tightening the wool wrap around my middle produced no comforting relief. My blistered feet hurt, which at least indicated they were not frozen.

Before peering over the edge of the crater to take stock of my surroundings, I discovered that I was not alone. In the bottom of the funnel-shaped pit, his lower half covered by oily water that had a skim of ice, was a burly and very dead German soldier. He lay on his side, face averted, so I didn't have to stare him in the

113

eye, as it were. The ice and remnants of melted snow on his gray overcoat said he had been there for quite a while: days, or, in winter's icebox, even weeks.

I took closer inventory of the bomb crater. Allied bomb or German? The only Kraut aircraft we had seen were fighters, and anyway, why would they bomb near their own community? So it had to be an American bomber, back when? The huge hole was a mile away from the objective. About par for our flyboys, I thought wryly.

The weathered guttering on the streaked sides of the crater indicated that the bombing had been a while ago. In addition to my crater-mate, there were other leavings: the bumper and grill of an American jeep, some of the white ID lettering from another division still readable; shattered building materials; and some emptied olive-drab cans that had contained GI C rations. Which side had partaken of the food would remain a mystery. The butt of the Kraut's rifle stuck up from the water, the gun as useless and abandoned as its one-time bearer.

Any humor in the situation remained drowned in the bile of excruciating discomfort and the absence of anyone with whom to share a thought, much less a light word. In place of all or any upbeat thoughts was an instinct that whispered I was mighty close to the end of the line. The silver lining in any cloud I could conjure up was peppered black with gunpowder. Almost indiscernible for the first time was that tiny flicker of hope that told me, way down deep, that no matter the odds, somehow I was going to make it. Even the knot of fear in the stomach that is the constant companion of combat soldiers was anesthetized.

Sliding away were chances for any escape from my plight. I was as frustrated and pissed off as I was destitute. There was no one to whom I could turn with my sad tale, and it was growing likely that there would never be opportunity to tell it, anyway. What would some third party think, to find the bodies of a GI and a stubblehopper in the same open grave?

With labored movements made more difficult because of chilled joints, I edged around the crater, opened the Kraut's greatcoat and went through the shirt and blouse pockets that were above the muddy water. Someone had collected my pal's ID packet and wallet, presuming he'd had one, so he was now an Unknown Soldier. I tugged on his overcoat to tip the guy partially upright, and fished out a hinged, brass tobacco box and companion lighter from his tunic. The ghastly face this exercise revealed caused me to drop him quickly back in his original, reclined posture. He sure as hell hadn't died yesterday!

The box was empty of tobacco or cigarettes, but a handy size for me to use for my own smokes and matches. The lighter looked like a fat lipstick, the top slip-fitted over a machined cylindrical base stuffed with cotton wadding. Wedged between the cotton batting and the cylinder were a half-dozen precious replacement flints. The wick was black and very short. I twisted the nub and lifted it to expose a short collar of white wick, spun the flint-wheel, and to my surprise the lighter worked just fine. I lit up a Chelsea and felt just a little better from the exertion and a good drag of raw smoke.

I thanked Fritz, or whatever the hell his name was, for the souvenir and resumed my station across the bomb crater. We sat in silence broken by shells passing overhead, as many coming from our side now as from theirs. Occasionally a round from one side or the other struck nearby, but none slammed into our bomb-created perimeter. Hours passed.

In the presence of stale death, I had renewed concern over my own imminent end. I definitely didn't want to share the fate of my uninvited guest. Or maybe I was the one who was uninvited.

Prompted by no single event, I started to recover from the doldrums. It was as though I slowly awakened from a fitful, nightmare-filled sleep. That tiny ember of hope flickered, however faintly. I rewrapped and pinned the scarf around my middle, further up over my kidneys, straightened the layers of upper clothing, hiked up my pants, and crawled up to see what lay beyond the German's watery grave.

I heard a voice, and Sergeant Wolcott suddenly appeared before me. I was so startled that my hands began to shake uncontrollably. The knot of fear was back, thank God. He was about as surprised to encounter me. Our ever-resourceful supply sergeant had a cardboard box of K rations, and had been tossing them to anyone he could find, wherever he could find them. "Where the hell you come from, Sarge?" he exclaimed. "I thought I had most of our guys spotted from back up there; but honest, I had you figured a goner back there in the woods when Foote got hit. Here, have breakfast, lunch, and dinner, all in one box. For that matter, I got most everyone covered. So, have two."

In addition to welcome sustenance, Wolcott brought word that we were finally set to move on down into the town. He also told me that Sergeant Foote had taken another hit in the ribs on his way back to the aid station, but that he would probably make it.

Whatever had ignited my energy and resolve in the past to step up and take charge came back to me, as my spark to live had revived moments earlier. I could scarcely recall the recent past; it was only after I dug out the brass cigarette box the next day that the episode with the dead Kraut came back to me. Maybe involuntarily censored recall is the best insulation of all.

I ducked back into the crater and ate the best part of both rations, tossing out the battery acid (powdered lemonade), wolfing down the spam from one box, the canned bacon-and-egg mix from the other. I washed both down with icy, chlorine-treated water from my canteen, ate the fruit bar and even the packets of sugar. I smoked with huge, lung-searing drafts the four Lucky Strikes from one cigarette box and stuck the other in my helmet liner with the toilet paper. Luckies! Maybe I was lucky, too; after all, I'd broken my string of two-dozen-straight boxes of Chelseas in the K rations that had come my way. The newspapers from home said that more doctors smoked Camels. Well, at the front, we needed a treat, not a treatment, and Luckies were a treat.

Heeding a distant shout to form up and move out, survivors emerged from hiding. We were still with the lead platoon, which meant that the other two mortar squads, inherited by me when my section leader was hit, were somewhere behind us. I accounted for everyone in my original squad except the malingerer, Fay. A nasty shrapnel hole in his lower back would allow Fartsack Fay's blistered feet to heal along with his wound, in a white-sheeted fart sack, a hospital bed in England. Lucky bastard! Maybe he and Foote would have adjoining beds, and could chat about the consequences of his boss forcing Fay into battle at gunpoint.

Imo's machine-gun squad, minus one ammo bearer who had lost his entire hand to shrapnel back in the woods, trekked along with us down the dirt road leading into town. My shoulders bunched in anticipation of resumption of artillery or mortars; as a few buildings became visible, I steeled myself for the sweep of enemy machine-gun fire. I was too done in to look for mines and booby traps. I didn't know whether we were just fortunate, or whether the Krauts had left in too big a hurry to lay last-minute traps.

After our chaotic, explosion-filled night and day we walked into town without a shot being fired at us or by us.

During my sojourn in the bomb crater, I had heard one gigantic explosion that I didn't comprehend at the time. I learned that the village had been treated to a special TOT (time on target) saturation by our artillery. For a TOT, the Big Brass identifies a critical target (our village objective) and plans a big surprise. They talk to the really heavy-duty 240mm artillery in the far rear, the 155 Long Toms, the 105 howitzers; and closer in, the SP (self-propelled) howitzers, the 4.2 rifled mortars, cannon company 105s, and the 81mm mortars in our own infantry heavy weapons platoon.

Figuring exactly how long it takes for the projectile to get from each gun to the target, the guns farthest away are touched off first, followed a few seconds later by the next closest group. If properly calculated and fired precisely at the designated times, the result is one deafening kaboom! The shells strike the target area all at one time. Literally hundreds of big explosions, nearly simultaneous, have a profound and demoralizing impact on those who survive, civilian or military. The attacking forces are supposed to pile into the impact area as soon as possible after the TOT to round up stunned survivors, so docile they might as well have been castrated, as indeed some of them might have been by the intense storm of shrapnel.

Our attack timetable had been upset by the destruction of our leading tanks and the devastating defensive barrages we had endured. Apparently no one told the Powers That Be that we were not prepared to conform to the original schedule. So, typical of Army methods, the artillery was called up as originally planned. We were fortunate that the TOT had been so convincing that any Germans lucky enough to live had crept out of town. A small bunch of defenders could have stalled us in our tracks. As it was, we limped and plodded down empty streets of rubble, smoking ruins strewn with the chewed-up bodies of German soldiers. It was already dark.

This late in the war, the German Army was bereft of adequate reserves. They simply could not muster the men or materiel to retake the town as had been done after previous American offensives. We established ourselves in the center of town in a huge, concrete troop shelter that had once been concealed by a camouflaged warehouse, earlier destroyed. We filtered into it not so much for safety, since there wasn't even sniper fire, but because it was the only structure in town not flattened by artillery fire, ours or theirs. We squatted against the wall on the cold, concrete floor. Badly wounded German as well as American GIs occupied bunks in the interior of the concrete monolith.

Working by candlelight and rays from almost-spent flashlights, the uniformed German doctor paid no attention to us milling invaders. He was too busy patching up patients from both sides. Space for new wounded was provided by those who hadn't made it. Bodies were moved from the bunks and lined up by the entrance, awaiting body bags. They didn't do much as a welcoming committee for stragglers finding the shelter. To my relief, I recognized only two of the shot-up GIs.

As the night wore on, other company members joined us, and more information trickled in. The town had been secured by a flanking attack that put friendly forces on the former enemy side of town, assuring our temporary safety. We spent the night taking turns out in the dark, obscured streets, calling to and locating comrades. When we finally called it quits, we took stock. As in our attack in the Bulge, we had again lost half the men in our company. I knew they couldn't all be the replacements, so our original nucleus had been reduced once again. By late February 1945, there were probably seventy or eighty of our original attacking company of 183.

Rumor had it that a lane free of mines was open and that the kitchen and supply trucks would soon reach us. We congratulated each other on being alive. The excitement of awaiting Christmas morning as a kid was no more exhilarating than our anticipation of hot coffee and warm chow in a rubble heap thankfully not under fire.

This phase of battle, possibly even more disastrous than our first action had been, did meld all of us together, including replacements, as battle-hardened veterans. Some of us survivors had been hardened longer than others, and a strange attachment still prevailed among the original company members. But like steel that is repeatedly tempered, perhaps our hardening was rendering us more brittle, leaving us less resilient than those who came aboard later.

No one had the answer to how far we had yet to go, nor what might be the breaking point for each of us before we could get that far.

Uniform of the Day

We were given little time to rest and recuperate in the big concrete shelter we shared with the Kraut doctor and his wounded charges from both sides. We were ordered at daylight to move on out. There were scattered villages to be mopped up, but for the most part we were deployed in open country to "take the high ground" that commanded a view, and hence military superiority, of the real estate below.

My childhood, tin-soldier conception of lines of troops facing each other across a battlefield was just that, childish. In real war, we rarely knew where the "line" was between the enemy and us. We were provided with dayglow-colored ID panels, which were to be spread on the ground along our position to inform friendly aircraft and prevent their strafing or bombing us. The panels were unceremoniously dumped along the way in favor of carrying more ammo or clothing. Anyway, we figured they might be used by the Krauts to point out our positions to strafing Luftwaffe planes, so screw 'em!

Fighting and traveling at the same time in unknown territory created new confusion and discontinuity. Because we were moving into his own backyard, on the way to the Rhine River, Jerry was able to make retaliatory fire efficient and effective. In an exercise I ran through my imagination, I knew damn well that if I had an armed gang to defend our farm back home, I could punish the crap out of any invading force by knowing so well every detail of the land I was defending. I'd have prepared plans and options to thwart his most diabolical plan. The retreating Krauts had that kind of an edge on us.

We had to pay close attention to what we wore and to the equipment load that went everywhere with us. The more experienced a frontline GI, the less baggage he hauled around. Now that I commanded a whole section, I had passed along the mortar sight in its fitted leather case to my new squad sergeant. His gunner carried the mortar, bipod collapsed, strapped with the base plate against the tube. The discharge end of the smooth bore was protected from snow and mud by a leather cap at the end of the carrying strap. The other three men in each of the three squads had their bibs of a dozen 60mm mortar shells slung on one shoulder, carbines dangling from the other.

I had swapped my M1 rifle for the handier carbine, and rigged an extra bandoleer of ammo clips across my chest, Pancho Villa style. Hanging from my neck were Coleman's field glasses. We had all fastened to our cartridge belts a trench shovel, trench knife or bayonet, canteen nested in a cup, and first-aid kit. Over the belt at the back was draped a folded, rainproof poncho, the Army's sensible replacement for the raincoat and tent shelter half we had first been trained to carry. Most of us still had an explosive charge to start foxholes taped to our shovel handles. Every item on the belt was used and useful. We just hoped not to have to get at the first-aid packet very often. And everyone had at least one grenade dangling from a buttonhole or lapel.

The late-issued poncho was welcome and useful, as were new combat boots with two-strap high-tops, sealed by dubbin grease, over which we bloused our pants. Like the old standard leggings, they kept the snow out and provided warmth. It was hard to keep pant legs bloused over boots if you didn't have a condom to tie and circle the boot top so the pant leg could be tucked under securely. That practice lasted over to peacetime, the best way to look sharp. They were not dual-purpose condoms. GIs cut or tore the end to avoid a bubble when tying, at the same time invalidating their intended primary use. Until they caught on, Quartermaster must have wondered about the persistent request for rubbers from a bunch of men miles from the nearest bed or bordello.

I let my pant legs hang outside the combat boots, free, not bloused. I took on less chilling snow that way, no matter how deep it was. Not very soldierly looking, but practical. And the free-hanging pants bottoms dried out more quickly than wadded-up blousing. Not many of us noncoms displayed chevrons. One remaining three-stripe buck sergeant emblem was still attached to one jacket sleeve. My recently awarded four-stripe chevrons never did get delivered or sewn on.

When the poncho was needed, a drawstring secured it tightly at the neckline to keep out a driving rain, and even for a tall man, it was long enough to keep clothing reasonably dry. Best of all, when not on the move, a soldier could squat, pull the strings to close the top opening completely, and hunker down under a little personal teepee that reached to the ground. It provided wonderful protection from snow, rain, and cold wind. Because danger could not be observed while you were enclosed under a tented poncho, a false but comforting feeling of privacy and safety was created.

We checked out each other's requisite equipment and arms, but individual dress had become optional according to what was available and what suited the individual. One ammo bearer stuck with his long overcoat, while most of the men preferred the freedom of a long field jacket over several layers of wool shirts and knitted sweaters, either GI or mailed from home. We all wore GI wool knit caps under our helmet liners. And each soldier tried to blend in and be invisible by wearing either issued white attire, or cobbled-up white covers of purloined bed sheets, tablecloths, any white fabric that could be scrounged. Steel helmets were draped in white cloth strips interlaced with the standard camouflage net cover.

Keeping weapons usable on the move was difficult. Even the meticulous Sergeant Imo had to struggle to keep his machine gun clean and shiny, and even more important, fully operative. I protected the upright muzzle of my slung carbine, which had a knobby grenade launcher, with a small, sample-sized Crackerjack box that had come up with the rations. It was worth a laugh, and it really kept out snow, water, and general moisture, allowing air to circulate so as not to cause the bore and chamber to rust. Not so with those who used condoms to protect rifle muzzles. True, you could fire a rifle through a rubber without harm, but it shut off air flow and promoted furry rust that rendered the weapon useless after as little as one day. We all used a muzzle cover of some kind. None of us wanted to risk plunging a rifle barrel into the mud and having it blow up in our face the next time it was fired.

Until committed to a fire mission, riflemen did not keep a cartridge in the chamber of their rifles, ready to fire. The brass shell casing was bound to turn green with corrosion and weld itself to the chamber wall, making removal of the fired cartridge very difficult at a time when fussing with a stoppage might mean your life.

I often spelled my gunners by carrying the mortar. I had learned early in battle to line both shoulders of my wool shirt with a folded sock, carefully sewed in place as a pad to protect the bony protrusion at the outside end of each skinny collarbone. That pad was an absolute necessity for me to tote a thirty-five-pound machine gun any distance at all. I never could find a soft spot on a machine gun receiver to ride my shoulder comfortably. Stateside, the supply room provided liners to ease shouldering large weapons, but GI pads were long gone; so was my sewing kit. I had to take good care of my makeshift pads.

Those who shoved the packets of toilet paper provided in rations into their pockets soon learned, on the move, that dampness or the wear from marching left them with a pocketful of mush unsuitable for its intended use. Toilet paper was safe and dry only inside the support straps of the helmet liner.

Few in Fourth Platoon carried any kind of a backpack. Ammo and heavy guns were all we could handle. We wore our warmth or relied on the poncho for last-ditch protection. My patented device for maintaining body heat was still that strip of wool, wrapped and safety-pinned around my kidney area and small of the back. Some of us didn't bother to button our flies; convenience for frequent emptying of a nervous bladder was preferable to warmth from pissing your pants that quickly turned cold, chafing, and miserable.

Tragedy was the irresistible urge for a bowel movement right on the verge of, or after the start of, a winter-weather attack. Equipment had to be shed, then resecured. Clothing had to be disturbed with resulting cold and discomfort. The act was hasty, too, with trepidation that a shell might arrive when you were in a virtually helpless position. It was the worst start for what was bound to be a bad day, but still preferable to filling your pants and living with that for hours or days.

I had left myself clearance to the snow, but the athletic feat of wiping without falling into the mess just made nearly did me in. I took a swipe at it, and struggled to my feet with that damp feeling that was to last for way too long. I stuffed, wrapped, fastened, jammed, and arranged my layers of clothing as best I could. Taking a dump had pretty well spoiled the day; I fancied that at least I smelled spoiled. I just hoped I wouldn't have to go again.

When our tattered company took off from a new LD toward its next objective, I stayed back with the company command group temporarily, to establish contact and control of the other two mortar squads in my inherited section. I fell in with the reserve platoon, which was posted at the end of a snowy valley that fell off toward a little settlement Able Company had been ordered to take. The two attack platoons were a good three hundred yards ahead. They were engaged in a lively skirmish, running, falling to shoot and back up other men, making zigzag patterns as they closed in on their objective. Their gunfire was muffled by the snowscape. We could not determine whether they were being met with resistance; if so, it was not slowing them.

The midday sun was bright, and despite white camo cover, the soldiers and their shadows stood out in strong relief against the pure white background. Their tracks, if translated to paper, would have represented textbook perfection for a small-unit infantry skirmish.

For the moment, my distance from the scene relieved me of personal anxiety and allowed me to forget the tension and fear that had to accompany every man in that brave advance. These men maneuvered with the sureness of professionals, and I felt a burst of pride at being one of them.

The Buddy System

————)《●》(————

He had a Mexican first name like Pedro or Pancho or some-thing, but he answered to Stocky or, when his last name was shouted at roll call, to Bourquez.

Problem was, frequently he was not there to sound off at forma-tions in the States. He inevitably ended up in detention after the military police picked him up back at his hometown in Texas, or on rare occasions when he came back on his own. So the moniker Stocky, short for stockade, was hung on him. He was the com-pany's perennial absent without leave (AWOL).

The nickname didn't describe his physique. He was five-ten and skinny, his spare frame topped by a narrow, black, Valentino-handsome face, framed in GI cropped, curly, black hair. He was plenty dark enough to be taken for colored, but his finely chiseled features put that notion to rest. When talk arose as to why there were no Negroes in the infantry, Stocky came up as an exception. The difference was his Spanish origin, same as my dark-skinned pal during basic, Pedro Munez. You had to have an old-fashioned American name, along with being black, to be excluded from the frontline infantry.

We relative latecomers to the division back in the States had our introduction to Stocky when he and a dozen others doing time in the stockade were released from shackles directly to the shipping roster as we boarded ships for Europe in New York City. The ex-prisoners were spread around all three regiments so they could not maintain old prison ties. All were assigned to rifle platoons, and whatever their rank when they went to the brig, they had all been busted to private. They were all assigned duty as riflemen.

It gave us college kids pause that Uncle Sam deemed combat against the Nazis sterner punishment than making little ones out of big ones at the prison rock pile. In the end, going "over the hill" countless times was somehow overlooked in favor of beefing the division up to full strength. We'd serve our sentences together in the infantry, the cream of college youth alongside scum from the tank.

Private Bourquez ended up in our company's First Platoon, where his last name, near the top of the alphabet, earned him automatic assignment as scout, first man in line at the head of a twelve-man rifle squad. Flat broke after a long stretch in prison, Stocky didn't get into any of the shipboard nonending craps or poker games. He was reluctant to make friends, spending most of his time in a claustrophobic hammock, part of a four-deep tier slung above the smelly bilge, way below the waterline in our section of D deck.

When our company was committed to combat, Stocky became known too quickly and too well. He was a reckless, fearless nut. On the very first attack, he took being out front as a scout so seriously that he was soon out of sight, ignoring the orders passed along by his squad sergeant or platoon leader. When his platoon finally paused to reorganize, his squad leader quickly relieved Stocky of the scout assignment, telling him in no uncertain terms that he was just another rifleman, charged with staying close to, and supporting, other squad members.

From the first day of Stocky's early training at basic, the rule preached by every instructor was to look to the welfare of your fellow soldiers. Every infantry soldier is imbued with the principle that survival depends on looking out for the men nearest you and generally observing the buddy system. In mortal combat, affinity to our fellow combatants strengthened our resolve to endure fear and hardship. Men often refused evacuation for wounds because they did not want to let their buddies down.

Stocky never exhibited this quality and in fact was so distant from his fellow troopers that it bordered on hostility. He never dug in and shared a foxhole, even when ordered to. He wouldn't dig one just for himself, preferring to forage while others dug and then make a lone nest for himself in the lee of a ditch, under a tree, or off some place where no one knew where he was. A real loner, that Stocky.

Stocky perceived his job of rifleman as a man who uses a rifle, uses it a lot. Before an attack was well under way, he was picking out targets, real or by guess, emptying a clip of eight from his M1, then quickly jamming in a full clip when the rifle clanged that it was empty. He bummed cartridges from anyone nearby after burning up the extra bandoleers criss-crossing his chest.

If the unit was held up either by tactical order or enemy fire, Stocky was wont to keep right on going by himself, right at the enemy. His brash actions won him a Silver Star medal, stirring envy, but also reluctance by any sane soldier to serve anywhere near the unpredictable Mexican. Because he shot his M1 a lot, he drew lots of enemy fire. Miraculously, he suffered not as much as a scratch in two months of battle, though he repeatedly exposed himself to enemy view.

Our shrinking group of veterans who had been in the line from day one of combat shared a particular closeness, except with Stocky. He remained aloof when we sought each other out to marvel at the phenomenon that we were still alive and together. He wanted no part of our sacred brotherhood.

To his credit as a savvy soldier, there was some merit in his contention that by staying well ahead of his platoon during attack, he didn't have to sweat the mortar and artillery fire aimed where the numbers of men were thickest. He had to pay heed only to small arms fire. He considered the Krauts lousy marksmen, and his own skills with an M1 adequate to shoot them before they could get him.

We were capturing new objectives. Replacements for our lost men continued to trickle in, but not in sufficient numbers to restore our original full strength. The rookies in their spanking-new green fighting garb were shuttled to us at the front from the replacement depot, termed disparagingly by GIs as the repple depple, through a regimental service company for in-processing, and eventually they were assigned to a combat company. With no idea of what they might face, their battalion-based rear-area jeep driver, out of rifle range, pointed in the general direction of their new frontline company and told them to march up and report for duty. The headquarters jeep then sped off. A replacement walked uncertainly toward us as we were underway with an open country attack on a tactically important crossroads that was protected by a hidden German machine-gun nest. Trying to report in to a new outfit in a hail of hostile machine-gun fire is a daunting task indeed.

Pvt. Frank Korda was one of those unfortunate new men, just off the boat and a long truck and train ride from Le Havre to the combat zone. Finally delivered to A Company and desperately seeking guidance and companionship, he almost literally clung to high-profile Stocky, who was the only one wandering about upright, with typical nonchalance. The rest of the platoon was proceeding hunched over and wary, scuttling ahead sporadically, apprehensive, hitting the ground when the enemy MG started to sweep their immediate area. The firefight ended abruptly when we dropped a lucky mortar round on the enemy machine-gun position. Korda was told to see the first sergeant, but stubbornly stuck with Stocky.

From that first meeting, Stocky and Frank were inseparable, an alliance closer than the buddy system the rest of us practiced. Foxhole buddies were rarely lasting relationships, most of them occurring by happenstance or proximity, as in a machine or mortar gunner bunking with his assistant, or two ammo bearers sharing a hole. Foxhole mates learned to share body warmth, even rubbing each other's chilled feet to ward off trench foot. We drank from the same canteens, shared ration bars, canned spam, and smokes. It was the kind of closeness you associate with mouth-to-mouth resuscitation, driven by desperate need; it was intimate, for sure, but involved no interplay of personal feelings. The

A young, carefree, and debonair John B. Babcock in his first year at Phillips Exeter Academy, 1938. *Author's Collection*

Civilian no more. Private John B. Babcock, May 1943 at Camp Siebert, Alabama. The enlisted collar device denotes his service in the Chemical Warfare Corps. *Author's Collection*

19 February 1944

SUBJECT: Reduction in ASTP

TO: Each Army Specialized Training Trainee

1. You were assigned to the Army Specialized Training Program because it was felt that the courses of instruction scheduled would materially increase your value to the military service. You have been working under high pressure to master as quickly as possible those essentials of college training of greatest importance to your development as a soldier.

2. The time has come for the majority of you to be assigned to other active duty.

3. To break the enemies' defenses and force their unconditional surrender, it is necessary to hit them with the full weight of America's manpower. Because of this imperative military necessity, most of you will soon be ordered to field service before the completion of your normal course.

4. The Army Specialized Training Program will be reduced prior to 1 April 1944 to 35,000 trainees which will include 5,000 pre-induction students and advanced medical, dental, and engineering groups, the USMA Preparatory Course and certain language groups.

5. Most of you released from the ASTP will be assigned to the Army Ground Forces for duty with divisions and other units. Your intelligence, training, and high qualities of leadership are expected to raise the combat efficiency of those units.

6. The thousands of ASTP trainees who have already been assigned to field service have set high standards for you to follow.

By order of the Secretary of WAR:

Thomas E. Troland

THOMAS E. TROLAND,
Brigadier General, U. S. A.
Commanding.

Letter of February 19, 1944 reassigning John Babcock and thousands of other unlucky ASTP trainees to the infantry. *Author's Collection*

The 60mm mortar set up and ready to fire. This was the weapon operated by the author during his tour in the ETO. *U.S. Army*

Member of an 81mm mortar crew listening to firing orders from the battalion command post. *U.S. Army*

American infantry moving through a village against German opposition.
U.S. Army

GIs prepare to assault a house held by German infantry. The soldier on the left carries an M1 carbine while the man in the center has a trusty M1 Garand with a grenade launcher on the end. *U.S. Army*

American GIs, in snow capes, advance during the Battle of the Bulge.
U.S. Army

German "King Tiger" tank captured by the Americans. Note the American insignia applied by the GIs to the turret and the front of the vehicle. This tank, weighing seventy-five tons and designed for defensive warfare or for penetrating strong lines of defense, made its combat debut in 1944. *U.S. Army*

One of the dreaded German 88mm anti-aircraft guns destroyed by the retreating Germans by splaying the barrel. This multi-purpose weapon emerged as one of the most publicized artillery pieces of the German Army during the North African campaign. It was primarily an anti-aircraft gun but was adaptable to antitank and general artillery use. Because of its fearsome reputation, most infantrymen thought they were under fire by 88s when, in fact, most German artillery fire came from guns of other, higher calibers. *U.S. Army*

A GI covers a German as he surrenders. *U.S. Army*

American infantry pass a dead German as they cross a stream. *U.S. Army*

Staff Sergeant John Babcock at a rest camp in Belgium,
March 1945. On his "Ike Jacket" he wears the Good Conduct
and ETO Campaign Ribbons below his Combat Infantryman's
Badge. *Author's Collection*

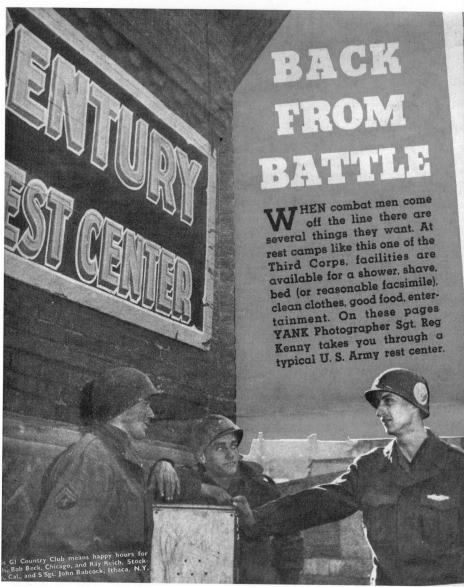

BACK
FROM
BATTLE

WHEN combat men come
off the line there are
several things they want. At
rest camps like this one of the
Third Corps, facilities are
available for a shower, shave,
bed (or reasonable facsimile),
clean clothes, good food, enter-
tainment. On these pages
YANK Photographer Sgt. Reg
Kenny takes you through a
typical U. S. Army rest center.

s GI Country Club means happy hours for
ls, Bob Beck, Chicago, and Ray Reich, Stock-
, Cal., and S Sgt. John Babcock, Ithaca, N.Y.

From the March 25, 1945 edition of *Yank*, the Army's weekly paper. This posed
shot depicts John Babcock (right) with two "buddies" at a GI rest center. He
had never seen these two men before nor did he again after the photo was
taken. *Author's Collection*

Author with dead German soldier in background, early April 1945.
Author's Collection

A portrait taken at the end of mortal combat in June 1945 hints of scars of the soul that will prevail far longer than the bitter lessons learned in *Taught to Kill*. *Author's Collection*

lonely, beseeching Korda made himself Stocky's buddy, adopting him as protector and companion, and Bourquez liked it.

Shorter than Bourquez, Korda was the one with the "stocky" build, and it didn't take long for inventive platoon brothers to label them Mutt and Jeff behind their backs. There was open wonder that lone operator Bourquez had a close pal.

Rest stops and pauses in battle are fertile breeding ground for gossip. Talk usually involved rumors of extraordinary good fortune to befall the company. Such escapism also invented impossible, cushy assignments awaiting us good guys. Stocky and Korda became a talk item. Stocky had halted his headlong personal forays. He showed Korda how to build a foxhole, and surprisingly took to the shovel himself. The two had little contact with others. Mutt and Jeff were missing during most forward actions.

We veteran noncoms were concerned with their closeness, having experienced personally the impact of the loss of an especially good friend or buddy. Some of us limited sharing a foxhole to only once or twice with the same soldier, careful not to get too close to one another as we experienced the random way lives were taken. When it came to Mutt and Jeff, we were uneasy about the obvious intimacy of their relationship.

During a chow break we watched the pair take their filled mess kits and head away from the knots of tired soldiers enjoying a warm meal. Korda handed a small pack of cigarettes to Stocky, who threw an arm over the youngster's shoulders and gave him a quick thank you hug.

"What them guys up to?" asked one grizzled ammo bearer.

"I got my suspicions," answered an assistant gunner with a little grey in his temples. "Acting like they do messes up the whole damned outfit. What was all for one, one for all, has turned into all for him and me, all for me and him. Think either of them guys would help one of us if we was in trouble? Forget it!"

"I've heard tales about this from the Navy where swabbies are out to sea so long they turn to each other," struck up another man. "Don't drop the soap in the shower is the way I heard it."

"I've made and lost some good buddies in this stinking war," asserted another squad member, "but back home or in the service

I never had the kind of feelings for any guy that I have for my girl back home. Do you think for a minute I'd ever try to save your butt if you were in trouble and I was somehow keeping company with her?" We all fell silent.

We pretty well agreed that there might be a place in this man's army for couple like Mutt and Jeff, but it sure as hell wasn't the combat infantry.

Less than two weeks after Korda and Bourquez began practicing their own brand of living close, we launched an attack on the Cologne Plains over a large field that had been planted to sugar beets harvested months earlier. A spring thaw had melted most of the winter snow, and the mud was so deep that no wheel-driven vehicles could accompany us. Even half-tracks and tanks ended up stalled in the sticky mess. We dogfaces were left to make it on foot to the heavily defended city two hundred yards across the soupy mire.

We feared an artillery barrage. We got one, a big one. Eighty-eights and screaming meemies poured on us from within the city that was our objective. Our only choice was to slog forward as fast as we could slog. Added to the confusion was 90mm fire from our new tank destroyers, stuck in the mud behind us. Their guns were leveled at the nearest buildings ahead of them and a short distance from us dogfaces. High-velocity rounds passed over our bowed heads by literally no more than a few feet. The muzzle blast and supersonic projectiles almost lifted us off the ground as they sped over. Our own 90s drowned out the warning whine of incoming 88s.

Soft mud directed flying shrapnel up from a smaller crater than usual, the explosions coughing globs of mud high in the air. The salvos were thick, and casualties mounted. This type of terrain yielded few million-dollar wounds that could be a free ticket home. You either escaped harm or were blown to bits.

Pvt. Frank Korda took a direct hit, right before the horrified eyes of his pal, Stocky. Those who saw the 88 strike were sure that its victim was a goner. Stocky threw down his rifle and jumped in the wet shell hole, screaming at Frank to get up and follow him to safety. He tried to lift him to his feet. Our attack pressed beyond and ahead of them. Yelling, wailing, crying out, Stocky sank down in the muddy shell hole with his slain buddy, struck with unspeakable grief.

By dusk, we had established a tenuous foothold in our assigned sector of the objective city and tried to reassemble our scattered company. At first so few showed up that we feared the shells had claimed over half our strength; stragglers kept trickling in, however, and by midnight, we had accounted for a good share of our outfit. There were harrowing tales of close escape, but little chat about our losses.

The next morning, snipers kept us close to protective walls and cellars while we awaited orders to continue the assault. I almost jumped out of my skin with surprise when Stocky slipped up beside me from nowhere.

"Sarge, I need a favor."

"Sure, Stocky," I replied, somewhat guarded about what his next move might be. During one earlier attack, he had borrowed my rifle, and when he handed it back the next day, it was filthy and starting to rust. I had reason to be wary of the wily Mexican daredevil.

"Take these, will you?" He squatted down to hand me his Combat Infantryman Badge, a muddy, blue leather box containing his Silver Star, and a handful of religious medals and battered photos. He placed in my hand a stained piece of V-Mail paper on which he had laboriously printed a name and Texas address.

"Why me? Why not your own platoon sergeant? Why have a stranger be responsible for your personal possessions?"

"I want you to mail this stuff to my old lady at that address. My outfit and sergeant don't like me. You an old-timer. You been a square guy, so I count on you to do like I say." His eyes held mine to underscore his request, to transform it to an unequivocal directive.

"Sure, Bourquez," I said, "but why now?" I thought of Korda's being blown up, and had to ask, "You going over the hill again? They'll catch you, and it will go hard for you. They shoot deserters."

"Don't worry about that, Sarge. I'm going no place," replied

Stocky, his eyes resuming their familiar shifting sweep. He rose and started out from the protection of the wall I had chosen, cradling his rifle to shoot from the hip.

"Hey, buddy, get your ass back here," I exclaimed in alarm. "We been getting sniper and machine-gun fire from that street all morning." Stocky shrugged and meandered down the street, out of sight. No one took a shot at him.

If he had been a one-man army before he met Korda, Stocky was now irrationally reckless. He made up his own missions. His platoon leader, a ninety-day wonder fresh from Fort Benning, simply didn't know how to handle him. His platoon sergeant had given up trying to get through to him, not a little intimidated by a perception of pent-up violence that threatened to erupt at any moment.

I placed Stocky's personal effects in an empty machine-gun ammo carrier and sent the metal case back to the mail clerk for safekeeping. Stories of his new exploits abounded. Whatever drove him, Korda's death was a big part of the equation. By himself again, Stocky might well have won a Congressional Medal. As it turned out, he was found dead by his platoon in the doorway of a battered house as they were mopping up after an attack. Stocky had forged out front of the advancing squad and had tripped a booby trap, an ignominious end for a soldier of fortune more appropriately fated for death in one-on-one confrontation with the enemy.

I sent Bourquez's stuff home without a letter. Weeks later I wrote Korda's folks and said he was a brave man killed fighting for his country.

Some Lose

O n the move in late February, toward the end of our second long battle in the forested Ardennes, two of our five-man light weapons squads hastily dug foxholes at the end of a short winter day. We hurried because dark in the foreboding pine forest was blacker than the inside of Dick's hatband (an old country-boy expression), almost as foreboding as the Hürtgen. From an exposed hillside, our machine-gun and mortar squads and remnants of two rifle squads stalled an enemy counterattack with rifle fire, our light machine gun, and one welcome Browning automatic rifle (BAR) manned by a nearby rifleman. The enemy was too close, the trees too thick, to deploy our 60mm mortar. Mortars aren't for close-in fighting, particularly when required to shoot up through tree branches.

I never played around with German ammo, but word was that after the safety pin was pulled by the gun crew, German mortar shells, maybe all German shells, would explode from a hard rap on the nose. We assumed that included dropping a round headfirst on the frozen ground. Our American mortar shell, on the other hand, had an ingenious safety device called a setback pin. It kept our mortar round safe even after the manual safety pin was removed.

When the round was dropped fin-first into the tube, the force of the exploding propellant that drove it high into the sky caused a spring-loaded final safety pin to release and press against the smooth tube of the mortar. As the shell cleared the tube on its journey upward, the pin that prevented the shell from exploding by mistake was ejected, arming the detonator on the nose to do its job on the slightest impact. We gunners could sometimes see that little pin "ping" away as the shell departed, but never settled the argument as to how far the actual projectile would have to clear the muzzle before it was fully armed to explode.

During preparation for their counterattack, shells fired by the Krauts had exploded in the trees above us, the detonators touched off by contact with branches as the rounds plunged toward earth. Those of us lucky enough not to be hit by plunging shrapnel remained pinned in our holes by unseen enemy machine guns and rifles intermittently spraying bullets blindly in the waning light.

Battle noise subsided as darkness settled in. In the silence, a frightened voice rose from nearby in the woods: "I'm hurt real bad. Please, somebody! Come help me. I've got to go home." The tree bursts had claimed a victim.

We determined that the voice had to be PFC Cecil NMI (no middle initial) Billings, "Seesaw" Billings, a runner/messenger recently assigned to our Fourth Platoon. He failed to respond to the hushed roll call. We had spared Billings being hailed as Cecil by twisting the sissy name around to "Seesaw," a label that somehow stuck. Seesaw wasn't much of a messenger, nor had he demonstrated aptitude for weaponry or any platoon task more demanding than running errands, stringing phone wire, and fetching supplies. He had taken on these jobs with no complaint. He was acceptably reliable. He had no close friends. He had no enemies. He was a name on the company roster.

Seesaw's pleas grew in frequency and intensity. Sergeant Imo, guided by the pleading voice, finally slithered over in the dark to the troubled boy's foxhole to see what was the matter. We could hear snatches of his words of comfort and assurance. Company medics were beyond earshot of the voices that relayed calls for a stretcher. It was pitch dark, and no one could find his way about, friend or enemy. We hunkered down, hoping the enemy was as weary and intimidated by the blackness as we, and wondered where the rest of the company was scattered.

For a few minutes, Seesaw was silent. Then, lonely, hurt, and scared in the dark, he groaned with each breath, his voice rising every minute or so to a plaintive shriek for help, interspersed with entreaties for his mother. The enemy had withdrawn, or at least ceased firing. The quiet pine forest hillside was filled with Seesaw's rising complaint at the expense of any other sound. Finally his loud cries diminished, and took on a whining, singsong quality that was as hard for us to bear as his more strident cries of pain.

Sergeant Imo felt his way back over to Seesaw's hole. The wounded youngster was oblivious to his presence. The rhythmic moans persisted with little change in tempo or intensity. Without hoisting him from the hole, Imo attempted to discover, with a brief flame from his cigarette lighter, visible signs of injury. He passed the word to adjacent foxholes that Private Billings seemed unharmed, except for a trickle of blood below the base of his skull, just above his collar. Imo guessed that a shard of shrapnel had penetrated the base of his brain or his spinal column. It didn't seem like anything that could be treated or alleviated in the field. We were fresh out of brain surgeons.

It was close to dawn before Seesaw's foxhole fell silent. Although the enemy had posed no imminent threat, none of us had been able to drift off for even a few winks. Imo checked again as we prepared to move out. Palms up in a gesture of futility, he left the curled-up body in the grave its owner had dug. We moved silently back to our distasteful task, relieved, no matter what danger awaited us, to be long gone from that sad locale and the haunting sounds of death in the making.

While his personality or military exploits were hardly memorable, Private Billings nonetheless left an indelible scar on the psyche of his fellow soldiers. Had he been blown to smithereens with nary a grunt, his name would quickly have faded. But his legacy of agony reverberates at the oddest times in the heads of those of us who can only imagine the pain and terror that energized his futile, vocal struggle against death. None of us infantrymen wanted to die, but many of us prayed that if battle death had to occur, it would be mercifully quick. If it were messy, so what? We wouldn't be around to clean up anyway.

Echoing forever in my memory are the moans that so painfully accompanied the lingering nighttime death of boy-soldier Private Billings in his lonely forest foxhole. His image pops back into my mind on the oddest occasions: the trembling groan of two trees rubbing together on a windy night; a woman in labor down a hospital corridor; the far-off bawling of a lost calf. Billings is gone, but he left a bitter, haunting memory.

Some Win

O ne of the biggest and most frustrating management jobs in
my war—maybe any war—was caring for the wounded.
There are five to six times as many casualties who live as who
die, and the odds improve with every war. The primary link to
professional help on our battlefield was the medic. Our medics
were officially members of Battalion Headquarters Company, assigned for duty in the roster of the rifle company they regularly
accompanied in battle. To the men who looked to their ministra-
tion, the medics traveling with each company delivered security
and compassion. The company medic was truly your "family"
doctor. The pejorative "chancre mechanic" or "pill roller," reserved for garrison doctors and orderlies, were never invoked for
the company medic, even in fun.

Most medics were corporals or buck sergeants, with a "T" under
the inverted "V" of their stripes to designate their skills as technical, medical in their case. A private is a seventh-grade soldier, a
private first class is grade six. A two-stripe corporal with a "T" is a
T-5, a three-striper a T-4. When things were tough or you had blisters on your feet that cried for treatment, they were respectfully
hailed not by rank, but as "Doc." And to many a badly wounded
man, they were addressed with heartfelt reverence as "Doctor."

Company medics deftly wielded a scalpel to whittle away calluses and blisters on feet too sore to bear weight. They applied medicine, painkillers, pads, and patented dressings to keep a man walking. While their contributions were accomplished with limited medical knowledge, no skilled surgeon or senior medical officer could match the infantry medic's skill in foot care. The infantry may travel on its stomach, but it gets around on its feet. The foot was a dedicated medic's primary concern. If there were a civilian counterpart to infantry company medic, his shingle would picture a bare foot with umpteen sores and blisters.

Trained Stateside to identify and render first aid for all sorts of injuries, they learned in battle to practice medicine far beyond the compress, tourniquet, and sulfa pill. Absent a physician, front-line medics improvised on uncharted medical ground, forced to treat emergencies the manual never described. After hastily performing first aid, they then served as pack mules to take their battered burdens to the rear and a real doctor.

Experience in the field beat out textbook knowledge; formal medical training took a back seat to practical experience, love of craft, and real dedication. I once suggested to our original medic, Ben Tanner, shot in cold blood during our first attack, that following the war he might think of making podiatry his profession.

He thought a long minute, and shook his head: "Nope, I think I'd like to get into foot care as a full-time job," he replied. Tanner was not long on book learning.

You couldn't miss the large red cross on a white background that medics displayed front and rear. It was accorded worldwide respect ordained by the Geneva Convention. This same international rulebook that decreed a prisoner of war need give his captors only his name, rank, and serial number dictated that each side would care for the other's wounded. After all, some rules and restrictions should apply in war, just as they do in a Spanish bull-ring, or did in an ancient Roman arena full of lions and Christians.

Except the war that engulfed us GIs grew to be grotesquely devoid of humane rules and customary amenities. Perspectives narrowed. The obsession was to kill or be killed. No place for Mr. Good Guy. No scoring markers, as in Stateside maneuvers, to designate make-believe casualties. We played for keeps. Rather than turn the other cheek, if the enemy deliberately harmed one of our medics, we short-circuited to pure revenge.

Incessant violence and the specter of our own imminent deaths blunted compassion. Some formerly clean, upright, and thoroughly ethical American soldiers occasionally took a shot at an enemy medic; our guys beat up or shot prisoners once in a while; enemy wounded were occasionally left untended for long periods, sometimes out of spite. But our own precious medics watched out for their own like a bear guards its cubs.

One strapping PFC in our outfit called Popeye (all muscles, he could chin himself while wearing a fifty-pound field pack) carried his thirty-five-pound, "light" machine gun diagonally across his shoulder with the same ease he would have toted a kitchen broom. When called on for a fire mission, he was flat in an instant, the bipod front legs of his weapon flopped out to support the jacketed barrel, the stamped-metal stock tucked and held firmly against his right shoulder with his left hand. He was ready with his right hand for service from his assistant, who closed in on his left. The number-two man opened the green metal box containing a web belt holding three hundred .30-caliber cartridges.

For easier accessibility, the assistant gunner would often ignore the personal safety afforded by lying prone, and sit cross-legged so he could better direct the three hundred-round ammo belt into the feedway, where a pull on the trigger sucked it in at rates as high as seven rounds per second. He'd place the end of the belt across the feedway already opened by the gunner, see that the first round was positioned on the belt feed pawl, and snatch his hands away as Popeye slammed the lid down and jacked the operating handle two times.

The first action of the bolt delivered a round to the extractor; the second pull slammed the first cartridge into the empty chamber of the barrel. Popeye would slap the cover to confirm it was latched and bang the bolt forward with the heel of his hand to be sure it was properly seated. If the target was obvious, he'd open fire, tripping the trigger briefly to deliver short bursts. More often, he looked to his squad leader for instructions on the target and rate of fire.

We American troops were moving rapidly across the Cologne Plain toward the great Rhine River. Highly fluid conditions were yet another test for a company that was gaining experience at various kinds of warfare at the expense of its own manpower. This was hit-and-run, with proficiency measured as harshly by the "run" as by the "hit."

Popeye had just "hit," firing a full belt of three hundred rounds at various suspected targets in a woodlot across a little valley of scattered homes. Range was maybe four hundred yards. He and assistant gunner Pvt. E. M. Buck had been at this one location for over five minutes. They were getting antsy to move on, to "run." Sergeant Imo was still scanning the enemy hillside from behind a nearby stone wall with German binoculars he had earlier "liberated." He did not feel that his gun was imminently threatened. But some instinct told Popeye to haul ass. Longevity for a machine gunner was to avoid becoming a sitting duck. A fire mission was noisy, drew attention, and inevitably attracted reprisal, usually mortars or artillery, or another machine gun. That's why it was essential to shoot and immediately move to a new location. The quiet after its own firing is particularly ominous to a gun crew.

So Popeye waved Private Buck and his fresh box of ammo away, rose to his feet, and cradled the gun in both arms, bipod swinging to and fro. Imo caught on to Popeye's instinctive tactic and smoothly signed his approval with a hand signal sending the crew toward the next fence line and another stone wall. As Popeye whirled and started to run, the blinding fast rip of a Kraut machine gun flooded the gun position that moments before had been filled with the din of outgoing fire.

This time, Popeye's luck ran out. By some miracle, Bucky ran unscathed toward new cover as Popeye spun and fell heavily, the machine gun tumbling from his arms. For a moment Sergeant Imo stood frozen in surprise and disbelief. Then he swept his glasses toward the source of fire on the right flank, and saw the enemy machine gunner slinking away for his own protection. He didn't want what he had just done to the American machine gunner to happen to him. Imo ran over to his fallen teammate. What he saw left him almost speechless, his throat dry, senses numbed.

The muscular, dynamic, invulnerable iron man was a pile of torn flesh. The white bone of his long, sturdy thigh, shattered just below the hip, protruded from his bullet-torn pants leg. He desperately clutched his lower stomach, arms and hands covered with blood flowing from somewhere higher on his body. At first glance, Imo figured Popeye for a goner. Miraculously, he was alive and cursing his bad luck, not yet aware of the damage he had suffered. His injured leg was bent grotesquely to the side, almost completely severed.

There was no hesitation on the part of Medic T-5 Charley Carpenter to join the squad leader and the new casualty. Imo's confident plunge into the gun position indicated that the enemy fire that had caused the damage no longer threatened. The two men looked questioningly at each other, Imo shrugging and nodding negatively. Doc immediately started his examination, ripping open Popeye's shirt and unbuttoning his pants.

The profuse bleeding was from a long tear made by a bullet slicing sidewise, teat high, across Popeye's upper chest. It was a flesh wound, grazing but not penetrating the breastbone or ribs. Lower down, another bullet had sliced open his abdomen, but without penetrating. Entrails protruded obscenely from a baseball-sized opening. A third bullet or bullets had done the real damage, shattering Popeye's femur.

Medic Carpenter pulled Popeye's web belt from its loops and wrapped it twice around the damaged upper thigh, not bothering to remove the torn pants. He swore softly when the belt would not make two complete loops and settled for one time around. Firmly, roughly, he jammed a fist-sized chunk of wood wrapped in gauze between the belt and Poppy's bloody inner thigh. Then, much like tightening the belly cinch on a horse's saddle, he took up the slack and drew the belt and wood block as tight as he could against the femoral artery. He wiped bright red blood from the ragged stump and stared intently for several seconds.

"Arterial bleeding's stopped. Lemme get a wet compress against this hole in his gut and a bandage over his chest. Then we'll see." He worked silently, grimly. Frustrated at our inability to lend a hand, Imo and I simply watched, as Popeye's eyes rolled back and his complexion faded to gray. Shock spread a streaked, yellow hue across his tortured, sweat-drenched face.

"He's not going to make it, is he?" I ventured.

"The hell he ain't. Just need four things," replied the medic without looking up. "Gotta have a stretcher, a jeep, plasma, and some of that-there penicillin. That's the new stuff. Not much around."

Imo took off for help. Carpenter and I moved Popeye to the lee of a farm wall where he could lie flat. The medic straightened out what was left of the lower part of his leg, but did not try to set the bone or even put the two ends together. It was a bloody, mangled mess. Popeye had not uttered a sound since his initial yell of surprise, but now he moaned softly. With two shots of the medic's morphine in him he drifted into the promised land of oblivion.

"He'll never make it, will he?" I repeated.

"Don't say that. He's got a chance," guessed Carpenter. "He's strong as a bull, not the type to go into irreversible shock, and I've about licked the worst of the bleeding."

"Won't you have to let up on the tourniquet once in a while?" I asked, this being about my knowledge limit of field first aid applicable to the situation.

"You do that to restore circulation to save tissue below a wound," Carpenter explained. "Not much use here. Nothing left of his leg that anyone can save. I may let up a little once in a while to serve the general area up above with fresh blood, but the leg below is *kaput*," he pronounced.

Meanwhile, darkness approached and we were ordered to dig in where we were. I busied myself moving the men around, establishing guard posts and watch rotations, and in absence of contact with our kitchen, advised everyone to make do with K rations or D bar chocolate. It promised to be a lonely night, but at least the temperature was above freezing. I scrounged up whatever blankets and extra clothing the boys could spare, and gave the pile to Carpenter to use as he saw fit to make Popeye comfortable. Looking in on him, Popeye appeared to me to be about gone. I had little hope. The CO appeared, briefly examined the wounded soldier, and sent riflemen on patrol to locate other units and battalion aid.

As I dozed late that night, I was brought back around by Imo's noisy arrival. He was dragging a folded litter and carrying a bag of equipment from battalion aid that turned out to be the kit and dispensing equipment for bottled plasma that Carpenter needed so badly for Popeye. He also brought doses of penicillin from battalion that Carpenter administered immediately in Popeye's good thigh.

"Well?" the medic asked Imo.

"Well, I'll tell ya' what," Imo replied. "There's a way out of this, but it's not going to be easy. I think I can make my way in the dark through the cross-country route I found, and avoid enemy positions and hopefully patrols. But it's a half mile, the terrain is rugged, and I'm pooped. But it's got to be me. I'm the only one who can find the supply jeep we got waiting to take Popeye on in to the aid station."

"The other end the stretcher's got to be me," grimaced T-5 Carpenter. "We'll finish this bottle of plasma, belt him again with morphine, and take off. Gimme a few minutes to get him ready."

Imo nodded with relief, taking a long swig from an offered canteen, catching his breath, lying flat to regain his strength.

T-5 Carpenter emerged in a few minutes to say they were ready to leave. His assessment was that the miraculously strong Popeye was stable. He was reluctant to allow his patient any more water than to wet his lips because of the stomach wound. He explained that the plasma had helped Popeye's terrible craving for a drink. He had Popeye bundled up and strapped to the litter, ready to go.

"Ya' know," Carpenter observed, "if this was World War I or any time in the old days, this guy would be a goner. Thank God for miracle drugs and plasma. If we can get him to the aid station in the next hour or so, he might just make it."

The T-5 "doctor" grasped one set of stretcher handles, Imo the other, and off they trudged into the dark countryside.

I felt strangely relieved that Popeye was out of sight, if not out of mind. To have seen such vitality and strength suddenly ripped apart was unnerving and disturbing.

I shivered, stretched to remove the kinks in my weary muscles, and moved over to the pile of cloth and blankets that had been heaped on Popeye. Maybe my blanket could be recovered. But no, it was drenched in blood, as were most of the other items. I stirred them with my foot, and uncovered Popeye's right combat boot. Not a bad idea, thought I. Leaving that boot meant one less thing to carry. I nudged the big shoe with my toe. It didn't budge. Poor Popeye's foot and most of his leg were still with us.

We got on with our work the next morning. Private Buck was made gunner. He was only one casualty short of being Buck Sergeant Buck, opening the way for more imaginative nicknames.

As for the indestructible Popeye, in three weeks we had our first letters to his old pals from a hospital in Paris. He reported that his chest was about healed, the hole in his gut was repaired, and his hand with the thumb shot off was coming along okay. His hip was in traction to draw skin down so that eventually he would have a covered stump that would accommodate an artificial leg.

As for the thumb, I hadn't known it was missing. Carpenter explained after we read the letter that it was chopped off cleanly by an enemy bullet, and that he had bandaged it with other wounds. He just forgot to mention it in the fuss of taking care of worse problems.

Popeye's closing line in his first letter was that he wished he was still with all us guys. He said it would be better than life in the hospital. We figured he was still on drugs, or better yet, booze.

The Reporter

Infantry divisions in World War II were organized in a triangular configuration in strategic design (the big picture) as well as tactical deployment (our smaller perspective). Roughly, this meant that two of three basic military units engaged the enemy, while the third element served as a backup, an uncommitted reserve. Two divisions would be on the line, a third held as backup. Next step down, two regiments would engage the enemy, often in a pincers-like encirclement, while the third regiment remained available to help where and if needed; eventually, the reserve element would replace one of the attacking regiments, which in turn would earn respite as the reserve.

Going down the size scale, the three battalions of each regiment were deployed, two up front, the third in support, and the three rifle companies, two up front, one in reserve. Then, tactically, of the three rifle platoons in each company, two attacked, one backed up. Finally, in each platoon, two of the three rifle squads would lead, the third hanging back for support.

It might appear that this three-legged stool approach left no role in the company for a Fourth Platoon. Not so. We were firepower designed to strengthen the basic rifle units wherever and however most helpful. Our squads were carefully parceled out and attached to the three rifle platoons.

Going back up the scale of unit size, there was a fourth entire company in each battalion designated as heavy weapons. Just as our light mortars and highly portable light machine guns backed up rifle platoons, heavy weapons companies were spread around to bolster rifle companies with their water-cooled machine guns and 81mm mortars. At battalion level, extra firepower was available from cannon company, whose 105mm field artillery pieces were assigned to the battalion sectors that most needed them. Regiment, one step higher, had artillery and tank units to call on for extra muscle. Then up at division level, you could call on heavy-duty help from the 155mm and 240mm big guns; or you could call for airplanes or other divisions from corps or Army.

Able Company usually assigned one 60mm mortar squad to each rifle platoon, First Mortar with the First Platoon, Second Mortar with the Second Platoon, and so on. The two MGs were deployed according to the task at hand. They might both go on the attack, or they might both remain with the reserve if we needed to be sure of an exceptionally solid pivot point if it appeared that we were vulnerable to counterattack. Just how our five weapons platoon squads were to be committed was resolved at the company briefing of officers and noncoms that took place before each action. The disposition was then communicated to us men by the company's executive officer, who also served as Fourth Platoon leader.

In the open-country fighting that took place after the Bulge, Able Company's mission changed daily, sometimes hourly. So, then, did its platoons and squads undertake different assignments.

The Reserve Officers Training Corps (ROTC) officer who taught military tactics in college would put me in the stockade for such a simplistic explanation of sophisticated military procedure. As we dogfaces saw it, however, that's about the way World War II organization worked on a day-to-day, practical basis.

When it got to the big picture, I had an unfortunate vision of a bunch of splendidly uniformed high command brass hanging out in a big plans room full of wall maps, colored pins, and clerks churning out reports. The clerks, majors, and colonels rushed about delivering the latest poop to ribbon-bedecked, gray-haired generals. With coffee cup or brandy glass in one hand, a general would unlimber a pointer and, for the benefit of the others, poke at the map and pronounce the next troop movement. Maybe it was to straighten out a squiggle in the line representing the front. Whatever macrodecision he made, however, profoundly imperiled the lives of frontline troops. Lives like mine.

We figured that the staff generals rarely got up into the front lines; otherwise, for instance, they never would have chosen the Hürtgen Forest as a place to do battle with anyone. What may have looked workable on a map had turned out to be a slaughterhouse for dogfaces and tankers alike.

Up where we were, tactics worked similar to, but more simply, than strategy. We saw the value in flexible deployment and appreciated how critical it was to have effective reserves that could be committed on a moment's notice. Our briefings were democratic exchanges that nonetheless maintained respect for rank. In other words, a minor noncom could advance a theory for an action, but he could be and often was overruled by a noncom of higher rank, or by an officer. But his ideas were weighed: "What you up to, dogface, bucking for a promotion?" and if rejected, a logical reason given: "Shut your 'tater trap. We do it my way and that's an order."

What we all dreaded was an edict from Above that was clearly impractical or suicidal. Such instructions were appealed by radio and phone lines or, if time permitted, by messenger; but rarely was the decision changed. Quite probably orders had come from an even higher authority than immediate command anyway. When an infantry unit is faced with a questionable or unattainable objective from a higher authority, it has one choice: Carry out the order.

On one occasion, after crossing a key river bridge that other GIs had captured intact, our clear and terse order was to turn left, proceed in a marching column two miles downstream, and then deploy to engage the enemy. Captain Goodspeed was right there at the end of the bridge waving his arms, typically akimbo when he was frantic, in the direction ordered. Suspicious, I dropped back in the advancing column to talk to Doughboy, our crack Sec-

ond Platoon scout. Doughboy had forded the stream and recon-
noitered enemy strength before daylight. It was his discovery that
was to guide our attack. He shrugged at my question, simply re-
peating what he had told Battalion S-2 (intelligence): The enemy
was two miles to our right off the bridge and up the river. I trotted
up to the bridgehead and told Captain Goodspeed Doughboy's
findings.

"Sergeant, these orders came from division," Goodspeed hissed
with obvious frustration. "I did everything I could to set them
straight, and this is what I was told to do. We'll go down here to
the left a few hundred yards and take a break. Maybe somebody'll
wake up. If not, we'll resume the march two miles to nowhere.
That's just the way it is, Sergeant." His eyes were dulled by fatigue
and frustration at our mission.

We took our ten-minute break after marching left a little while,
and sure enough, a speeding jeep from the rear brought urgent
orders for us to reverse the field and head out in the other direction past the bridge and up the river. By the time we did our two
miles, Doughboy's reported enemy force had gone elsewhere. We
lucked into a small village with its buildings pretty well untouched
by war. It was near dark and in no time flat we had set up a perimeter guard and burrowed into the warmth and shelter of real
buildings. There were no civilians to greet us.

That's where I met Scribe.

With the chow jeep, after dark, arrived three replacements, a
familiar occurrence when motorized contact with our rear area
headquarters was practical. Captain Goodspeed talked briefly with
one man and pointed at me. Apparently, they knew each other.
Since I was usually part of the process of choosing weapons platoon candidates, I wondered briefly about this arbitrary assignment, but dismissed it. A body was a body, and long ago I had
given up hope of securing trained weapons operators. This me-
dium-build, slightly stooped man just didn't look like the kids the
repple depple had been sending up. I moved out to greet my new
man, determined to give that instant reassuring welcome we had
finally learned that nervous new men needed when they first
came into a combat area.

My first impression was right. This was no boy. I extended a hand, and when he gave me his, I sensed a polite and cordial grasp, a hand too soft for a new recruit or a transfer. Even kids fresh from home were exposed to enough manual work to possess meat-hooks callused and chapped in varying degree. Looking into his face, it was also immediately evident that this "boy" was really old, maybe forty. Older than the captain. Way older, even, than our battalion commander. We called men ten years his junior "Pop" in the combat infantry.

His clothing was not quite right, either. He had the usual bright olive drab newly issued field jacket, regulation helmet (no camo netting), and GI boots. But his bloused, wool pants had a gray-pink cast: officer's twill, by gum! And the carbine slung on his shoulder was not only new; it hung at a clumsy angle that belied its owner's familiarity with bearing, much less using, a gun. He had one fresh stripe on each arm: another PFC. Had someone "hung one" on me?

"Soldier," I directed at him, "I don't know where you came from, but not many replacements hit here and call their new CO by his first name. You and the Old Man friends from way back?"

"Well, Sergeant," he replied as directly to me. "We actually had not met before, but I knew of him, and frankly he was expecting me. Can I explain?"

"Explain away," I invited.

"Some place we can talk?" This man did not lack self-confidence or presence.

"Sure," I invited. "Step into my office here. The reception room is to the right." I waved him into a small, low-ceilinged livestock shed I had chosen for my personal retreat. It was half filled with hay, my usual objective for dry warmth and comfort. I had used my rank to nail this spot down for individual use and a good night's rest. With the door closed, the shed was pitch dark. I could risk showing some light. I set a flashlight on its base, shining straight up between us. The lighting was a little eerie, but adequate. I had earlier checked that it did not send a single ray outside.

The old fellow sank gratefully into a cushion of hay. "I'm not so sure this was a smart idea," he puffed. "Not much use my playing soldier with you. Fact is, I'm a newspaper wire service freelancer, up here on my own to see if I can put together an account of just what sort of life you guys lead in the infantry. I wish now I was back in a saloon in L.A." The old duffer was sincere, and refreshingly honest at least.

I tried to be direct in turn: "I didn't figure you for a commando in disguise or anything. But why pick on me, Ernie Pyle? Or are you a Bill Mauldin? Or maybe a visiting Walter Winchell?"

"None of the above," he said patiently. "I write, I submit copy, I try to be honest. Your boss, Captain Goodspeed, said you were college trained, wrote a good letter, and would probably understand my mission better than anyone else in his outfit," my guest allowed. So Captain Goodspeed was the one who had been censoring my mail. Despite his avowed impartiality as a censor, he obviously knew a great deal about me, my family, and my innermost thoughts, from all those letters I churned out. He'd never mentioned them, never would. I suddenly realized they constituted an intricate and comprehensive tie between us. Given our difference in rank, such intimacy could not otherwise have been attained.

I was given solemn assurance from Scribe that my name would never be used in any of his written accounts, so I opened up, delighted to have someone from the outside world to whom I could unload some of the impressions and feelings I was saving for the day when I might arrive home to describe this unusual and indescribable war. I was too exhausted at this first meeting for such talk. I gestured toward a pile of hay to indicate where he could sack in. I fell asleep immediately and left Scribe with his thoughts, and maybe fears.

The next morning, our kitchen jeep arrived with coffee and a main course of S.O.S. After no hot meal for forty-eight hours, I wolfed down an almost-full mess kit of the steaming, lumpy, pepper-laden mess. Delicious! Scribe stirred his serving around, ate enough to stem pangs of hunger, and contented himself with several cups of coffee, already laced with condensed milk.

Company A was ordered to wait for other units to catch up on our left flank before resuming the advance, so, in effect, we had at least the morning off. I felt pretty good after a deep and dreamless night. Scribe said he simply wanted to hang around, be part of the routine. I told him I couldn't believe our good luck at the huge rest break.

We wandered out of our shed and I started to poke around in one of the houses at the crossroads. The building had been abandoned in haste; I concluded it had been occupied by civilians. Plates and cups were scattered about the kitchen table, and a pot on the stove indicated that someone had recently heated water for tea or the ersatz grounds that the Krauts called coffee. No booby traps. At least none I could see. Sometimes I threw a grenade in to cleanse a room of possible tricks like that, but this looked like a purely civvies' evacuation.

Scribe looked on as I opened kitchen drawers and cupboards, rummaging through the contents, tossing items on the floor, finding nothing worth taking. I turned my back to employ a boot heel to bust open a locked lower cupboard. Scribe winced. Again, standard household wares; nothing of particular interest.

"How come you treat the place so roughly?" Scribe inquired.

"Why not?" I replied carelessly. "Looting's part of the game. We don't often find anything worth carting away, or small enough to pocket, but we look anyway. Who knows, you might run across some real jewelry, silver coins, a pistol, Nazi flag, or some other souvenir you'd want. We guys don't do 1 percent of the damage. Wait till the MPs [military police] and the military government get here. There won't be a stick of wood left worth keeping when the Lootwaffe gets done."

"Lootwaffe?" Scribe inquired.

"Yeah, that's what we call the guys who follow up us dogfaces after we capture a town. It's a takeoff on Luftwaffe, the German Air Corps. Only these guys don't fly. They just take everything that isn't nailed down; and if it is, they take it apart with a wrecking bar. You think I'm looting? You ought to see this place a week from now—if we're still holding this part of the country," I explained.

"I've heard about the atrocities the Germans and even the Russians commit, but I didn't realize our guys were into looting and all that sort of stuff," Scribe said in mild wonderment.

"Hey, buddy, a soldier's a soldier, and soldiers loot," I explained earnestly. "At first we treated the countryside like it belonged to someone else. Then we captured a distillery back there where they have all those grape terraces. Sure, we hustled a few bottles of good stuff, but we didn't wreck the place or anything. The headquarters office was a real showplace, solid wood paneling, fireplace, furniture. We wiped our feet before we went in.

"Then ten days later I had a chance to go by there again on an ammo run with the supply jeep. You should have seen the joint! The office area had been completely razed, and the place was crawling with MPs and GIs hauling out the booze in Army trucks. After that we figured we'd better get our licks in first. We had taken practically nothing. Only thing we left to show we'd been at the distillery was a Kilroy," I said, shaking my head.

"'Course we wrote down what outfit we were, too," I added.

"A Kilroy?" Scribe asked.

"Yeah, you know, a cartoon drawing of a round-eyed, baldheaded guy peering over the edge of a wall, holding himself up with three fingers of both hands. Anybody can draw one. Under it you print: 'Kilroy was here,' the date, and your name or outfit or maybe hometown. You find them every place soldiers have been.

"We leave a Kilroy to show we were there first. I'll bet they're still talking about the one at the booze factory. Me and another guy got the old heinie who was tending the tunnels to lead us clear to the end of the farthest cave. That's where we left our Kilroy sign. They never could have guessed any GI had been that deep into the joint before. I'd like to seen their faces when they found our Kilroy!

"Now, when we first arrived in the ETO we drew the same cartoon character in unlikely places, but we called him Otis. 'Otis was here.' Tell you the truth, I liked Otis better than Kilroy, but Kilroy was what other outfits used, so that's what we use too. Shit, who'd know what we accomplished if we didn't make ourselves part of the written record," I said earnestly.

Scribe shook his head in dismay, and made his way out among the other looters from A Company. Good fortune reigned and we remained in position through the entire day. Another hot meal and a second night in my haystack, and I felt almost human. Scribe reviewed his copious notes and I commended him for having the balls to come right up front where the fighting took place when he didn't have to.

"When the shooting starts, Sergeant, count me gone," Scribe said seriously. "I'm not the one with balls. Real balls is being unable to pick and choose when you want to experience combat. You poor bastards go at it day after day, with no choice, and from what I have learned, no letup, save occasional pauses like I have been part of these couple of days. It's the not knowing and the relentless threat of death that makes you special. I'm outa here, but you can count on one thing: I'll bust a gut to tell as forcefully as I can just how it is. Count on it!" Scribe grabbed my hand with warm sincerity.

Why did I feel that his good-bye handshake had an overtone of finality? Scribe really didn't think I'd be around to meet again. I had allowed myself to start thinking he might be wrong. But then, it's easier to challenge the law of averages when you are rested and well fed.

Basic Training: ETO

The first two of three battle stars ultimately awarded our division were earned at the price of rows of pine boxes, and wards full of wounded. The Bulge claimed many early victims because of our overall inexperience, our innocence, really. The Hürtgen Forest and wooded hills beyond brought even heavier losses among both veterans and new men, proving that no one was exempt from random harm.

During the winter of 1944–45, some ten thousand infantry replacements poured off boats from the States into the ETO every week. Training cycles had been drastically shortened. The cannon fodder was either very young or very old. The new men were also justifiably very scared.

That almost all of them went to the infantry was a given. Forty thousand replacements coming into our ranks translated to ten thousand men per week leaving the front lines for hospitals or for Dutch and Belgian cemeteries.

The conventional Second World War rifle platoon lined up in four ranks. The first three rows were rifle squads of twelve men; the fourth rank was made up of automatic rifle, bazooka, and flamethrower teams, messengers, and "basics" who had not been assigned specific duties. The unassigned, private rifleman was at the bottom of the infantry pecking order, about as close as you could get to military anonymity.

In combat, the supernumerary role didn't last long. The extra riflemen moved into menial jobs, as surviving squad members moved up to fill the more specialized roles of evacuated comrades. The confused newcomers sometimes inherited duty they had never heard of. One late joiner told me, after combat was over, that he had carried a flamethrower for three weeks without the haziest idea of how to use it, nor did anyone in his platoon, including his sergeant, declare any knowledge of the lethal device. He was surprised to learn that he should have had a teammate bearing fuel and trained to assist in the instrument's fiery discharge.

Pvt. Richard Reynolds, like Stocky's Private Korda, joined Able Company under pitched battle conditions. Korda had found Stocky as his bosom buddy; Ferret Reynolds found in me a twenty-two-year-old daddy. After he earned acceptance in our group, he confessed his terror on that first night of his arrival.

Dubbed Ferret, because of his rodent-like, narrow features and intense stare (caused by bad eyesight, not rapt attention), yardbird Dick Reynolds had spent Christmas on POE (port of embarkation) leave at home, drinking beer with the few chums from his high school senior class who had escaped military service. He'd been rushed to Europe after a crash course in how to be an infantryman. The bruises on the biceps of his right arm from firing the M1 for record that had awed his pals at home had not fully disappeared when he was delivered to our less than tender care in Germany.

The distributors of fresh men had no notion of current conditions at the combat unit to which their charges were to be delivered. If things were quiet, fine. The recruit would be delivered to the company CP, introduced around, and maybe even told a little about what was expected of him. He was what the old noncoms called "orientated."

In Ferret's case, our company kitchen truck was on the move along with its coterie of rear-area personnel. When his escort discovered that our unit was on the move, Ferret was simply dumped and told to head "that way" to find Able Company and report to the first sergeant. His host was then long gone, back to his sack in the rear. Ferret was abandoned, helpless as a baby left on someone's porch.

Following tracks the company had left in the snow, and desperate for any kind of companionship, Reynolds caught up with our stragglers just before dark. A heavy barrage of German 88s and mortars commenced. The first man he encountered told him to dig a foxhole as fast as he could, and worry about reporting in later. Ferret dug with the energy of desperation and the panic of loneliness.

The abrupt commitment to the cacophony and din of battle stunned the youngster. He was caught up in an overwhelming nightmare that seemingly would go on forever. His mechanisms to reason, to measure time, to take care of himself were turned topsy-turvy. When morning finally came, he fully expected to crawl out of his hole and find himself abandoned and alone forever in a limitless wasteland of snow and blackened shell holes. He was sure everyone around him had been blown to kingdom come. Being alive was a miracle. War was exponentially worse than anything he had imagined.

That's when I was found by the hapless youngster. He was at my heels like a lost puppy as I made my rounds. No choice, I figured, but to join him up with my Fourth Platoon, though at that juncture I doubted that the forlorn little fart would ever be very useful. He was already developing that vacant, zombie look. Then, that very morning, someone in authority determined we had so many green men that our company should come off the front line long enough to teach new arrivals how to stay alive and become useful to others.

In our rifle company, light weapons platoon was still given first pick of replacements, hopefully to find men trained to shoot mortars or machine guns. Absent experienced candidates, we sought volunteers, figuring that willingness was half the game. Somehow, maybe because movies portrayed the work as extra dangerous, replacements rarely volunteered for mortars, and never for machine guns. Most trainee newcomers had an MOS (military occupational specialty) number 1812—basic rifleman. Legend persisted that the average combat life of a machine gunner in battle was bare minutes. So we came up empty and got our volunteers GI style: "You, you, and you. Fall out for duty with the Fourth Platoon." Then we had to teach Ferret and the rest their craft.

Poor Private Reynolds had missed a lot. In our good old days Stateside, after basic training came weapons familiarization, bivouacs, field exercises, and, for some, weeks-long maneuvers simulating battle conditions. We originals found that advanced training very helpful in the transition to real war.

These new kids were something. They didn't know from sic 'em. Our seasoned line riflemen were assigned to teach new men one-on-one about, of all things, the rifle. Some of the older members were surprised themselves at how much they remembered from their earlier, repetitive training with the infantryman's best friend, the Garand M1. Experienced dogfaces taught dry-firing with no ammo, describing for their pupils the proper sight picture, how to squeeze off rather than pull or jerk the trigger, how to break the rifle down for cleaning.

The regulars sat back in amusement as the hapless rookies tried to put their rifles back together again: "Look, boy, that there bolt goes up here. Keep the extractor and firing pin toward the front. Be sure the tang's on top the receiver bridge and it just about falls into place. Here! Gimme, goddamn it! I'll show you one more time, yardbird."

For real practice, instead of a firing range with white paper targets at two hundred yards, with Maggie's drawers to flag misses, various terrain features were picked out for the new men to shoot at. Repetitious firing familiarized them with the noise, recoil, and how to press in a new clip when the last of eight shots caused the bolt to remain open. Every replacement rifleman had to prove he could handle and shoot the M1.

The standard limit of a few live rounds allotted in the States for each trainee was waived. There were crates of cartridges. Concentrated firing exercises produced confident, instinctive shooters. In two days, many were handier with an M1 than peacetime trainees with weeks of formal instruction. Like hitting buckets of golf balls teaches a player that game, lots of shooting with an experienced coach makes a rifleman.

If you could handle an M1 Garand, you could work its little brother, the M1 carbine. The carbine was assigned to GIs who carried big loads or who required high mobility. Compared to the hefty Garand, carbines were more than two pounds lighter, shorter, and accommodated a fifteen-round magazine of smaller .30-caliber cartridges below the receiver rather than the Garand clip fed in from above. The powder charges were smaller, the lighter bullets slower, effective only up to three hundred yards compared to more than one thousand yards for the heavier piece. If you knew the right artificer back in supply, you might get a magazine that held thirty rounds and have him file the sear to modify the carbine for full-automatic, so it would perform like a tiny machine gun.

Functionally, the M1 carbine was, like its big brother, a gas-operated, air-cooled, shoulder weapon. You had to keep it a little cleaner, dry of excess oil, and rust-free, to avoid stoppages. It was designed to fire semiautomatic, one shot with each pull of the trigger, and that's the way it stayed for most GIs. It was a swell little weapon for close work like house-to-house fighting, and amazingly accurate in the hands of a dead-eye-dick marksman.

When it came to mortars and machine guns, we tried to pick the smartest and most trainable men. Smart might mean a little college; trainable was a fellow who knew how to fix motorcycles or trucks, or any farmer because he'd know how to fix about anything mechanical. Rifle platoon sergeants looked for the same qualities for Browning automatic rifle teams. If one of our chosen students turned out to be a dud, he was shifted to a bazooka or flamethrower team, not that those weapons didn't require equal proficiency. It was just that they were less frequently called on. I never did see anyone in our company put a flamethrower to use.

Training just to the rear of the front lines was different from putting in time goldbricking at Stateside classes. We demanded full attention and were impatient with slow learners. We required lots of self-study and practice. The recruits learned to place a mortar into action, setting its legs and base properly, sighting the aiming stake, leveling the longitudinal and traverse bubbles, preparing rounds for fire. Then, firing and adjusting fire. A constant reminder for new men to pay attention was the persistent rumble of artillery not far from our improvised training field.

At night, we old-timers tended to stick together, although we knew forming new bonds with our men was as important as it had been when some of our present regulars came up as replacements themselves. It was a camaraderie akin to men of the world sharing their worldliness among each other to the exclusion of virgins yet to prove their manhood. It wasn't a class thing. We just felt uncomfortable with the new arrivals, uneasy with their questions, and horribly inadequate to articulate what awaited them. We wanted them to know all we could tell them about the tools and techniques of war but we felt, universally, that none of us could provide the mental or psychological armor that each man secretly has to contrive for himself.

I was Sarge. I led. Men followed, some of them sticking as close to me as possible, hoping to have rubbed off on them some of the magic or charmed life they perceived had kept me alive this long. That's the way Ferret saw me.

The problem was that my "charmed life" was completely illusory. I felt as vulnerable as the rankest rookie, the pervasiveness of my personal trepidation enhanced by the random slaughter and chaos I had witnessed week after week.

I was getting grumpy back in our training area. I didn't want to return to combat, but with each passing day away from it, I feared for my ability to gird my loins for yet another round. We were to end up spending a whole week training new troops off the line. The difference in our lessons here was that they would all be put to use not three thousand miles away but just over the next ridge. The rookies were gaining confidence. I was gaining nothing but anxiety and self-doubt.

Learning Curve

W hen crack fighting units like the Airborne or Rangers were brought up to strength after battle losses, replacements came aboard with the necessary training to make them immediately useful. All that was needed was a little battle seasoning to blend them into a well-oiled machine. The people refilling our ranks were about as useful as tits on a boar hog.

Uncle Sam sent us three thousand miles to wage war, not just live through it. We veterans needed competent help. We were like a football team that suddenly loses half its starting lineup. Instead of a "bench" to call on for backup help, our reserve players were plucked willy-nilly out of the stands. The best chance we could give the raw rookies for survival was to teach them to use our killing tools. That old soldiers never die is bullshit. They just live longer when surrounded by other old soldiers who know their trade. We were grateful to have had a little time to teach new boys how to use a military rifle under comparatively safe conditions, but we were a far cry from transforming our replenished outfit into a capable fighting force. We had to compress weeks of more sophisticated weapons training into hours, and then refine techniques under battle conditions. We didn't want someone being killed during a lesson on how to deploy a machine gun or mortar.

Our MG virtuoso Sergeant Imo had taken on the training of those "volunteering" for machine-gun duty. I taught the kids we had picked out as potentials for mortar duty. So here, a few hundred yards off the front, I started from scratch my own brand of instruction. From the weeks of mortar training I had received, I had to carefully choose priorities learned in war that would most quickly qualify a bunch of neophytes.

Assembling my class of five freshly uniformed repples in a clearing near the CP, I hoisted a mortar by its strap from my shoulder and lowered it to the ground before them. I must have made a pretty picture as a teacher: bearded, bundled up in a ripped field jacket, a grenade dangling from my lapel, a German SS dagger secured along my shin under a boot-top strap. The net on my helmet was torn and awry, awaiting white camouflage if snow returned. I had removed my cartridge belt, adding to a picture of gross sloppiness. The gun was strapped neatly in its carrying mode. "Ever seen one of these before?" No response. No flicker of recognition.

I reached down and grabbed the shoulder loop of a loaded ammunition bib and swung it with practiced ease to lie next to the mortar.

"Well, men, if you never saw a mortar, you probably never have seen this either. This is an ammunition bag with twelve 60mm projectiles in it. You *will* get acquainted with this carrying bib." (The emphasized *will* is honest-to-God noncom talk.) "All of you are from this moment on mortar ammunition bearers. Gofers. Mules. Haulers. Carriers. Grunts."

I removed from the bag a black cardboard cylinder, peeled off the sealing tape around the lid, removed the top, and slid the mortar round into my hand. Pretty neat, actually. It looked like a little aerial bomb. The shiny, machine-tapered nose rising from the button-like PDF (point detonating fuse) was shiny-smooth, save for a thin safety wire to be pulled off before firing. Below the fuse was an aerodynamic steel body painted yellow with black lettering to signify an HE (high explosive) round.

What made the three-pound projectile resemble an airplane bomb were the four fins at its tapered base. They looked like an aerial missile whose fins stabilize it so it will drop straight down. And indeed, that was their purpose for this projectile, which eventually would fall almost vertically to its target. In the recess between each of the four tail fins was a shiny little plastic sac containing a precise measure of propellant powder. Visible through four holes drilled in the bottom of the "V" behind each powder charge was a red cylinder in the core of the base about the size of a shotgun shell—which it was, minus the pellets. The primer was visible in its brass base, awaiting contact with the firing pin.

The idea, I told the class, which by now was paying close attention, was that when the round was dropped fin-first into the mortar tube, a firing pin sticking up from the tube bottom would set off the shotgun charge, which would ignite the propellant powder. The whole mortar projectile would be tossed high, toward a target as far as a mile away. Anticipating the question, I added that if all four powder charges were removed, the .12-gauge cartridge by itself was capable of sending the mortar shell two hundred yards at the closest range setting, and as far as four or five hundred yards as the tube elevation was declined toward its maximum range at 45 degrees.

I explained that while the combined four powder charges produced maximum range of over a mile, as each bundle was removed the distance the shell would carry was decreased. Other variations in range came from changing the vertical angle of the tube, which we would get to later.

I dangled the little mortar shell with two fingers gripping a rear fin, and growled: "What happens if I drop this?" The little class recoiled, except for one compact, athletically built fellow who remained seated as he was, elbows on knees, eyes alert.

"You." I directed, pointing at his still figure. "Want me to drop it?"

"Long as I don't have to clean it up, go ahead," he replied, no challenge in his tone. "I never saw one before, but I bet it doesn't help it to get dirt all over it. With that safety wire I see there, it's not likely to go off. And if it would go off, you're not boob enough to drop it anyway."

I tried to retain my stern training-cadre look. No way. I broke up. I shook my head, and smiled at my star pupil.

"Name, soldier?"

"Harry Holley, Sergeant." I liked that he had the poise not to call me "Sir."

"Want to be a mortar gunner?"

"It hasn't been a lifetime ambition," Holley said evenly, "but given the hand I been dealt, why not?"

"Well, I'm about to show all of you how you get to be promoted to combat mortar gunner. You do it like my helper here, Sergeant Beales. You learn the trade. You hang in there until there's an opening. Those squareheads out there (I waved generally toward the enemy lines) make the openings. And I guaran-goddamn-tee you I'll pick the best qualified man," I concluded grimly, arms folded on my chest (shades of the late Sergeant Coleman, back Stateside).

"Now," I continued with the lesson, "There's only one gunner in a four-man mortar squad. But your army requires that everyone in the squad knows the gunner's job, right down to the last ammo bearer. Why's that?" I was pleased that my new guy didn't pop off, like I am sure he could have. A timorous voice from elsewhere:

"In case someone gets hurt?"

"Right," I replied, biting my tongue not to add "or killed." I picked up on the lesson:

"So if any of you ever shot off a Roman candle, you get the idea of how this here mortar works. You waggle the Roman candle around and point it straight up, that's where the colored ball goes. Lower it a little, and the lighted ball goes out in an arc, just like a mortar shell. You point the mortar tube the right direction, pick an elevation, drop this mother into the tube, and bang! Out she goes. A half-minute or so later, wham! She drops in some Kraut's back pocket. Or at least that's the idea. Now let's get busy and learn how to work this stovepipe."

I motioned to Rube Beales, who knelt to the left of the grounded gun. He went through what for him was an automatic routine to demonstrate how the mortar is set firmly on its three contact points, ready for action.

"How far's it going to shoot?" asked Private Holley.

"About a thousand yards, as it's now set up," I replied. "One thousand twenty-five with Charge-2, sixty-two degrees, according to the firing table that comes in the container with each round. Far enough to be sure not to hurt our guys out front of us, and close enough for the squad leader to observe the impact of the round.

"Let's see. Anything I left out?" I queried. Again my new protégé spoke up.

"If that's a trick question, Sarge, I guess you want us to say the safety wire has to be removed before dropping the round down the barrel."

"That's right," I replied. Actually, I had simply forgotten to mention it. Another point for my new man.

"Back in training," I went on, "you'd have an aiming stake stuck in the ground out toward the target, and all range and deflection adjustments would be made from that base point. In combat, we usually are not in business long enough to screw around with such refinements. Your squad leader or I can read the situation and tell you what to adjust so the next round is on target, or at least a hell of a lot nearer.

"With the base plate driven firmly into the ground from the first round, adjustments in range and direction can be made with as much effectiveness as your squad sergeant is capable of. Some of us are better than others, but as gunner you simply follow orders. You'll be out of sight of the target anyway, in order to keep you and the gun safe, so you simply concentrate on what you're told.

"Let's say that first round was pretty much right on for direction, but for the sake of argument, too far over the enemy target.

"For distance, you'll be told to move the elevating screw up or down and how many powder charges are required, usually one or two. If you're hitting out there too far, your orders will be for fewer charge bundles, higher elevation. You'll rarely use Charge-4, so get used to the idea of removing at least two powder bundles before firing."

"What you do with the unused powder packages, Sarge?" asked one student.

"Just toss 'em," I replied. "Without a detonator, they're as harmless as a pack of sugar from a K-ration box."

Continuing the lesson: "For direction, we'll tell you in numbers of turns of the traversing crank over there on the right side of the gun. There's one trick to gunnery, and that's keeping the leveling bubble centered as you move the tube right or left. Otherwise, you simply pivot the tube on the base and range changes unpredictably as you move in an arc, right or left. Keeping the sideways movement level gets you on target a whole lot faster. One turn of the traversing crank moves the round sideways fifteen yards at one thousand yards. Of course the change is fewer yards closer in, more yards at longer range. It's confusing now, but you'll get the idea. Rube, show 'em how you crank the barrel right or left." I paused in my discourse, sure I had gone too fast too far, but now I had reference points to start filling the lesson.

Rube smoothly cranked clockwise and the barrel moved to the left. At the same time, with each rotation of the crank, his left hand turned the leveling nut on the left leg a practiced twist clockwise. The leveling bubble never budged, remaining securely centered. Then Rube reversed the process, moving the barrel right, all the way to the end of the horizontal brass screw, his counterclockwise twists of the leveling screw maintaining a level bubble without his even looking down at it.

"Now I'm going to tell you the most important thing about firing the 60mm mortar, and it doesn't appear anywhere in the instruction manual," I told the class. "The procedures I have described are all shortcuts to speed up getting into action, how to fire, adjust fire, and hopefully destroy your objective. Whether you hit anything or not, you've only got so long in any tactical mortar mission. Then you must move out," I emphasized.

"Rube. Out of action!" I barked.

The experienced Farmboy cranked the elevating mechanism back into the guide tube, removed the sight and secured it in its case. He centered the nut on the traversing screw, slapped on the muzzle cover. After loosening the bipod locking clamp, he lifted the left leg, and shoved it against the right one. As the gun collapsed on the ground, bipod feet positioned under the base plate, he tightened the carrying strap and stood up, the gun clear of the ground. Elapsed time: fifteen seconds.

"Why the hurry? Well, men, mortar, like machine-gun fire, draws enemy counterfire like honey attracts bees and shit draws flies. You can bet from the very first round, some Kraut mortar squad, just like yours, is calculating range and angle to take you out. Or some squarehead with a machine gun is scrambling into a place where he can hit you. Or some crazy bastard with a burp gun is circling around to get a crack at you. The rule is: Shoot and run. That way, you might be around to shoot another day." Too bad Popeye hadn't heeded that advice, I thought silently.

"So endeth the sermon today," I intoned. "Lots to learn, men, but you seen it all. Now you just got to do it all." Late afternoon light was dwindling. So was I. Student Holley looked perplexed. He started to ask a question, thought better of it, and wisely awaited the next lesson to satisfy his curiosity. He'd make a good one. I hoped I'd have time to teach him before he (or I) was killed.

We were through schooling, and off the next day to the real thing, destruction and new fears. How much longer could I win the odds game?

CHAPTER **4** | # REMAGEN: MY BRIDGE TOO FAR

Regret to Inform You

—————————————⟨⟨◉⟩⟩—————————————

The calm I felt was something a hunted animal must experience when all signs of pursuit finally fade, and a haven has
been reached that instinct signals is safe and invulnerable. For too
many weeks, the threat of being maimed by a small arms bullet,
grenade, artillery shell, mortar burst, air strafing, huge aerial
bomb, or enemy bayonet sustained towering levels of dread. Con-
stantly. Apprehension varied in intensity, but was always present,
its hand on the throttle of that human mechanism that generates
adrenaline.

Now, for the moment at least, my system was producing no
adrenaline. I was slumped on a pile of blankets in a corner of
the cavernous basement of what had once been a huge German
foundry. Rising at least twenty feet toward the high ceiling above
the concrete floor were two gigantic furnaces, long since abandoned and cold. I lay close to one of them, the heavy mass a satisfying bulwark capable of warding off the most dire enemy missile,
if indeed anything could first penetrate the concrete roof of our
deep, deep refuge. This was pure, baby-crib safety.

The site had been chosen as battalion aid station because of its
obvious sanctuary, and because it was only hundreds of yards
from positions up the steep cliff that had been scaled by our rifle
company. The big furnaces aside, it more resembled a ramshackle

dormitory than a foundry. Canvas cots and litters occupied by casualties lined the floor parallel to the furnaces. At the far end of the cavern was the heart of the field aid station. I fantasized that the bright white light from the operating arena replicated the glow from flowing, molten metal that at one time must have illuminated the factory floor.

My present peace of mind derived from more than the structural protection of the stolid building. Major Al Leonard had stuck a needle in my butt as he was looking after my wounded hip to remove the shrapnel, clean it up, and apply a dressing. Almost immediately, a special warmth suffused every nook and cranny of my aching body, and gently bathed and numbed each frazzled nerve end. I marveled that a skinny, shiny needle could so quickly deliver such complete freedom from anxiety.

The battalion aid station on the Rhine River was safe as long as we held the heights commanding the enemy shore of Ludendorf Bridge at Remagen. We had scratched our way to the peak at night following a forced march on March 10 that took us across the beleaguered railroad bridge. Now, secure on enemy soil, I recalled only the fear of climbing cliffs under fire in the pitch dark.

I had traveled full circle back to the formidable black-iron bridge, which was now only a few hundred yards upstream. Our factory building muffled the constant sound of antiaircraft and machine guns shooting at enemy planes bent on destroying the single thread of access the Allies had to inner Germany across the Rhine River. Ack-ack units were parked along the shore back-to-back, as far as the eye could see. It was to be days before aerial bombs so weakened the huge trestle that it collapsed into the black water below.

In my fingers I rolled back and forth an acorn-sized nugget of shrapnel that Doc Leonard had handed me a few minutes earlier. It was something special, mined from the flesh of my very own body. My filthy fingertips recorded the sharp edges and tiny spears on the fragment, born of the powerful explosion that had burst the thick walls of the shell into thousands of lethal missiles, each of them as unique and different as a fingerprint. My God, I thought wryly, something like this could kill a fellow.

I was sure that the shell that had wounded me had been misdirected friendly fire. Dreamily, I speculated that the steel fragment in my hip had once been a LaSalle or Ford V-8, or a worn-out railroad switch, or the yield of a community metal drive that included the wrought-iron fence in front of the courthouse. Maybe it was part of an old mowing machine our farm had donated for scrap. Why hadn't this speeding piece of steel torn me in half?

Doc Leonard explained my good fortune as he went about exploring the damage, finally extracting the fragment by working it out of my flesh with big tweezers and rubber-gloved fingers. It was only a little over an inch below my skin.

The ragged steel shard had struck at belt level, right above my left rear pants pocket. Doc ticked off an inventory of the tough fabrics it had passed through before penetrating my soft flesh: Several layers of rubberized rain poncho folded over my belt, the web cartridge belt itself, field jacket, wool pants (it missed the slightly higher, narrow web belt that held them up), wool shirt, wool sweater, undershirt, and long johns. Many of the clothing items were haphazardly tucked in various thicknesses or folds. Without those tough materials to slow its flight, Doc said, the slug certainly would have spelled the end of my hip, pelvis, and, he speculated, possibly my genitals.

Doc guessed that the shell had struck pretty close to disperse fragments with such force. I confirmed that, and told him about my companion who was not in his care and never would be.

We had just taken "the high ground," a familiar objective for foot soldiers in every war. At the peak of the objective rock-quarry hilltop, it had been impossible to dig a hole, so one of my new ammo bearers, Pvt. John Cotes, and I piled quarried rocks in two ovals around side-by-side depressions we had grubbed out between the stones. We hunkered down in these fortified depressions when artillery started to rake the hilltop.

Not muffled by trees or soft earth, the shells that skimmed just over the hilltop were deadly banshees that wailed and warned. The projectiles screeched their dire threats as they sped by a scant foot or so over our heads. I don't recall hearing those that passed us up exploding in the rear. Since they were on high-velocity paths at the crown of their flight over us, they went far beyond to explode in valleys we could not even see. The artillery fire was coming, inexplicably, from our side. I yelled at Cotes that this was friendly fire, and that we'd better seek protection on the enemy side of our peak.

That's when we took a direct hit.

Sprawled on the hard surface amid the dust of crushed rock, burnt powder, and falling rubble, for the moment I could not breathe. It was not exactly like having the breath knocked out of you. It was like trying to catch your breath in a vacuum. I gasped, but air refused to come. Then great rushes filled my lungs. The acrid powder and dust provoked retching coughs, and set off a display of bright spots before my eyes. Looking about, I was completely disoriented. I couldn't locate the wall of my protective, partially aboveground foxhole. My helmet was missing.

Facing Cotes's crude foxhole, I finally realized that my shelter no longer had a wall on his side. It had disappeared in the explosion. Nor was there any Cotes. His entire little nest was gone, scrubbed clean off the earth by the blast of a U.S. Army 105mm shell. I recognized part of his ammo bag, noting that the mortar rounds he carried had been blown apart, some chopped into pieces, but apparently none of them detonated by the exploding 105. Cotes's rifle lay unscratched where he had lain. Scattered around the impact area were patches of clothing, red shreds of Cotes sticking to some of them.

Cautiously, my hands started to explore my upper body for signs of damage. Searching fingers encountered a warm, wet glob stuck to the front of my field jacket. Pulling it slowly off, I discovered close-up a hairy patch of skin with a lump of flesh attached. The sticky mess turned as I peeled it off my coat. A human ear took shape before my eyes. Feeling a little foolish at my immediate reaction, I touched both sides of my head with my free hand to confirm it was not me. A small part of Private Cotes's head was my unwelcome companion.

Breathing in shallow, quick gasps, I grabbed the sling of my carbine that lay outside the remaining partial wall of my foxhole and tumbled down the hillside I had recently climbed to secure our forward observation post. I did not head, as I had just advised the late Cotes, for safety on the lee side of the shelling. Like a wounded animal, I instinctively headed for home base, toward our men, down the cliff-like gravel slope.

The sensation of my carbine banging along the ground after me made me realize that my trusty weapon had been blown in two, the stock broken off just behind the trigger guard and receiver. I let go of the sling attached to the battered parts and redoubled my effort to distance myself from the killing peak.

Inside an old quarry machinery shed that now served as a temporary company shelter, I gradually became aware that Captain Goodspeed was wiping my blackened face and hands with a rag, Talking in earnest tones, his voice came from way behind an echoing wall of sound still roiling in the caverns of my empty head. I sat very still, feeling neither heat, nor cold, nor pain. I felt strangely outside the person the captain was examining so diligently.

Goodspeed was explaining that he had jumped on the radio to stop the artillery fire. The artillery forward observer, Lt. Charley King, didn't realize some of us had reached the top of the mountain, and had called in what he thought was support for our attack. Usually he was right up there with our leading elements, but this time he had slipped up, not realizing that Cotes and I had gotten so far ahead of him. As a rule we were almost side by side, me seeking a vantage point to direct our 60mm mortars, King doing the same to adjust fire for his artillery battery. It never occurred to me to blame King for my plight. The error was unintentional. It was not the first or last occasion we would be victims of friendly fire.

T-5 Medic Charley Carpenter scuttled into the CP. He grasped and rotated both my hands, and asked if I hurt anywhere. I gave him a brief negative headshake. He pulled me to my feet.

"Hey, Captain," the medic exclaimed. "Take a look at Sarge's keister. The seat of his pants is all ripped up and bloody."

Carpenter and the captain unbuttoned my pants for a closer look. Without exposing me to cold and shock by removing any more of my clothes, they informed me I had been hit and that it was my blood. Carpenter sprinkled sulfa powder on the wound from my first-aid kit, and placed a gauze bandage over the angry red hole before refastening my pants. Only then did I experience a slight burning sensation, an awareness, but no real pain. I started to tremble as I recalled Lount and the shock that had killed him when he realized he had been hit. But this wasn't bad like his, was it? I willed myself to calm down.

Carpenter said the darker blood meant no arterial bleeding. Then he had to take off. There were cries for "medic" and "stretcher," elsewhere on the hillside. He told me to stay under cover until dusk when the weasel would come from our kitchen to the bottom of the mountain with chow. A weasel is a jeep powered by tank-like treads. He told me to ride with the cooks back to battalion aid. He reassured himself that I could navigate, that I could qualify as "walking wounded," at least until the wound stiffened up. The crackle of small-arms fire outside also grabbed Captain Goodspeed's immediate attention. I was left alone. Well, almost alone.

In a darkened corner of the shed was a crouched form, so motionless that I thought he might be dead. I crawled over, the pain more annoying than hampering. It was little Hubba Hubba Derrick, Second Platoon rifleman, hugging his knees to his chest. His ineptitude with weapons and general consternation during combat had relegated him to the company CP, where he was supposed to perform less-demanding tasks as a runner or messenger.

While we finished our desperate attack up the mountain, Hubba Hubba had been impatiently shoved into the shed and told to remain there. He had deteriorated mentally, unfit to carry out the most simple assignment. A clear case of battle fatigue, diagnosed Medic Carpenter. Priorities of caring for and evacuating combat wounded temporarily prevented an escort to the rear for Private Derrick; he was simply ignored.

I sat down by Hubba Hubba, comforted to have companionship, however uncommunicative. Hubba Hubba was actually a pretty good guy. He'd been hung with that appellation way back in training days. When a platoon on informal route march had nothing better to do, nothing to say, no songs to sing, no cadence to count,

someone would shout out "hubba hubba" and like peacocks or-
chestrated to echo their leader's call, everyone in the outfit would
sound off "hubba hubba" for several seconds. An enthusiastic par-
ticipant, Pvt. Fred Derrick finally inherited Hubba Hubba as his
own handle.

All you had to do was say "Hi" to Derrick, to draw a cheery
"hubba hubba." Say good-bye, same thing. Ask a question: hubba
hubba. Give him an order: hubba hubba. Tell him it's chow time:
hubba hubba. Ask him his name: Hubba Hubba. He drove everyone crazy. Now it was Hubba Hubba turned fully nutty. Hubba
Hubba had suffered all the war he could handle.

The firing died down, and dusk formed. Critical action elsewhere on the hillside left the CP empty, and me with a decision.
Before I got stiff, I should head down the hill where the track-
laying chow weasel was scheduled to come. Should I take Hubba
Hubba along? Why not? If my hip didn't hold up, maybe I could
lean on him. And he certainly needed someone on whom he could
lean, mentally.

So off we started, me still without a helmet or rifle, Hubba
Hubba carting an M1 almost as long as he was. I had to order him
to his feet and lead him by the hand like a little kid as we made
our way down to the path. He said nothing. There was not even a
glint of recognition in his eye. But when I had sharply commanded him to move out, the trained response, conditioned by
the repetition that makes military discipline what it is, stirred him
to his feet.

In relative calm, the chow-carrying weasel arrived like a little
tank, just about when we did. Soon we were clanking our way
down a winding dirt road to the "doctor's office," battalion aid.
Sharp pain had set in.

So, here I was, all comfy and feeling swell, safe in Doc Leonard's care. Poor Hubba Hubba had been shoved into an empty six-
by-six headed for the rear. He was denied the dignity and comfort
of ambulance evacuation in favor of those with threatening,
bleeding wounds. But I sensed, sadly, that Hubba Hubba's injuries
were altogether as deep and serious as a sucking chest wound.
There was to be no quick remedy, maybe no cure at all. The best

doctors in the world might not be able to put Humpty-Dumpty-Hubba-Hubba's head back together again.

Still euphoric and a little intoxicated, I took stock of my own surroundings and condition. Doc Leonard had said he'd look me over more closely when the stream of incoming patients subsided, and for now I should just stick around. I liked that. No place I wanted to go, anyway. I dozed, sipped on Halazone-flavored water from my canteen, and wondered how the guys were doing back on the hill. I couldn't rid myself of the vision of Cotes's disappearance. Hardened as I was to seeing men hit, killed, there was something particularly unnerving about evaporating into nothingness as had Cotes.

Poor Cotes, I thought. Lend me an ear. Suddenly I felt dizzy and nauseated. Forcing deep breaths, I vowed one day to find out who Cotes really was and to tell his parents he had died a noble death. Because there was so little of him left to remember, I wanted desperately to recreate him as he was, as he had been, before this lousy war. I needed to form a picture of the whole Cotes to assure myself that he had ever existed. While I knew his name, we really had never talked. He was part of a stream of faceless replacements.

How many other replacements would come and go and be recorded only briefly, quickly forgotten names among comrades in arms who somehow would survive them to carry on?

"We regret to inform you" was the opening line pasted on the Western Union telegram forms to inform families back home of wounded, missing, and killed in action. That's all Cotes's people would be told. That's all my grandmother and my mother ever knew about my Uncle John, who died in the infantry on the western front on November 1, 1918. I had wondered as I grew up what really happened to him. We'd talked about it. My mother had wanted desperately to have some description, a letter, any word at all, on how and exactly where he had died.

These thoughts alerted me to my present state. Greatly agitated, I told a passing medic that I had to see Major Leonard—not later, but right now. Puzzled but sensing real concern on my part, he brought Doc out of the treatment area.

"What's up, young fella? Something wrong? You hurting?"

"That's not it, Doc, it's a whole lot more important," I said anxiously. "You haven't sent a telegram home that I been wounded, have you?"

Major Leonard smiled, relieved that it was not my wound that concerned me. "No, no, not yet. We usually authorize that when you ship out of here by ambulance to a rear area or base hospital. We'll probably send you back to the hospital tomorrow. That's when the telegram will be sent."

"Let's put a lid on it, Doc," I begged. "I'm not that bad off, and it would scare my mother to death. Let me hang around back here for a little while, and when I start feeling better, I'll simply go back to the company. No need for a telegram," I pleaded.

"If they check you into a hospital, the wire goes out automatically," admonished Leonard. "For now we'll keep the record open. But you are forbidden by me to return to your unit till I give you permission." His eye regained its characteristic twinkle. "You and I have been together too long, Sarge, to break up that old gang of ours just yet."

I heard those last words, but acknowledged them simply by falling fast asleep.

Kitchen Commandos

———————————— ⟫⟪⟨⬤⟩⟫ ————————————

Having avoided medical evacuation and the scary official telegram that would have been sent home, I favored my wounded hip by riding the ammo jeep or chow weasel when a long march took place. Otherwise, I participated in the village-to-village skirmishes that characterized the fighting after the Remagen bridgehead was secured. The weather was improving. The snow had given way to mud. While layers of clothing had limited its penetration, the heavy blow of the shrapnel left my hip numb, so it was not pain from the wound that made me gimpy. It was swollen glands in the groin below, irritated by infection, aggravated by exercise.

I hitched a ride with the visiting battalion operations officer (S-3) back to the aid station every day or so for a change of dressing, and returned to the front with the chow weasel. The weasel was a jeep-size carrier with tank treads. It was the only reliable transportation in mud that bogged down anything on wheels that ventured off a roadway.

That's where I had my first glimpse of able soldiers ducking wartime hardship. They were hanging out at the company mess in the safe battalion headquarters area, near the aid station. What a discouraging revelation!

A rear-area refuge was the appropriate base for our supply sergeant, mail clerk, a few soldiers assigned to lay phone wires and run messages, jeep jockeys, the company clerk, first sergeant, and of course the kitchen crew, including our tipsy mess sergeant and the great cooks who had shipped out with us from the States. The cooks were "family," all first-name acquaintances.

Actually, our chief belly-robber had shaped up pretty good himself. The mess crew he ran was commended high and low for consistency in preparing hot meals, but more important, for delivering them to us dogfaces on the line. They had really gone the distance in feeding us during many a dangerous artillery barrage. The crew was understandably pooped out, and always shit-scared while filling our mess kits; but they could go to sleep in the rear echelon for a few hours each night, satisfied they'd done their jobs.

The mess sergeant issued his orders from a field kitchen transported by the ubiquitous GI six-by-six transport truck, and set up where it was temporarily safe and convenient after each move. He rarely ventured to the front to dish up the meals. On the occasions he did, he was so jumpy and nervous that he could scarcely handle a stew ladle, much less dispense coffee. When he had a chance to fortify his bravery with booze, he came up half drunk.

But then it was not the chief chef's lot to be a combat soldier. His mission was to provide life-sustaining fodder for us cannon fodder. There was no opportunity for him to follow his primary calling, gambling. So, instead of buying poker games with his ample bankroll, to his credit, he concentrated on being a good mess sergeant.

Company headquarters and the kitchen were placed far enough to the rear to be safe from enemy artillery. Headquarters personnel usually enjoyed comfortable rooms in commandeered houses that had survived shelling. At present, two such billets were near the open shed that served as Company A's kitchen. Personnel at the rear had to eat too, and usually did so just before the chow run to the front. That's when I first saw Technical Sergeant Oaks again, shining mess kit in hand, working his way toward the steaming food containers.

The noncom, who had been our steadfast Stateside training

taskmaster, had not been up front with the platoon since opening day. Now he headed a straggling handful of soldiers of various ranks, including another five-striper, John Schoen, also one of our former Stateside training noncoms. I thought Platoon Sergeant Schoen had been wounded and evacuated. He and Oaks skulked away with filled mess kits, disappearing into one of the nearby houses.

While awaiting the ride back up to the front with the night's hot supper, I sought out my favorite cook, Cpl. Ivan D. (ID) Wilson. ID had salved my hunger more than once with a nighttime snack when we were in garrison. In combat, he was one of the faithful delivering chow to the front.

I buttonholed ID and told him to level with me about how regular line noncoms got to hang out back of the lines. I was flustered and getting madder by the minute as I contemplated these kitchen commandos.

"Well, the way I get it, Sarge, they're not injured bad enough to evacuate, but they are harmed enough not to stand full-time combat duty up with you dogfaces."

Looking down at the ground, ID did his best to explain. "Now, Sergeant Schoen there, well, he's managed to last out here for a long time. He's taken on the job of orienting and assigning new men as they come through the repple depple. He says he can help out best by wising these kids up as to what they can expect up front with you guys, and recommending jobs after he sizes them up. Says he can tell whether a man ought to be a rifleman, BAR man, machine gunner, bazooka man, whatever," ID finished lamely.

"And he's designated an invalid?" I asked. "Sounds to me like he's got yellowing-of-the-stripe down his back."

"Well, it's hard to say. Like Oaks, he was reporting to the aid station regular-like to get some injury worked on, but actually none of us ever seen what was wrong with them. And lately the two of 'em don't even bother to go on sick call. So how sick are they? You tell me," the cook finished.

I caught up with S. Sgt. John Wolcott, one of our original Stateside group, and still company supply sergeant. We had grown close as time after time he had come forward with his jeep to find my platoon and replenish mortar and machine-gun ammo. He also passed out extra bandoleers of rifle cartridges, K rations, and cigarettes. I doubly appreciated his effort, since I knew Wolcott as an extraordinarily mild and noncombative fellow who paled in the face of violence. It had been a harsh transition from working at a retail fruit stand in civilian days.

As tough as it was for any of us to face enemy fire, it was more gut wrenching for John than for most of us regular soldiers on the line. Our jobs gave us no choice. Wolcott could have found a million excuses not to go that extra few yards toward danger, and no one would have been the wiser. When I told him of my admiration for that kind of balls, he beamed all over with pride. I later feared my expression of approbation might goad him into venturing too close, and get him killed. His trips to the front lines were already what citations termed "above and beyond the call of duty."

I put pretty much the same question to him that I had posed to ID. How the hell did these high-ranked noncoms get to live the good life while the rest of us fought their battles and insulated them from the odds?

He replied that some of them had been permitted to stay back there by the captain himself, who worried that they had lost the crucial will to fight, and just might get someone else killed by pushing from behind rather than leading out front. Others had nagging wounds or old injuries like a trick football knee, and hung out promising they'd go up any day, as soon as they were "better." They snowed the medicos and staff officers who questioned them, their clever inventiveness born of fear and self-preservation.

After a few months in combat, Tech Sergeant Schoen had come alone on foot to the rear, blubbering that he hurt all over and that his ears couldn't take any more artillery. It was either bust him down to private and send him back up to spread hysteria as contagious as the plague or, as it turned out, use his background and training skills to process replacement green men from repple depple. The frightened transfers were impressed with his five stripes, Combat Infantryman Badge, military manner, and commanding voice. He was good at it. Instead of an indictment for desertion or conspicuous cowardice, the judgment ironically was to let him remain safe himself, while he told rookies how to "go up there and fight like hell."

Among the more promising replacements were technicians and noncoms rushed in from other branches of the service where weapons were typewriters and mechanical devices. Because they had already proved capable of rank, it made them more likely candidates to master complicated automatic weapons, antitank bazookas, and mortars. The kitchen commandos taught them.

These two old Regular Army pals, Schoen and Oaks, were doing what they did in the States: training recruits. The pace of war had slowed now to accommodate this activity in the rear echelon, as opposed to pulling us off the line as had been done earlier, to qualify replacements as fighting men. I resented deeply that these bozos had been able to persuade our officers to exchange the peril we experienced daily at the front for this cushy life. Maybe I was just plain envious.

I thought of my aching hip, swollen glands, and growing mental fatigue. Not a bad set of credentials for a similar job in the rear. Then I thought of Farmboy, Imo, two new gunners, and the ever-smaller band who'd been with me since day one. Something told me that if I ever got separated from my frontline gang, I'd never make it through. I would dissolve in a gibbering mess if I some-how got transferred and had to fight alongside strangers.

Wolcott aced my decision for me: "I wouldn't give him the sweat off my balls, he was dying of thirst," Wolcott went on about Oaks. "He tried to pull rank on me. So I asked him to ride up to the front and deliver ammo to you guys one day when things were hot up there. When he started hemming and hawing, I told him off big time, and now he stays the fuck outa my way."

Would as simple a thing as disdain from a supply sergeant be enough to keep my sorry ass on the firing line? I set off toward the chow weasel to hook a ride back to the lines.

CHAPTER 5 | MOP UP AND FINIS

Let's Roll

—————————— ««◉»» ‑‑‑‑‑‑‑‑‑‑‑‑

O nce it developed momentum, the final battle of World War II in the ETO was a roller-coaster ride with parts of the track missing. It was satisfying to take great chunks of land with relative ease. But about the time we got used to surging through villages with white surrender flags hanging from the windows, we'd encounter a strong point of dug-in Krauts firing rifles and machine guns at us. Sometimes the defenders, kids and older men, would come out, hands up, when our skirmish lines approached. On other occasions, we'd encounter remnants of the regulars and deal with vengeful fire as only we old-timers knew how: hit them from three sides. If they didn't surrender, they displaced to the rear, which is military for taking a powder.

This last battle past the Rhine River, starting in early April 1945 deep in the heartland of Germany, was called the Ruhr Pocket, pocket implying correctly that the remaining armies of industrial Germany were hemmed in on all sides. It was a heady experience for us, accustomed as we were to stubborn resistance.

Brand new replacements experienced a different, and far more benign, introduction to combat than had greeted us veterans of earlier pitched battles. They sensed growing relaxation of tension among the seasoned soldiers they joined. And with snow and sub-zero winter behind us, they could concentrate on watching out for their own asses without freezing to death. Trench foot was a faded white memory.

But the big, big difference was relief from the relentless 88 artillery barrages that for weeks had inflicted on us combat fatigue and butchery. War without that giant boom just wasn't the same monster.

If we seized a community that had been evacuated, we learned to expect booby traps and mines. Some were diabolical. Others were the standard trip wire connected to a doorknob to pull the pin on a Potato Masher hand grenade. (The wooden handle for throwing it, plus the grenade on the end, looked like, well, a potato masher.) The warning pop of the timed fuse gave the surprised intruder the same few seconds to duck for cover that the Kraut would have had to throw it and take cover.

If we had a compelling need for support, we could call on TDs (tank destroyers) or self-propelled (SP) guns mounted on tank-like vehicles. They had the mobility to keep up with our advance. Our own regimental cannon company and division 105s had their guns mounted on two wheels, towed by trucks or half-tracks. They could not go cross-country with the infantry, nor anticipate where we would be. Because they moved by jeep or on foot with us, the heavy weapons company took the place of howitzers, lobbing their deadly 81mm shells; and our little 60mm tubes also provided fast and reassuring support. We rarely dug foxholes, convinced that heavily armed counterattacks were unlikely. Our spotter planes observed enemy artillery being towed by trucks or horses in retreat. We had reason to suspect that, even if they had time to stop and shoot, their caissons were probably empty of ammunition.

Some of our seasoned soldiers became downright cavalier about personal safety. Spared regular pounding by artillery, they indulged themselves with forays into homes and businesses in towns that had largely escaped destruction by bombs and shells. Sporadic fire from a bunch of kids and their grandpas slowed them only temporarily. Once small arms fire died down, indicating that defenders were bugging out, they resorted to the conquering soldier's cruel sport: looting.

Rube and I did our share of picking through ruins—looting, to put it plainly. But we grew uncomfortable with the excesses of some of our comrades. Dependable soldiers, even very good soldiers, seemed to go a little bit crazy the first time that reduced combat pressure allowed options other than simply staying alive.

Accountability to family, friends, and neighbors is a strong tenet among American high-school-aged boys. These guys were a long way from home, in an environment that embraced violent death and encouraged brutality. Recklessness surfaced where caution had reigned. There was no one from their home scene to hold them accountable, or to tell on them. They reacted like little kids left unattended for too long at home. They ran wild.

Groups of stubborn inhabitants, unwilling to abandon hometowns, huddled in cellars during our noisy invasion. Their emptied homes, some with warm food still on the stove or table, were easy prey. Practiced looters soon learned that valuables were not likely to be out in plain sight, or located in bedroom drawers and kitchen cupboards. They headed straight for attics, obscure trap doors, and the cold root cellar dugout used to preserve potatoes, sugar beets, and turnips. The most unlikely places yielded occasional silverware, jewelry, schnapps, wine, or family valuables. Sometimes there was even a pistol. There were some remarkable fabrics, but even the most delicate lace or embroidery was relegated to such grubby tasks as cleaning guns, or squirreled away as toilet paper and handkerchiefs.

If any inhabitants were still somewhere in town, it was unlikely they would have booby-trapped their own homes and thereby invited vicious reprisals or risked killing their own people by mistake.

As for me, I'd had it with souvenirs. Just more baggage to carry for us weapons platoon types, already overloaded with heavy guns and ammunition. At one point I had a nice World War I Luger pistol, an engraved SS dagger, some watches, and a pocketful of German medals that I was saving for later identification. But one nightmarish night, we were surrounded and imminently to become prisoners of war. I unloaded and buried all the foreign loot except the SS dagger. Discovered with such items, my captors were not likely to deliver me unharmed to one of their comfy stalags. For sure, if we had found American souvenirs on a Kraut prisoner, he would have been long gone before he ever made it to our POW cage. We never did suffer capture that day, so I didn't have to toss the dagger away. Lord knows where in the dark woods my cache remains buried.

On our headlong plunge into the heart of the fatherland we took one charming creekside village by storm, and were told to hold up to allow another division unit to leapfrog us and take the next town. That meant several hours of time off and, since it was already afternoon, a rest until the next day, when we in turn would be the leapfroggers. Preparation, a euphemism for whacking the hell out of an objective with heavy shelling, preceded our sweep into the community. Its recent denizens had all been scared off. A few buildings were still burning or smoldering.

That very day I'd "liberated" a 5.35mm (.25 caliber) automatic pistol from a cabinet in a public-type building, along with a lunch-pail-size wooden box chock full of the cartridges that were made for that little personal weapon. This was one souvenir I meant to keep. It was small enough to fit in a shirt front pocket, no more conspicuous than a cigarette case. To shoot it in battle outdoors would have been ridiculous. Too little. Too light. But in the confines of a room, it could be effective and deadly. I liked my new-found peashooter.

Halfway down the main drag was the local tavern, the neighborhood watering hole traditional in every German community. The windows were broken, including the thick pane in the heavy front door. While the main barroom had been turned upside down by our looters, it took only minimal effort to right a comfortable chair and set the room in reasonable order. I was alone, although I could hear my comrades shouting, shooting, and passing by the doorway from time to time. I loaded the pistol clip, slammed it home, snapped off the safety, and took aim at a hand-carved wooden figurine above the back bar. Bang! I missed it by three feet.

I lowered my gun hand to lap level and pointed the pistol roughly in the direction of the little wooden figure. Wham! Just about as close. Still not sighting down the barrel, I pointed and emptied the clip of seven, one shot coming pretty close to the target. In the next hour, I loaded and reloaded and banged away offhand at various targets lining the interior wall and back bar. A few platoon members sauntered in to watch and set up drinking glasses, mugs, china plates, pewter goblets, even empty C ration cans. I became proficient at "instinct shooting." The theory is that you point a pistol just like you point your finger and develop remarkable accuracy at centering up a specific target. I got to where I could shoot from the waist to plink about any target my pals picked out. When I finally pocketed the pistol and slipped a few extra rounds in a spare pocket, it was dusk, and I had my own personal defense system.

Hot chow had arrived: veal stew, the cooks asserted, although those of us who had to eat it figured it was butchered goat or maybe Great Dane. But anything hot was good, and partly mixed in a mess kit with canned fruit cocktail and reconstituted mashed potatoes, the hot-sweet-sticky mess was a gourmet delight. The coffee was hot. That was good. But as usual it was premixed with condensed milk and sugar. That was bad, and would lead to a lifelong preference for black coffee. But on balance, no complaints and no questions as to whether there was to be any dessert. There wasn't.

Done eating, we swished the empty mess kit in a drum of water boiling over a fresh wood fire. We washed our cup in the same GI-soap-laced water, then the usual rinse tub for both utensils. After refilling our canteens from the Lister bag, we fitted them into the cups and inserted both into the canvas covers hooked to our cartridge belts. Meal and dish washing were complete for the day.

Down the street an isolated frame house was burning fiercely. There had been no recent artillery barrage from either side, so I wandered down to see what had happened. It was getting dark and cold.

A squad of riflemen had picked the house for shelter and, failing to find blankets or other fabrics in the house to keep them warm, they smashed a delicate little wooden bric-a-brac shelf on the floor, and set it afire. The welcome heat from the varnished fragments grew, as did the smoke, so they withdrew to the next room. In a few minutes, flames from the fire they had set spread across the floor, up the tinder-dry walls, and threatened the rest of the interior. Driven out into the street, the squad was now standing around watching the flames consume the house, basking in the heat, retreating step by step as its intensity grew. When the fire peaked and started to die down, the GIs became bored and wandered off to find a place to bunk for the night.

Spring had turned snow to mud, subfreezing cold to bone-chilling wet. The newer replacements suffered more from the early spring chill than we old-timers who had grown accustomed to being so cold that even a slight improvement in temperature was welcome. Some of us could scarcely remember being warm, as in at-home warm in a comfortable kitchen, cheery living room, or a bed with familiar, worn blankets.

Then came still another product of our brief respite from incessant enemy threat.

S. Sgt. Edward Hart had come up as a replacement private back in the Bulge. He had his problems, like all new men, but he had the resilience and adaptability that helped him adjust to life as a combat dogface. He evidenced moments of terror, as did we all, but still stood out as a potential leader. A Steady Eddy type. That's why he made rifle squad leader and was awarded four stripes. He was a pretty fair noncom.

In our forlorn, conquered creekside village, he came alongside me while we both idly watched the dying embers of the torched house. He poked me in the ribs with an elbow and in a conspiratorial whisper, allowed that he had just "knocked off a piece."

"Piece?" said I. "Knocked off a what? What the hell you been up to, Hart?" I sensed that "piece" didn't refer to a military rifle.

"I mean a real piece," Hart replied triumphantly, "as in a piece of ass." I didn't know what to say, didn't say anything.

"Yeah," Sergeant Hart went on. "I was snooping around over a couple of streets there when I heard someone down in the cellar. I started to toss in a grenade and then figured it might be one of our guys looting. So I gave out with the old '*Hande Hoche*,' and up the stairs comes this big mama, scared half to death." I remained silent. Ed couldn't stop talking.

"Well, it was getting dark, but I got a good look at her, and she wasn't so old after all, and not half bad. So I had her right there on the kitchen table."

"You what?" I said incredulously.

"Just what I said. I screwed her. Screwed her good." His lined, dirty face peered at me in the flickering light.

He made no attempt at justification: "Well, she had it coming. They all do, them fucking creeps. For three months they been trying to kill my ass. Three months and four days, come right down to it.

"I told myself back at the Rhine that if I ever lived long enough to do it, I'd get my rocks off just one more time, 'cause it still looks like the odds don't favor me, or you, Sarge, ever getting back home where you can hump your girl in the back of the old family Ford, or up in the sack. I couldn't face dying without at least one more notch on the old gun. So it wasn't exactly a movie romance. But by God, it was a piece of ass! I swear, it wasn't rape. Shit, 'fore I finished, I think the old gal was really enjoying it much as me."

Mumbling in a tone that still invited approbation, S. Sgt. Edward Hart wandered down the street. He never mentioned his terrible misdeed to me again; I suspect he never told anyone else. Sergeant Hart escaped death by war. In his later life working in the family hardware store, I wonder how far down and for how long he was able to bury his shabby transgression. I never bothered to look him up to find out. He never attended a veterans' gathering.

That night in the creekside village frightened me about myself and my fellow soldiers. Given even a brief pause in the intensity of war, what we sought for release did not paint a pretty picture. I knew that conquering soldiers were a rough lot throughout history: rape and pillage. Should I expect that we citizens-turned-soldiers would be any different?

Prolonged battle had changed us profoundly, although we didn't really know in what ways. Some innate mechanism allowed us somehow to erect a protective screen that compartmentalized our sensitivities and sensibilities. Fundamental values and moral qualities survived to emerge when called on by many of us, no matter the degree of trauma we had experienced.

Basic behavior values didn't prevail for everyone, and were topsy-turvy in greater degree among the new men who had not been humbled by bitter combat. For some among the battle-hardened, Hart one of them, relentless pressure had permanently eroded or erased norms of behavior and respectability. For some, those precious values never fully returned.

Would we ever be able to return to the lives we had once known, to lifestyles that dimmed in our memories more with each passing day of combat? Was I, like that neanderthal Hart, becoming depraved? Would new and shoddy values replace those implanted in our schoolrooms, churches, living rooms, locker rooms, and clubs? Would we sink, or had we sunk, to enjoyment and satisfaction in practicing brutality? I didn't want to dig too hard for the answers.

Getting Even

—————⟨⟨●⟩⟩—————

A boy growing up during the 1930s and early '40s had his share of conflict and competition. After a playground wrestling match and shoving matches in the school corridors, you found your place among your peers. If you were really enterprising and assertive, you could take those Charles Atlas ads for his body-building course to heart, in the hope you might resemble old Chuck one day, with his rippling muscles and bulging chest. Bet your ass no bully would kick sand in your face at the beach. He'd take one look at your torso, and you wouldn't even have to lay a hand on him. But the Charles Atlas course was too much like work. Looking and talking tough was the easiest way to avoid violent conflict.

Kids, like wild animals, tended to stare each other down, and rare fights were brief and inconclusive, rarely producing bodily injury. "Step outside and we'll settle this," was confined to comic books and movies. Kids just didn't seek out serious trouble all that much.

There were exceptions in the service. Some of the toughs from big cities had lived harder, more combative lives. They'd had to scramble for bare necessities and prove their manhood in street athletic contests, fistfights, or wrestling matches. But again, rarely did they attempt or render lasting harm to each other.

Most of us had never attended a funeral nor viewed a dead body before the war. Violent death was abstract; the guy in a black hat who fell without bleeding to the ground after being beat to the draw by Hopalong Cassidy, Tom Mix, or Buck Jones.

Then, suddenly, with no warning, our comfortable limits on real-life conflict and violence were escalated beyond our wildest imaginations. War was not a confrontation conducted by two stiff-legged opponents circling while sizing each other up. There was seldom a visible opponent. But someone out there was bent on serious hurting and killing. For me the stark reality of killing on purpose had been my first look at Sergeant Coleman draped over that barbed wire fence, ripped to pieces by an unseen enemy machine gun. It took time to get angry, to hate; my first feelings were awe, confusion, fear.

Who was this evil enemy? Even after we closed with him, came face to face with surrendering prisoners, and witnessed fallen enemy bodies, we did not feel we were actually seeing the very individuals who had shot at or shelled us. Some of the riflemen did have the satisfaction of routing out and capturing or killing the very adversaries who were trying to kill them, when they conducted house-to-house fighting. (They called it "house to house." Actually it was house. That's where the action was: in one house.)

As our number of wounded and killed added up, hatred of the Germans grew apace. They became pejoratively Jerries, Krauts, squareheads. If we discerned an especially gross wrong, like one of our medics shot by the enemy, the next few surrendering stubblehoppers, despite their having had no connection to the heinous deed, were not always given a pass to a cushy prisoner of war camp in New Mexico. One vengeful sergeant spun the unlikely tale that a prisoner had tried to escape and he had to shoot him. His act was pure revenge and spite, and did not endear him to his comrades.

The Ruhr Pocket was our final battle, and it took us into the very bowels of the homeland. Attrition had produced my final promotion to five-stripe technical sergeant. Our veteran machine-gun section sergeant was wounded on our way to Remagen. He had doubled as platoon sergeant since Oaks dropped out the first day of combat. We had not enjoyed a close relationship because he didn't care for mortars.

In addition to running the Fourth Platoon as its top-ranked non-com, I also did double duty as platoon leader. Lieutenant Jewell was long gone, finishing his military term as a prisoner of war. Captain Goodspeed had invited me to accept a field commission as a second looie. I demurred, preferring to be the company's senior noncom rather than its most junior officer. When Goodspeed was wounded by shrapnel at Remagen, the whole hierarchy of Able Company had turned over. A platoon leader was then promoted to company commander. This final battle was far easier for us than the grinding combat of earlier days.

We would often arrive at the objective without artillery preparation and find the German soldiers formed up in the street, their weapons stacked in front of them. There were so many that on some occasions we did not bother to provide an escort, simply pointing in the general direction of prisoner holding areas that grew in size and number so fast that hapless captives could not be properly fed nor provided shelter and latrines.

Mass surrenders did not provoke vengeful treatment. These didn't seem like the guys who had been shooting at us. Mostly they were old men, young boys, dregs of the military. There were too many Sad Sacks to take it out on them.

Then one day we caught up with the whole German Army! Or that's what it looked like. Proceeding village to village, we went into the next town on our route without encountering a single enemy gunshot. As we advanced warily to the middle of town over a ridge that was its main street, we could not believe our eyes. Spread out like a picture-book military tableau of an entire army were enemy troop truck convoys, trucks trailing artillery, marching formations of men, antiaircraft carriers, even a few tanks, as far as we could see over a vast valley. Closest to us were horse-drawn caissons trailing artillery pieces like the ones I had seen in ROTC back home, only with two instead of six horses per gun. The tail end of the retreating column was barely eight hundred yards in front of us.

Quietly and quickly, I ordered one of our 60mm mortars into

action right there in the middle of the main drag. As platoon sergeant, I told the machine-gun teams to hold off. Too far. As observer, I customarily directed mortar fire from a location where I could observe our hits and relay adjusting fire to the crew back under protective cover. This time, even the gunner and his assistant could see where those rounds were going to strike.

Rube Beales was the squad leader, but he chose to serve as gunner, quickly pointing the tube in the direction of the enemy, and making a practiced guess to set tube elevation at the right angle to reach the target. Without my instruction, he had his assistant drop in a round to settle the base plate. I pointed my glasses toward the German column. A puff of smoke erupted just behind the last caisson.

"Not bad," I observed. "Give her three cranks to the right, two down, charge one, and try one round." The mortar sounded off again. This time it struck just to the left of the second caisson from the rear of the German column.

"Charge one, hold the elevation," I sounded off to Rube. "Boys, it's payback time!" I crowed.

"Roger, Sarge, that's about where I got her." Rube's assistant gunner pulled the safety wire and dropped the three-pound projectile into the tube. Twenty seconds later: Boom!

"Bingo! One more turn right. One down. Three rounds," I sounded off. My next words: "Fire for effect," were drowned by the explosions of outgoing shells as Rube anticipated the order. Seeing where his rounds were falling, he simply took over. He didn't stop at the three rounds. An entire bib of twelve shells was dropped into the tube one after the other. Cranking the tube small steps lower, and nudging it to the right, Rube ran a picture-perfect string of explosions right up the diagonally arrayed Kraut artillery formation.

"More ammo," shouted Rube. His two ammo bearers hastened up from behind a house. "Where the hell you guys been? Where's everybody else?" Rube asked in a cross voice.

"We been under cover back there," the ammo bearer replied. "Shit, Sarge, you firing right up through a bunch of telephone lines. Hit one of them with a round and you're long gone."

"Now you tell me!" Rube said, peering heavenward. "Geez, you're right! We're putting rounds up right between those fucking wires. Shit, man, we coulda been killed," he yelled.

It was little wonder that the area was cleared when our mortar went into action. Battle-savvy soldiers saw the overhead wires, and fearing a freak, accidental explosion, they dove for cover, not from anticipated German counter-battery but from a misdirected explosion of our own lethal weapon. The excitement of the moment had shut off Rube's usual good judgment about such matters. Mine too. I had not seen the wires in my haste to lay down fire.

Rube lifted the mortar, moving closer still to the enemy and out from under the threatening wires. As he prepared to resume the barrage, a rifleman ran up waving his arms frantically and shouting "Cease fire."

"What the hell you mean?" challenged Rube. "First time this whole fucking war we got them guys where we want 'em, and you want me to quit shooting?"

"Take a look," the frantic soldier replied. "You got two horses down, and one hobbling around with a broke leg. Screw them Krauts, Rube, but jeezus, don't hurt no more them poor horses."

We focused our glasses as smoke lifted from the artillery column. Indeed, horses had been hit, and several men were down, others trying to crawl to a nearby hedgerow for protection. Two men from the column, one with a shattered arm hanging useless, had found a white cloth and had hoisted it on the end of a rifle to wave us off and declare surrender.

"We gotta quit, Johnny," agreed a disappointed Sergeant Beales. "Shit, we been waiting for a moment like this since the first time these bastards caught us in an 88 barrage. Never could find the bastards for sure. Now, here they are, gray uniforms, big guns, everything they need to fight with, and we let 'em off the hook? Wasn't for the horses, I'd shoot every fucking shell we got."

Fighting rising bile in my throat, I quietly ordered an end to the carnage. The exhilaration of a few moments earlier was extinguished by the devastation we had wrought among faceless troops who had made not a single gesture of resistance or defiance. No enemy guns were unlimbered and pointed our way. Other retreating German units appeared oblivious to the fate of the horse-drawn artillery column we had decimated, continuing their weary retreat.

We stood silently, soberly, as the mass of men and machinery slowly crept toward the horizon. We were watching the remnants of a great war machine crawling back to its source, not to lick its wounds and return, but to await inevitable destruction if they did not surrender.

We had taken out four months' of frustration in the meanest and cruelest way it could be exercised. We had killed for the sheer sake of killing. It had been payback time, but any satisfaction was submerged in the blood and twisted corpses of the defenseless, and the pitiful image of the horses struggling, writhing, dying.

We could almost smell the end of war; and it was not a good smell at all.

Prima

———————— ⇒«(●)»⇐ ————————

The pins on the Supreme Headquarters American Expedition-ary Forces (SHAEF) grand strategy map must have been moving fast as the German opposition crumbled. We wondered if they kept up with us. The end was in the air, in our hopes, in our hearts. But then, experts had thought Germany was crumbling back in December, only to get sandbagged by the Battle of the Bulge. We were wary this time, but increasingly confident that the enemy had lost depth.

In our earlier pitched battles, we GIs had the impression that behind the forces fighting us were limitless supplies of reserve infantrymen, tanks, and those ubiquitous 88s. We saw Hitler as capable of moving huge divisions like dominoes, at the flick of his baton. Sometimes when we were gaining objectives quickly, we wondered uneasily if we might be inviting Hitler's personal atten-tion and further wrath. But now we were privy to a peek at the mysterious inner Germany. It was no longer a limitless arsenal.

Surrender had a sour stench. Those giving up were a sorry look-ing lot, uniforms muddy and tattered, faces expressionless, heads bowed, movements listless. In marked contrast to surrendering soldiers, hordes freed from slave labor camps, farms, and factories were happy with their lot, despite being just as hungry and de-prived as their former masters. They were no longer escapees.

They were neglectees, abandoned to shift for themselves. They were caught between the tide of the retreating German army and the unruly advance of our infantry. They begged for food. They mooched smokes. They were cheerful, smiling, warm in their welcome. The displaced persons (DPs) were a tattered destitute lot to us invaders.

When we could not hitch rides on U.S. half-tracks, jeeps, trucks, or tanks, in our rapid advance, we commandeered German trucks, cars, motorcycles, bicycles, any wheels our men could lay their hands on in the territory we overran. Sometimes even a simple two-wheel cart was pushed along to haul ammo and guns. All of a sudden, we also had willing help, cheap help. Cheap as in free.

DPs were easy to spot, speaking out boldly in their native tongue, calling us "Joe" and always stating up front: "*Nix Nazi.*" American uniforms were enough to forge an instant bond, and the handout of a cigarette or part of a ration cemented an instant relationship. We were freedom. We were food. We were smokes. We were medicine. We were protection. We were all Joes.

Many of those freed from slave labor camps were too debilitated to walk along with us, or do much more than stare in disbelief and relief. Newly arrived military government units were established in the rear to care for them.

Others had labored as live-in slaves on farms or worked in factories, some for so many years that they knew no other life. Many of them were healthy, game for anything, and deliriously happy. Thanks to the melting pot that makes up America, our company had native sons who spoke or could understand Polish, Russian, Italian, and French, those being the predominant nationalities among the DPs.

As we marched our way into what was the Ruhr Pocket in the spring of 1945, we dogfaces found willing helpers walking alongside, begging to carry any burden we cared to share. Sure, we fed them and passed out smokes, but abundantly evident was their pure joy in friendly companionship and the security of being among armed friends. When we were fired upon by the Krauts, they displayed an innate ability to melt into the landscape instantly, only to bob up again when things quieted down. A few were wounded, one killed, as they practiced newfound volunteer-ism. The joy of working in freedom left no room for regrets.

The one universal word of bonding and mutual understanding? *Prima!*

Everything was prima. Americans were especially prima. Hand-outs were prima. Work was prima. A cigarette butt was prima!

Their German ex-masters were *"nix gute."* Being in our presence prompted an immediate counterpoint, a spirited "prima," directed toward any of us, and anything that was going on in their circle of saviors and new friends.

In the American Regular Army back in peacetime, a command-ing officer—major, colonel, general—was usually entitled to a per-sonal servant, an enlisted man assigned to serve his every personal whim. Some aides even sported noncom stripes. Those glorified valets were called dog robbers. Now, here in inner Ger-many, even a lowly private had his own DP dog robber. We re-frained from referring to them as dog robbers. They were our pals, our buddies, our helpers.

The chickenshit brigade finally caught up to us. Strict orders came down to rid ourselves of any foreign vehicles we had ac-quired. Reluctantly, my mortarmen gave up a little command car they had liberated that ran just fine on GI gasoline. To deny the vehicle to others, particularly the enemy who might again use it against us, we shoved it into a ravine and sadly watched it self-destruct. For a while we pushed bicycles along to carry machine guns and blanket rolls but, eventually, the officers made us aban-don them, too. It was back on foot, and the marches were long. The DPs were shooed away, but always surfaced again when the officers were out of sight, to carry ammo and, under close watch, even our weapons.

I had forged a unique bond with one DP when we happened on a blown-up German command car at a country road intersection. Our unit was under orders to continue down the left fork of the Y in the road. Movement had been so rapid that we worried that those following might miss the turn and lose contact. Best to leave a sign. In the ditch beside the little Kraut jeep were two dead crew members. Draped over the windshield of the open-top car was the officer who had apparently been shot as he stood in command.

I called on my dog robber Jon ("Yon") to give me a hand, and the willing Polish DP sprang to action. Together we straightened up the dead officer so that he appeared to be standing. We managed to lean his stiffened body forward against the windshield frame (the glass was shattered). Jon found a forked stick to prop his right arm so that it pointed down the correct fork in the road. We replaced his campaign cap to cover the hole in his head. He didn't look very lifelike, but he was a memorable sentry to point the way for our followers. We hung a GI battalion designation sign on his outstretched arm.

Our platoon file was almost out of sight when the following unit approached as Jon and I were finishing our handiwork. We were a hit. Pointing and guffawing loudly, everyone had his chance to be a comic:

"Hey guys, take a look. That's what happens when you drive drunk!"

"Hey, Adolph. Which way's Berlin?"

"Hey! You guys with the jeep. Take ten. Smoke if you got 'em."

"H'yo, heinie. Come on down and mix it up. We're ready."

"Need a jump start? My uncle's got a garage."

"Yaahh! Your uncle sucks eggs."

"Wanna wax job? We'll Simonize that bus of your'n for fifty marks."

And on it went. Some of these were the same men we had admonished to look the other way just weeks ago as we filed by an American machine-gun squad massacred at a similar intersection. Times and tolerance had changed.

Jon basked in his role as co-architect of the unique highway directional. He told the story to other DPs so often in Polish that I didn't need PFC Stan-the-Polack to interpret any longer. We all knew Jon's tale by heart. I was prima among the DPs.

Jon must have hung around with us for a full week. He learned enough GI slang to stay well fed and well treated. Rube was impressed, and asserted that Jon could understand everything. I argued that he had a keen awareness of what we were saying from

the way we acted and reacted, but that he really didn't comprehend. I proved that to Rube and some mirthful onlookers.

Taking my new asshole buddy aside, I put an arm around Jon's
shoulders, and with the most cordial smile I could summon, spoke
warmly as follows: "Yon, old buddy, how's about I take you out
back of that truck over there, find me a club, beat the living shit
out of you, and leave you for dead. Deal?" Jon smiled broadly and
nodded vigorously in assent.

Next, I removed my arm, affected a deep frown, and swinging
my head threateningly in prolonged negative sweeps, I somberly
intoned: "Yon, you simple prick. I want to feed you the best meal
you ever had, get you laid, and give you a jug of wine and a whole
carton of cigarettes. You'll be in hog heaven," my tone becoming
ever more threatening and serious. Jon looked dolefully back at
me, wagging his head in the negative, and muttered: "*Nein, nein.
Nix gute. Kaput.*"

"I rest my case," I said to Rube and other delighted onlookers.

None of us ever really mistreated Jon. As military government
grew overnight like all newly authorized governmental agencies,
guidelines came down on nonfraternization with other nationals
and all German civilians (including and emphasizing women).
What happened to Jon? I have no idea. But I'll bet if he ever did
get home to Poland (if indeed he still had a home there), he still
looks back fondly on his first few days of freedom from Nazi rule.
I can barely remember what Jon looked like. But then, that also
goes for dozens of men who fought beside me. I recall names and
actions, but the three-dimensional images fade away.

While we were corralling crestfallen military prisoners and trying to help the DPs, the German natives stayed in quiet background. They were deferential, courteous, sometimes fawning. A
few professed to be glad we had "liberated" them. Most of them,
of course, were female. All able-bodied men, and then some, were
serving in the armed forces. While alliances and dalliances were
bound to develop, and did, after combat, GIs stayed a cautious
distance from the hausfraus during the fighting. Any German was
a dangerous German.

Funny thing: We belligerent GIs inquired of surrendering soldiers and natives alike as to whether they were Nazis. Not a single person admitted ever having been a member of the party. Seeking swastikas for souvenirs, we found that the countless banners and flags had all been thoroughly hidden or destroyed. There were still enemy troops contesting our advance, but those admitting to being Nazis were gone. All of them!

Follow Me

———————⟫⟪●⟫⟫⟫———————

An immense American supply system dubbed the Red Ball Express hurried food, guns, ammo, and fresh troops into the Ruhr.* Battle-savvy defenders could still exact a toll and slow our progress, but they could not stem the tide. They lacked our guns and butter.

Red Ball stood for the swinging red lanterns that directed the traffic as deftly as New York City cops during rush hour. These experienced rear-area support personnel labored day and night to see that supplies and replacements kept moving. While they were no longer suffering heavy losses, many infantry units in the Ruhr still had not been brought back up to full strength. Remarkably, some of the replacements we received were our own. Their relatively minor wounds healed, they had been discharged from the hospital to return to their former unit. Experience had proved that returnees felt more at home among old friends.

Ironically, high turnover often left them among more strangers than familiar faces.

* Actually, the Red Ball Express was officially retired on November 16, 1944, but as David P. Colley explains in *The Road to Victory: The Untold Story of Race and World War II's Red Ball Express* (Washington, D.C.: Brassey's, 2000), "the Red Ball never really died. Its name and mystique was so embedded in the mythology of Wold War II that, even after its termination, most of the men who drove the trucks until the end of the war believed that they were part of the Red Ball."

"We anywhere near jump-off?" asked a replacement.

Rube Beales peered out of the rear of the bouncing six-by-six. "Not even close," the mortar sergeant estimated. "Still being moved around by the rear-area traffic people. They wear helmets, but this far back, believe me, there's not much need for them. When we run out of nigger Red Ballers and find our own armed infantry troopers at the crossroads, that's when you can get ready to off-load," Beales advised.

We had wondered at the induction center what would happen to all the Negroes isolated from us in their own barracks. We finally concluded that, at least in the ETO, they were assigned to run motor pools and direct traffic. Some of them carried M1s, but none were members of our frontline rifle companies. That's just the way it was. It was rarely an item of controversy.

In our mixture of scarred veterans and raw rookies, victory after easy victory fostered an infectious spread of complacency, and a festering tendency to avoid risk. The artillery and mortars that usually punished us when we were on attack seldom took a stand, adding to a sense of well-being. Seasoned veterans who had resigned themselves to prospects of a crippling wound or death from an 88 shell started dreaming of more attractive alternatives, like surviving and maybe even returning home in one piece.

Behavior changed for the worse. Command in combat has to be absolute, orders followed instantly. We depended on each other. Through weeks of combat, despite being sick with fear, our rank and file nonetheless had followed orders consistently, without pause or question. But now, direct tactical orders were met with challenging stares, hesitation, petulance. It had become unpopular to court death this late in the war.

Signs of reluctance among the veterans they looked to for example spread and were amplified among untried replacements. They already resented being treated like outsiders by the closed-mouth fraternity of survivors. Skimpy training, immaturity, and a short, soft Army life made them more vulnerable. Their brief Stateside training had been long on "You'll be sorry," and short on hard-nosed discipline. We guessed that the retreads who trained them were themselves cynical and tired, or too old and infirm to ship out themselves. Some training cadres were rehabs (rehabilitated following hospitalization) whose recollection of combat was too horrifying to permit them to teach killing with any enthusiasm.

A stern test for our odd mixture of men occurred during a forced march into enemy territory that was uneventful until mid-afternoon. Plodding single file along a grassy path that followed a meandering stream, the men in the Third Platoon had sufficient intervals between them to prevent surprise damage from unexpected enemy fire: "Spread out, men, one shell could get you all." But it wasn't mortars or artillery that struck. From a hilltop to our front, a German ack-ack (antiaircraft) gun opened up on us.

Fired simultaneously from four barrels focused to converge on a distant single target (called a coaxial mount), a flurry of small caliber shells, a third the diameter of our 60mm mortars, exploded like huge firecrackers all around us, hundreds of them in just a few seconds. My first reaction was relief that the aim was panicky and erratic—probably an inexperienced gunner or he would have chewed us up much worse. My second reaction: Get the bastard.

Projectiles meant to shoot down a speeding airplane were directed downward, spraying us ground-pounders. One rifleman lay helpless or dead, face up in the path; others had leapt into the creek to seek cover, including one of my mortar squads attached to the Third Platoon. Frightened boys all but drowned, their panicked faces buried in the cold spring water of the stream bottom.

When surprised by enemy fire, the common response is to get as flat as possible as soon as possible. We vets had learned there was no percentage in staying frozen in the first place we landed. Peering around cautiously often revealed a better place for cover. Selfishly, I had also learned that looking around relieved the fear of the unknown that looms uncontrolled when your eyes remain closed. It's like being in a dental chair. Eyes open, it doesn't hurt as much.

No sooner was I prone than I observed that the bursts of enemy fire were marching along the path to our rear. No doubt the shooter would rake back toward us. Right now there was a brief opening to seek safer haven. I quickly chose to leave the path and head straight at the hill from which the fire was coming. The shooter wouldn't expect anyone to come at him from his front, and there was just a chance that the angle required to fire straight down the hill would not be practical, or, since ack-ack is designed to shoot straight up, it might be mechanically impossible to decline the half-track mounted gun that sharply downward.

It was a good guess. Once on the forward slope, I couldn't see the hilltop, so the gunner couldn't see and shoot me. In fact, if the gunner's supporting foot soldiers were not too tough, the gun would be takeable. Holding my right arm straight aloft, I waved it stiffly toward the hilltop, rotating my hand at the wrist to indicate assembly, a standard signal for troops to join me to assault the hill.

No one moved. Some still had their faces pressed to the ground. Others, those with experience, pretended not to see my signal, except for one helmet that came into view from the creek bottom. Sergeant Beales gave me the high sign and started to run zigzag toward my position.

"Move out. Move out, men!" the veteran noncom yelled. "Let's go. Come on. Up and out of here. The hill over there. Assemble up with our platoon sergeant. Let's go!"

Two of his mortar men within earshot rose, crouched infantry-style, and dashed toward me on the hill. My tactics changed on the spot. Assault, my ass. I'd be lucky even to get a mortar in position to retaliate. Meanwhile, the ack-ack swept back toward the foot of the hill, and a couple of men who had started to follow the order dropped back flat on their faces.

If anyone thought I was going to storm that hill alone with a carbine and a few lightly armed mortar men, they were nuts. Ignoring the ack-ack bursts, which were not threatening now that he had ascertained their pattern and limitation, Rube wearily climbed up to join me on the open slope.

We sat together on the greening spring grass, elbows on knees, looking down at the prone soldiers scattered alongside the path, a few of them stirring as the clatter of the ack-ack subsided. We saw no obvious paths or road leading down the enemy-held hill toward us, so our guess was that the squarehead could not improve his position to deliver effective fire. More likely he was out of ammo or nerve and "displacing to the rear."

"Want to set up your mortar and toss a few his way?" I asked.

"Oh. I guess I could," Rube replied laconically. "I wouldn't know which way or how far to lay down fire without hilltop observation, and I'm too pooped to climb up there. Anyhow, who wants to support them guys down there? Don't even know most of 'em."

"They give you shit when you tried to move them out?" I inquired.

"Said they weren't taking no fucking orders from you or from me. Said they don't work for us. Said they are Third Platoon, not weapons types," Rube lamented.

"How 'bout the Third Platoon noncoms?" I asked. None of them were from our original roster either.

"Way up or way down the path, they're outa sight. They was a day when guys didn't question which noncom give the order. We all worked like one outfit. Now we got a bunch garrison pansies setting their own damned rules." He paused, stirring the dirt with a stick, peering down between his knees. "Sarge, back on the Cologne Plains I saw you threaten to shoot a rookie rifleman if he didn't get out of his hole and move. You said you learned it from Sergeant Foote. Think it would work here?"

I thought for a moment. "Rube," I replied wearily, "these green bozos would simply think I was off my rocker. They look at you and me like we are crazy-dangerous. They think we're trying to get them hurt or killed. What more can I say?" It was "us" and "them." And by this point, there were more thems than us's.

After a few more minutes of musing, Rube said: "Ever wonder if one of these dinks might take a shot at us for ordering them into dangerous situations like this?"

"No way," I replied. Then I remembered the staff sergeant squad leader shot by our own people just as we first jumped off into battle.

"I don't think they got the balls, Rube. But I see what you mean. We got an armed gang of rookies here. Might be someone in that bunch who thinks he can be a big fish in the pool. Tell you what.

You kind of watch my ass around these ginks. I'll look out after yours," I said.

"You got it, Johnny. 'Nuff said," Rube concluded.

There was no resumption of ack-ack fire. Rube and I wearily trudged back down to what we called the Third Platoon, lacking any other name. The soldier on the path, a newly arrived private, was indeed dead. Whatever his thoughts and trepidation about joining an active, combat rifle company, I bet his imagination never embraced being chewed to pieces by a gun meant to shoot down airplanes. I didn't recognize his name; it's somewhere in our long list of KIAs.

Sandbag

W e could almost smell the end coming. It had been too easy, too long. I regretted that Captain Goodspeed could not be along to see the end, after having looked to our welfare for so long. Maybe it was lucky that he had received some puncture wounds from stone fragments striking his face and neck; they had resulted from an enemy machine-gun burst that hammered the wall where he had taken cover. Lucky, because he was so close to collapse from sheer exhaustion. What kept his old bones going was raw courage. We'd been around together so long that, notwithstanding our difference in rank, we were first-name friends out of earshot of the men. I regretted never visiting him after the war. He died within a few years of cancer.

To us old ground-pounders, it didn't seem right that Able Company took objectives riding on tanks, jeeps, and trucks, often not even dismounting to lay claim, but it sure was nice. We scarcely turned our heads as unarmed German soldiers wandered disconsolately to our rear, seeking a place to surrender. We didn't have the slightest idea where to direct them.

The previous afternoon and night had been spent outside a slave labor camp, liberated without a shot being fired. The compound contained maybe two hundred sorry-looking, emaciated men of various nationalities, Poles, Italians, a few Frenchmen.

Our resident Polack, Sergeant Mandichak, found out that many
had been imprisoned for years. Some of the younger ones could
not remember their childhood homelands. They were literally
men without a country, suffering a dreary existence of endless
pick-and-shovel work. They slaved long hours filling the countless
Allied bomb craters inflicted to impede rail traffic. Their "rations"
were potato peels and turnips. Any self-respecting hog would have
rejected the shacks they were allowed for shelter.

One man in particular caught my attention. So wizened by
hardship that his age could only be guessed, there was still an
unmistakable air of authority about him. Eyes burning bright from
deep in his emaciated face, he approached me, inviting response
to German, Polish, Italian, and finally French. I encouraged
French, having honed my limited schoolboy proficiency every
chance I got. We hit it off right away, improvising with gestures.

A history professor from Florence, Italy, my new pal said he
had been in the camp for two years, swept up as a suspicious
person because of his academic credentials. Mussolini's Italian-
Nazi thugs considered him a dangerous intellectual, even though
he wasn't a Jew. He was tearfully grateful that we had liberated
the camp, and as spokesman for the compound, he thanked me
for the rations our kitchen truck had dispensed. Then he shyly
asked a special favor. I told him he and his people deserved just
about anything, but that we were limited in what we had to give.
I knew that substantial help from the military government was
not far behind. His immediate request was simple, however, and
granted without hesitation.

The professor and his companions had peered for weeks
through the concertina barbed wire barrier at a horse tethered to
a stake in an open field, the property of one of the farmer-guards
in charge of the slaves. He said his comrades and he had dreamed—
fantasized might be a more appropriate term—about turning the
horse into a bountiful feast. Could his people, he asked, eat the
horse?

"Hey, buddy, be my guest," I spoke up. "Be our guest, all of us.
You want the horse, you got the horse. Hell, man, you're free to
do anything you want, including working over your former cap-

tors. I'm not much on eating horsemeat myself, but hell, you guys go right ahead."

I didn't put it in exactly those words, but my Pidgin French got the message across. The professor bowed his way out and returned to his eagerly waiting colleagues.

Within minutes, a clique of six ragged men slowly approached the horse. As we watched from fifty yards away, one of them took out a bayonet from under his coat, sidled up to the unsuspecting victim and drove the two-foot-long blade into its soft underbelly, at the same time giving the handle a mighty rip upward. The startled and mortally wounded horse reared, breaking his halter, and in terror tried to run, entrails tangling in his rear hooves. The bedraggled ex-prisoners chased after the gaunt animal, trying to head off the crazed beast so their butcher could get another crack at him.

Farmboy Beales watched the unexpected action in horror, his rural roots upset by the distressed animal. He yelled at the men to stay clear. When they paid him no heed, Rube steadied his M1 rifle barrel against a tree, watched for a safe opening, and with one loud clap, shot the horse through the head. Dobbin shuddered and slowly settled to the ground. The six men closed in like ravenous coyotes on a slain deer, none of them harmed by or mindful of Rube's chancy shooting.

Others from the compound swarmed onto the scene, and in minutes the horse was reduced to a bloody skeleton and pile of guts. Chunks of meat were borne away with gleeful shouts. The long wished-for feast was to become a reality. They hadn't bothered to skin the beast; we could only hope they would remove the hide from the pieces before barbecuing, boiling, or whatever preparation they could manage.

We pushed off shortly thereafter and learned later, from the kitchen truck that followed us, that the camp did indeed devour the horse, every last bit of it. Many were sick from having their first rich food in months or years. Three, in fact, died from overindulgence. The professor? I just hope he made it back to Florence and his classroom. We never did exchange addresses.

Our platoon mounted the six-by-six truck that arrived to carry us deeper into the heart of the Ruhr Pocket. Improving late April weather allowed us to dispense with the canvas cover that had shielded us in cold weather. As we left the prison camp area, a gangly, long-legged rabbit, startled by our noisy vehicle, shot across the road ahead of us, out into the same open field occupied by the horse skeleton. He didn't get fifty feet before someone took a shot at him with a carbine. That signaled everyone else to open up, and, as the truck pitched down the bumpy dirt road, a virtual fusillade was directed over its side racks at the hapless rabbit. Uncle Wiggly made it unscathed through a hail of high-powered rifle bullets. Amidst laughter and bantering about rotten marksmanship, we careened down the alien country road.

As our truck rolled down into the valley below the camp, other troop carriers from Able Company fell in line, and after a mile or so, the convoy halted for piss call. Lt. William Emerson, promoted to company CO after Captain Goodspeed's evacuation, called in his platoon leaders and sergeants. He had the "skinny" on what was up for us.

First we were told that the kitchen truck had stayed back to help feed the prison camp, and that meant K rations for the rest of us. Some of the rookies were pissed off. As for us vets, it wasn't the first time we had been screwed out of a hot meal. No big deal. What with the lack of enemy pressure lately, we'd had our share of hot rations.

Then the briefing. Lieutenant Emerson said Battalion S-2 had told him the Krauts were all but done, and that this might be our very last push. We were to convoy thirteen kilometers to the outskirts of a factory suburb of a key Ruhr city, Wuppertal, a cultural center that had itself been spared damage from our bombers. We'd occupy the town, and it might be right there that the war would end for us. It seemed too good to be true.

"Hot damn!" said one of my new ammo bearers. "Sarge, how's about dumping half these shells? Won't likely need 'em, and my fucking back's about broke." My scathing glance silenced the green man and discouraged further outbreak of that kind of talk.

We wolfed down our K rations and mounted up for the afternoon drive through the countryside. I hadn't felt better or more relaxed in weeks. The bouncing truck rode like a limousine as far as I was concerned. I gloried in each field, hedgerow, and village we passed, any one of which would have cost us a bunch of casualties just a few days ago. Man, this was the way war ought to be conducted, thought I.

At dusk we pulled up at the outskirts of the objective, a manufacturing suburb. Rubble in the streets attested to choice of its factories as an aerial target. Still standing were long stretches of tall, dark brick walls, the paved street a cavern between them. No quaint houses. The place seemed as deserted as any big plant complex after quitting time.

We formed up in familiar units alongside the trucks, me sticking with the Third Mortar Squad attached to the Third Rifle Platoon. As platoon sergeant, I assigned the other MGs and mortars to rifle companies as they off-loaded. Weapons and ammo seemed to weigh a ton. But off we started, bitching in good spirit.

Suddenly, out of the dim, early evening light appeared a motorcycle with a sidecar. A civilian was astride the bike. We halted. In the sidecar stood a green-uniformed official, bedecked with epaulets, a fruitcake load of service ribbons, and a fancy, wreathed military cap. We stopped short, gripping our weapons in momentary apprehension. The smiling official stepped down from the car, and with a sweeping bow, confronted our lead scout.

"Your commanding officer, my good man," he said in only slightly accented English.

The scout, one of our old-timers who had remained a PFC throughout combat, didn't know what to say. His immediate reaction was to grasp his rifle in a bayonet-fighting pose and stand his ground. The smiling official wavered slightly but maintained his demeanor.

"Yo! Bill!" shouted the grizzled scout. Not lost on the rookies was that the battle-tested vet could get away with calling an officer by his first name.

First Lt. Bill Emerson hustled to the head of the column. The rest of us laid down our heavy guns and ammo, and typical of all field soldiers, stood around, waiting for the next event. It was clearly up to the CO.

"Who the hell are you?" were the CO's choice words of instant diplomacy. He'd never met any officer, friend or foe, as fancy as this. Emerson disguised his unease by spreading his feet, arms folded, back stiff, more like a defensive football lineman than the negotiating ambassador of a world power.

"I am here to welcome the American Army," stated the German official in measured terms. "I am authorized to declare this an open city, and invite your men to proceed in safety and in friendship," he recited, words obviously well rehearsed to avoid stammering or mispronunciation.

Lieutenant Emerson looked at the welcoming committee, glanced back over his shoulder at us, shrugged, and muttered: "Kiss your ass if that ain't a fair deal. Let's get on with it." He waved toward the cobblestone avenue leading into town. "You first, General."

"Not general, sir, Burgermeister. And again I welcome you." This was no clown. He was the by-God, no-shit mayor!

The motorcycle did a 180 and slowly putt-putted down "Wall Street." Emerson signaled for us to mount up again, and we turned to the nearest available vehicle. Everyone grabbed a seat, handle, foothold, anything handy, and a parade of assorted jeeps, trucks, half-tracks, and tanks crept down the street behind our splendid host. He receded into the darkness. Our stream of human-laden carriers moved along behind him, neglectful of the separating intervals we usually observed for safety. Suddenly the street erupted in a deluge of explosions.

The Headquarters Company soldier manning the .50-caliber machine gun on top of the cab of his half-track crumpled over his gun, struck by a burst from a burp gun. The ripping chatter was grotesquely amplified by the brick cavern in which we were trapped.

Grenades pitched at us from factory windows sent sprays of shrapnel in their indiscriminate paths. Rifle fire came from other windows, and far down the street, the throaty roar of a heavy German machine gun hammered our lead element. We had been had! It was a perfect ambush.

I had been lucky enough to have picked a TD 90 tank destroyer as my transport into town. The generous, flat, rear deck was handy for carrying a mortar and our ammo, and there were plenty of handles to hold onto. The ride was chosen for convenience, but it turned out to be a godsend in the confusing and distracting cacophony. With the first salvo, the open top turret closed with a clank, then cracked open cautiously as the tank officer took stock and ordered the big gun aimed down the street toward the heavy MG. Seconds after the attack began, our tank destroyer opened fire straight down the street.

There is nothing like the report of a huge 90mm rifle, packing high velocity armor-piercing ammo, in a narrow stone canyon. If you happen to be even a hundred yards in front and under the cannon, the concussion lifts you right off the ground, and if your ears are not covered, you may never hear again. Here, in the echo chamber made up of factory walls, the blast of the 90 was awesome. The TD fired once without taking time to change to high explosive antipersonnel ammo. In the breach had been the solid, tool-steel bullet that could pierce the toughest Tiger tank. There were no tanks out front, but the round must have been effective, because Lieutenant Emerson, riding the lead jeep, came back toward us, unharmed. The heavy MG was silenced.

The Krauts down that street disappeared, including the square-head manning that heavy MG, if indeed he had survived the anti-tank missile. Such is the message sent out by a tank destroyer round.

Our tank could not move because of vehicles cluttering the street, so we hunkered down behind it. The riflemen behind us were blazing away at factory windows above us and to our rear. We decided to take our chances staying put. The biggest potential threat was a Panzerfaust (hand-held antitank rocket) that might come to bear on our TD.

I set the mortar up on the street, not bothering with the sight, useless in the dark anyway, and ran the elevating screw up as far as it would go. The tube was pointed "by eye" down the street. Rube saw what I was up to and appeared with an armed round in his hand. I saw him strip off all four powder charges and the safety wire. One final quick calculation: None of our people were more than fifty yards ahead of us, because we were the lead unit into town. Looking skyward, there did not appear to be any overhanging roofs or wires that might intercept a round on its way up. And the tube was pointed in the right direction with enough angle to ensure that the projectile would not fall back among us. "Drop it," I hollered at Rube.

He slipped the shiny shell into the barrel, fins first, and swept his hand downward so as not to have it chopped off by the exiting round. Pow! The little piece discharged its cargo, the base plate bouncing off the cobblestone surface. I redirected the tube, steadied the base plate, and Rube dropped in a second round. Other than our tank, there were no big booms, so the mortar hits a few seconds later were easy to distinguish. Where and what they hit, we never knew. But they were in the direction of the enemy, and I fervently hoped a shell would drop squarely into that son-of-a-bitch sidecar. We lobbed up four more rounds, range about two hundred yards, and went out of action. A nearby doorway beckoned, and solid cover was too inviting.

As the ringing in our ears subsided, so did the small arms fire. There was the muffled bang of an occasional grenade (ours) as rooms were cleared. Under ticklish circumstances, our old-timers didn't ask who might be in a room, big or small. The technique was to roll in a grenade, take cover behind the wall, and swarm into the room after the grenade went off. That way, there was no unexpected welcome.

I looked at Rube in the dim glow of our cigarettes. "My God, buddy, what're we doing out there?" I asked. "This could be the last day of the whole goddamn war, and there we are, hanging our asses out in the cold, shooting like there's no tomorrow, begging to be blown up. Shit, man, we coulda been killed!" Rube nodded soberly toward the now quiet street, with its hanging fog of spent gunpowder.

"That's Jack McFarland out there on the sidewalk," said Rube. "Been with us since Christmas. Just made sergeant. Good man. Good leader. Good soldier." He bowed his head and tossed away his cigarette butt. "Dead soldier. Too tired even to bleed, looks like."

"This war may be over tomorrow," Rube mused. "God, how I feel for Jack's family, and that poor bastard manning the 50 on the half-track. So close to making it. He and I talked just this afternoon about his family back in Idaho; how he'd walk in on 'em from the bus stop. The presents he was going to bring. How he'd go back to running the garage with his dad. Man. It's really tough shit."

"There could only be one thing worse, Rube," I commiserated. To Rube's questioning gaze: "It coulda been you, or worse yet, me."

As it turned out, the last week in April was the last firefight of our war. The next day we occupied high ground over the final objective, and again a mayor welcomed the conquering troops. Only this guy delivered. He better had! I had positioned a machine gun, zeroed in on him, with orders to cut Herr Burgermeister in half if he budged one inch out of line.

CHAPTER **6** | **ENDING WITH A WHIMPER**

Punching Bags

A fter the fighting in the Ruhr Pocket wheezed to an end in May 1945, the division was scattered widely to secure the conquered nation among Western Germany communities judged to be of strategic importance. Nonfraternization enforcement was spirited at first, but it was difficult to forbid or regulate communication with a populace whose homes you have appropriated, and who gather to peer longingly at the mess kit scraps discarded after chow call. And when a civilian begged to do your laundry and keep your mess kit sparkling for a couple of cigarettes a day, it was hard not to take advantage.

The military government charged with restoring order, and doing so with as little taint as possible from members of the Nazi regime that had recently been in control, was frustrated and unsure of itself. While no one could find any avowed Nazis, there was paranoia that they were all lurking someplace, ready to spring out and take back their Third Reich.

A July 1945 post-combat assignment was conjured up. Like many military exercises, it had a code name: Tallyho. The mission was a two-day hunt conducted throughout the Western Military District of Germany controlled by the United States. We troops were told to look for phony German IDs, possible war criminals, pilfered GI goods, and our own AWOLs. As long as the war and time for planning had been, no one really seemed to have a clue about how to handle the peace that was suddenly there on a platter for us conquerors—surely not us at infantry company level, anyway.

Tallyho involved a platoon, or company, depending on the size of the geography to be checked, sneaking up before dawn and establishing armed roadblocks at every possible exit from the targeted town. Then, discharged from a variety of converging Army vehicles, riflemen burst into town at daylight and started a house-by-house search. This involved rousting everyone out into the street in whatever clothing they could grab, while the troops trampled through their premises.

On our particular Tallyho, the people flowed quickly into the streets, doubtless forewarned by grapevine of the procedure from actions the day before in other towns.

GIs stomped room to room in each house, looking into every nook and cranny for anyone who hadn't formed up out in the street and particularly for anyone in uniform. Out on the street, any male in a uniform was singled out, whether he was a firemen, policeman, or discharged soldier. Joining the segregated group, too, was any male appearing young and able-bodied enough to have been a soldier. IDs were checked, but most of our soldiers really didn't know good papers from phony.

Company A riflemen were required to hustle quickly through each building, but that didn't prevent some selective looting, and woe to any locked door or closet. They were bashed in with rifle butts, or if that proved too difficult, with a grenade. Occasionally bashers were rewarded by a food larder, wine cellar, and sometimes a hidden person. Most of the people thus uncovered were too old and frail to go out in the street on short notice. But there was sometimes a hiding and terribly frightened Kraut soldier.

Grenade door openings were specifically ruled out at Tallyho after some innocent civilians (and a few overzealous soldiers) became victims of concussions or fragments. Some stalwart American soldiers appeared to relish this search-and-seize mission, glorying in their first taste of raw, unchallenged power and domination. It would be self-serving to say that they were all late joiners; the fact is, some seasoned soldiers joined in, motivated as much by revenge as self-aggrandizement.

"Shit, man," complained Sergeant Mandichak as he walked around his roadblock machine-gun position at mid-morning. "Them new kids would like to spend the whole day here being big shots. They get their kicks out of looking for women's underwear, or copping a jar of jelly or loaf of bread. They wouldn't know a Nazi if he stepped up and threw 'em a 'Heil Hitler.'"

I gave the word for Stan to take his machine gun out of action and report to the gray, official-looking town hall, mayor's office, or whatever it was. Stan went on down. I followed.

Older than most of us at twenty-five, the grizzled combat veteran entered the main room, which might have seated fifty villagers for a town meeting. Now it featured three German soldiers and three nondescript able-bodied males dressed like farmers. All six were lined up against the wall, and a staff sergeant Stan did not recognize had seated himself at a small table in the middle of the room. Ten or twelve dogfaces shuffled around behind him, feeling a little foolish to be brandishing rifles and automatic weapons before such a motley bunch.

"Let that middle kid go," the sergeant said, indicating a squat peasant boy in tattered shirt and pants. "Interpreter says he's a Polack slave laborer. Been here three or four years. Tell that next civvy to step up to the table."

Trembling, a large, plain-faced man in his late forties limped up to the table.

"You a Nazi?" snarled the sergeant.

"*Nein. Nix Nazi,*" the frightened man jabbered, and looked desperately for someone who could understand him. The GI interpreter, sitting out of his sight in the background, told the sergeant that this man had been a soldier, claimed not to be a Nazi, and that he had been home several months after being shot up on the Russian front. Reluctantly, the sergeant told him to take off. The third civilian claimed that he had been discharged for wounds and was unfit for military service. He waved a withered arm to make his point. He too was released.

The imperious inquisitor turned next to the uniformed soldiers.

Two were low-ranking volksgrenadiers, thin, disheveled, scared to death. The sergeant impatiently heard out their claims not to be Nazis; then, with atypical astuteness, he liberated them as non-threats currently, or probably in the future.

"I guess if a man pisses his pants from being asked a few simple questions, he's not likely to start World War III," was his insolent dismissal.

The last uniformed German was a large man, thirtyish, with unmistakable presence and an almost surly demeanor. He stepped up to the table, came to attention, and clicked his heels.

"What's this guy's rank?" the sergeant-inquisitor asked.

"About what we'd call a master sergeant," answered the interpreter. "He's sticking to Geneva Conventions, just giving his name, rank, and serial number. Still and all, he doesn't look to be a combat type."

"Jerk his papers," ordered the self-appointed inspector. "Let's find out who this guy really is."

Inquisitor: "You a Nazi?"

Interpreter: "He's sticking to name, rank, and serial number."

Inquisitor: "His papers say what?"

Interpreter: "From what I can see, they seem standard enough. I think he's been at the Russian front, and from some of the wording, he's probably a quartermaster type. No indication of medals, awards, combat record, or recognition."

Inquisitor: "That's just the kind we're looking for. Big, tough-looking gink. Phony papers. Let's rough him up a little and see if he changes his tune."

At the sergeant's direction, two GIs grabbed the hapless Kraut by his arms and backed him away from the table. They released him. He braced at attention.

"Let's loosen this fucker up a little," said the sergeant grimly. "He's just suckin' for a bruise. Any of you tough enough to deck him? You floor him with one punch, I'll see you get an overnight pass."

Most of the men looked down at their feet, feigning disinterest to cover embarrassment. One big lad in a fresh replacement uniform finally stepped up to the table and told the sergeant he'd take a crack at cold-cocking the big squarehead. Prompted by a nod of permission, the big kid adopted the classic boxing stance and loosed a vicious, looping right hand. Whether the Kraut ducked ever so slightly or the executioner simply fanned a strike, he ended up swinging at thin air. The GI staggered several steps to catch his balance.

Red-faced with humiliation and frustration, he charged the erect figure and blindly unleashed another right and then a left. One blow caught the big man high on his cheekbone. A trickle of blood caused by the big GI's ring was the only visible sign that anything had happened to the stolid German sergeant. He quickly regained his rigid stance. The attacker sucked his knuckles, shook his injured hand, and melted into the group of bystanders.

Looking around, the bemused questioner spied Sergeant Mandichak.

"Hey, Polski. You a big man. I hear tell you're a fighter, gonna try out for the regimental boxing team. How about you showing these shitheads how to put a hurt on this big old Nazi?"

Stan looked down at his knuckles, thickened and rounded from brawls and punching bags. Who was this guy? What were these men doing hanging out with him? Were these A Company people? Had to be. He recognized only two or three by name, and could not remember ever having seen the other rifle squad members. Most of them wore unsoiled, newly issued uniforms.

"I'll pass, Sarge," Stan said quietly.

"You Mr. Chickenshit, or you just afraid you'll show these guys you're a powder puff puncher?" As soon as he spoke, the American sergeant sensed he'd overstepped his bounds. Burly Buck Sergeant Mandichak lumbered to the table, fingers flexing, the skin on the back of his neck growing dark red behind his thickened cauliflower ears. He leaned slowly over the table, seeking to meet eyes that were now cast down at the table surface.

"Hey, sorry, buddy," mumbled the sergeant, and just-resigned inquisitor. "No harm meant. Just joshing, having a little fun. Hell, this guy's dog meat, a phony, one of the pricks we been fighting against in this man's war. I don't really care if you cold-cock him or not."

"And you care if I'm chickenshit or not?" Stan said quietly.

After a pause and a large gulp of air: "Well, put it this way. I'm not about to try out in your weight class for the regimental championships." Smirking and self-conscious, the sergeant looked around for a sign of empathy or support; neither was forthcoming. He rose from the table, hiked his shiny, unused carbine over his forearm, and indicating the remaining men in the room, said: "Come on, you people. Time to move on out." Carefully avoiding a single step closer to Stan, he sought the door to the outside. The room remained filled, this time with silence.

I came from the back of the room and told the stolid German noncom to take off. I couldn't think of anything to say to Stan. As we slowly worked our way back to the jeep on which his machine gun was mounted, the stoic Detroit battler mumbled something in a foreign tongue, Polish likely.

"What say, Stan?" I asked.

"It's too ugly to translate, John, and would probably take a page and a half. Son of a bitch but I'm homesick. Sarge, we just got to get our asses out of here or I'll go crazy as a shithouse mouse," Stan said, his eyes misty with frustration and helplessness.

"Tell you something else," he said as we climbed aboard the jeep. "This Polack ain't going to China, Asia, or any other unfinished fucking war. When you guys take that boat for China, you can look for me in Hamtramck, Michigan."

Our World War II was winding down as unbelievably as it had started. Sadness drowned the relief and joy we had long anticipated when the shooting and killing was finally over.

"Fuckin' A right," I agreed with great insight and infinite wisdom.

Ignoble Death

─────────────《●》─────────────

After a month or so, occupation became a real drag. We all took pleasure from not being shot at, but the Damoclean threat of resuming mortal combat on some Asian shore persisted. It didn't seem to bother the men who had not done hard time on the lines nearly as much as it preyed on us who endured the crucial battles, or had been wounded and returned to the company. Between lectures describing how the Japs would pound bamboo slivers under our fingernails and field training, idle time dredged up memories of lost comrades that had been on hiatus.

While I often lamented our first casualty, Sergeant Coleman, there was no respite during combat to luxuriate in deep, real grief. You need time and a proper environment of love to experience that gradual and unique release. None of us had the emotional endurance to grieve over death, upon death, upon death.

Every KIA jarred surviving comrades. The irresistible identification of self with the individual who died perfected the there-but-for-the-grace-of-God-go-I syndrome. It became practical and essential for me, at least, to submerge vivid images of dead comrades. I tried to cram, force, push, compress the ugly pictures into a special recess of forgetfulness behind my memory bank. But painful recollections, like confined elastic, pressed relentlessly to pop out unexpectedly from its confines.

The piling up of bodies that followed blurred my recall of the first man killed. Coleman joined a montage of dead men who were slain at our very sides, and others discovered already dead, their demise possibly not witnessed by anyone. The dead became confused with those sorely injured. They also left permanently, as gone as though they were KIA.

The deliberately neglected list behaved like a pack of flash-identification cards curved tightly in your hand. When the pack squirted loose and scattered helter-skelter, a bewildering panorama of faces, names, and bodies suddenly materialized. The unwanted and unexpected flood of images left me dizzy, disoriented, lonely, so desolate that I moaned aloud.

The fighting war over, I had to lay down the casualty cards slowly and deliberately. My own macabre game of solitaire. Because I could type and parse a simple sentence (fully one-third of the company was functionally illiterate), it fell to me to write letters to the closest kin of our company losses.

Back during combat when we were briefly in a rear area, preparing to attack in a new sector, I recall wandering alone along a deserted dirt road. Out of the blue, I experienced a rush, an exaltation that made me scream aloud my intense joy at being alive. I felt blood tingling in every extremity, a hot blush in my cheeks, tremendous well-being, flexing my muscles, rising repeatedly on my toes. I took huge, gulping breaths of fresh air, virtually drunk on my own vitality. The exhilaration struck and then receded, like an athlete experiencing a mighty second wind.

I never told anyone of that heady moment; I was ashamed that my supreme feeling had burst forth. I was momentarily celebrating the providence that had spared me at the expense of other lives. I was mortified that I could take such enormous gratification in being unharmed as others took the rap for me, and for all those who survived them. The odd incident remained on my conscience, a mean and selfish indulgence best left untold. In its best light, maybe it was my private, joyful thanks to them for their sacrifice. Maybe these letters were my penance.

Hunched over a dusty German typewriter, its inked ribbon dry and dim from long disuse, I picked a record card from the company KIA file and faced the task of addressing his family.

Pvt. Lester Corbett. Rifleman, First Squad, Second Platoon. Didn't know him. He was part of a band of eighteen replacements who had been delivered to the company just before we crossed the Roer River.

Our company command group had piled into abandoned German troop barracks where the staff luxuriated in the comfort of a roof over their heads for two days. Other than scouting patrols from both sides, nothing was going on. In the absence of artillery barrages, some of us old-timers still hung out in foxholes, distrustful of such spiffy quarters that close to the enemy. A large detail of men just off the boat arrived, milling around outside the CP in their fresh, new ODs and out-of-place overcoats. That's when the enemy played its trump card.

Because the lodging was an established military installation, it was precisely located on enemy tactical maps. The Krauts did not even have to adjust fire to zero in on it. They simply loosed pre-aimed heavy mortars, which crashed down on the replacements and the noncoms who had emerged to process them. Pvt. Lester Corbett was one of several casualties. In the confusion of prioritizing wounded by need for treatment, the arteries severed when Corbett's arm was ripped open at the shoulder drained away enough of his blood to leave him dead before he could be tended to.

Questioning members of his platoon, I could not find a single person who had met Corbett. One of our kitchen commandos who had assigned him and the others their positions in the company thought he remembered who Corbett was, but could not recall why he had assigned him as he did. The corporal who led the group on foot from the kitchen area to their slaughter was himself badly wounded and evacuated to the States as a hero instead of a slacker.

So I was left with a name from his dogtag, Lester Corbett, and a name and address in a town I had never heard of in Oklahoma. Mrs. Leanne Corbett. What to say to her about a man (more a boy) whose war started with a short hike, and ended abruptly when he was blown apart before he had even first loaded his new M1 rifle?

I knew how the letter would end. Like most of them, right out of standard "awards" terminology:

"The exemplary courage, aggressive spirit, and devotion to duty shown by (insert rank and name and unit) in attaining difficult and important objectives against determined enemy resistance during this period (or certain date) are in accordance with the highest traditions of the military service." That last line was the clincher: ". . . in accordance with the highest traditions if the military service." Couldn't go wrong with that one.

This was the accepted tag line on every military citation, condolence, or letter of sympathy from On High. I used it in the hope that some poor family quoting it would prompt a response from sympathizers that they were the words of tribute reserved for deeds of the most heroic.

For the body of the letter? "Lester was liked by everyone in the company, and a generous friend to many." Nope. Even his folks would know that his tenure was too short for such attachments to have formed.

How about: "I got to know Lester during his brief service with our fighting unit. His great attitude and bravery were right up there with any soldier in his platoon. Through no fault of his own, a random enemy artillery shell struck his position. There was no opportunity to save him, nor for him to save himself. He died instantly, in the midst of carrying out his duties." Well, trite, but all I could dredge up for a poor lad I never met.

Next on the list: Cpl. Shirley S. Wilson, Company Messenger. Family address: RFD, somewhere in Louisiana. This time I had a face and a form. "Shirley" was an unfortunate name for a guy. He needed a nickname badly and earned the tag "Slick" Wilson for his prowess as a card player.

"He good at cards?" asked a GI who was skeptical because of Slick's plain-as-day demeanor.

From a card player: "Maybe he don't look it, but that guy in a poker game, he's slicker'n snot on a china doorknob. Ever seen him deal? Time I look for the second card, he's dealt a whole hand, the tickets smack-dab in front each guy. Made me wonder maybe he knew all them hole-cards, too."

After he decked a couple of guys for ragging him about his sissy name, those who he could beat up found it best to call him Slick. So did others, out of genuine fondness and respect.

Slick's two corporal chevrons had the letter "T" positioned under the two stripes. He had been a T-5 technician in the signal corps. He joined us during the early days of our combat, rudely transferred as were others from noncombatant services, to fill the fast-thinning ranks of the infantry. He didn't know an SCR 536 radio from a sound-power phone, but his signal corps MOS (military occupation specialty) won him the title "Messenger."

Slick hung on for two months, and was one of my reliable favorites. Given a message for delivery to me from the CP, he was prompt, accurate, and often performed under fire while we were dug in or under temporary cover. He was also pretty funny, finding some excuse to make a joke when the message otherwise was terse and grim.

"Got a message from the coach, Sarge," he might say. "Move your men out right now. Got it? Recess is over. Anyhow, you guys need some exercise. I'd go along with you all, but I got to get back to my sack at the CP. Duty calls, you know. Have a swell time!"

Now, dealing with his death, I could and did recite the general judgment that Slick (I wrote of him as Shirley) was a valued and dependable member of our first team. I described him as a crack soldier, a valued friend, liked and respected by all.

But could I tell his folks that he was caught by a shell while he was going to the latrine, pants down, completely helpless? A stretcher crew reached him almost immediately. Those first to arrive found Slick stooped, pulling up his pants with one hand, trying to tuck in his shirt with the other. He was pushing intestines from his ripped-open belly down with the shirt tails, as though packing them away in his pants would make everything okay.

Slick turned up his bloody palm in a gesture of futility, beseeching others for help. He slowly sank to the floor of the farm outhouse, shaking his head and moaning. The two medics moved in to tend him. One caught him under the armpits and lifted, as Slick's unfastened pants slipped to his knees. The medic relaxed his hold, and let the limp, now-dead form slide slowly back down. He signaled to his helper and quickly joined us under protective cover, the stretcher empty.

"No use staying out there for the next shell. Can't do nothing for that guy. He's gone. And a good thing too."

"What you mean, a good thing?" I said angrily.

"Balls shot off. His dork's gone. What would he have had to live for?"

I chose for my letter an occasion when Slick had courted real danger and sacrifice to deliver life-saving battle intelligence to his comrades in arms. My account to his family of his bravery conveniently replaced the lethal artillery burst and omitted any description of the horrible damage done to his fragile body and precious body parts.

I pecked out a few more letters, finally giving in to a pounding headache and deep depression.

Difficult as it was to write the letters, more wrenching were the replies. All wanted more detail, names of friends, offers to have me as a family guest after my return to the States. One grieving father, as only immediate family can grieve, hoped I might permanently join his clan if I had none of my own.

I decided not to write a second time. Too much familiarity could only demand more words . . . empty words, as are the words of consolation from any but those with bonds of blood and love. Nor did I keep their letters. It was too painful to reread them.

Meaningless End

N o more than a boy knows for sure when puberty is over does a young man recognize his passage from layman to warrior. But by the cessation of hostilities, as the government liked to call it, we few from the original company who had shipped out in the fall of 1944 were legitimate battle veterans. Old soldiers. Combat hardened. Cynical. Arrogantly proud. We possessed awesome knowledge of life-and-death strife that most fellow servicemen would never know. We required no service medals or decorations to affirm that aura. In its presence outsiders were uneasy, and we gloried in their discomfort. Bravado was a predictable if not attractive replacement for the abject fear we had stomached for so long.

Our company "fraternal order of survival" embraced at its core the fifty-some remaining charter members of our original roster, those who had gone the whole nine yards. We were an exclusive brotherhood, excluding even those original members who had sat out parts of the conflict in hospitals. Our meetings were quiet, congenial, and drowned in too much wine. There was no talk of war. The small size of our club was a somber reminder of the unique good fortune we shared.

War in the ETO was over on May 7, 1945. It took until the second week in August, however, for us to savor victory and celebrate the real end. I was in my first sergeant office, the orderly room, when Captain Emerson, sporting silver railroad track bars on his collar in recognition of his promotion to company commander, stepped up and bent over my desk to inquire: "Sergeant? You ready to fall the company out for that Jap tactics exercise we scheduled?"

"Yes, sir," I replied wearily.

"Well, forget it, John." I looked up to see a broad grin and excited eyes. "Our guys just dropped a humongous bomb on Japan, and guess what? The bastards surrendered. The fucking war's over! No shit, John." Bill Emerson started for the room that served as his office, shaking his head, chortling loudly. He executed a precise, military about-face. The smile remained, but tears steamed down his cheeks. "Can you believe it, John? This man's war is really done. No boat to China. We're heading for home."

I was stunned, unable to believe my ears. On the corner of my desk was the freshly prepared manual we were following to prepare for battle in Asia. I picked it up, slapped it smartly on the table, and with a yell of triumph, threw it as hard as I could across the room. "Take that, you fucking yellow monkeys," I shouted. The captain and his first sergeant looked at each other foolishly. I had a sudden urge to give him a big bear hug. Bill spared me.

"Step into my office, John. I got just a half-bottle left of my whiskey ration; that is, if you haven't snuck in and quaffed it already." He took the Johnnie Walker Red Label out of his desk drawer, took a big swig, and handed me the bottle. No time for glasses. I downed a belt that left me gasping, and with an excuse for tears in my eyes. Yes, the fucking war was over! And, by God, I was alive!

Wait till I tell these peckerwoods that there's no training this afternoon, I thought with glee. And wait till they find out why. I had the company fall out, and Captain Emerson delivered the astounding news to the ranks. My twenty-third birthday on August 10 only added to my celebratory mood.

The delirium was understandable, the celebration typically GI, with booze and wine turning up out of nowhere (the men were forbidden to possess alcoholic beverages). The newer men were boisterous. A lot of the vets became quietly drunk. How long the party went on, I do not know. I threw up from drinking too much good whiskey too fast, and retired to my bed. I passed out, finally, with a smile on my face.

Division command had put together a rigorous training regime. Chickenshit? You bet. Bad behavior had bubbled to the surface, particularly among the newer men. Pillage, drinking, fights, shacking up with DPs and German frauleins, AWOL, even rape. By making troops accountable for every minute of the day, and bringing down harsh punishment on those who broke the rules, order was restored, morale improved, and fighting capability regained. The prime enemy? Idle time.

During combat, sleep had been my fondest sanctuary. Of course physical exhaustion helped me slip away, but fatigue took second place to the escape itself.

Until the atom bomb dropped, my chief worry in the dark of night was shipping out to fight the Japs. I imagined a long, gray beach, water so shallow the landing ships left an almost-endless stretch of cold water to be forded to the distant shore. Approaching land, the lethal chatter of machine guns, swishing mortar explosions, and somewhere out there, buck-toothed little Orientals with funny-looking rifles and big-Jesus machetes.

There was no way I could pull myself together for yet another war in an even more alien scenario. I'd quit, damn it! I'd fake an injury. Maybe I could contract battle fatigue, though it was a little late for that. The thought of going thousands of miles to engage a new enemy in a new and endless war was crushing.

Now the whole war was over in one big bang!

It took a while to sink in, and we still had to cope with a spirited and unruly bunch of kids. We had to drag them back to the reality of military discipline, devised duty, drill, exercises, anything to keep them busy and accountable. It was hard, unrewarding work, and being in charge was no fun. The war had been lousy, and winding it down was almost unbearable boredom and futility.

Plans for our division were changed from shipping out to Asia to preparing for a key assignment right in Germany—securing and guarding the plum the whole Allied world focused on as the supreme objective of the entire World War II crusade: Berlin.

Berlin

―――――――――《O》―――――

It was a somber, slow procession of six-by-six trucks in early
November 1945 that funneled our division from the American
zone in Germany, single-lane, through miles of Russian zone, to
the bombed-out city of Berlin. We ran a gauntlet of Russian soldiers, stern, armed with machine pistols, and stationed only a few
yards apart along the entry route. Our guys seated at the tailgates
of the trucks soon learned there was to be no friendly banter with
our Rusky allies.

Meanwhile, my seat by the tailgate as first sergeant had been
improved by my "top kick" rank, six-stripes-with-center-diamond.
I now rode in the warm cab of the truck with the GI driver. I
looked with misgiving at the endless row of Russian honor guards
along the road ahead. Or were they "honor guards," as the briefing
described them? One false move on our part and they looked like
they'd be all over us with those machine pistols. Our trucks were
too strung out for us ever to be able to assemble a defense.

It was eleven months to the day since we had jumped off at the
Bulge. Cold November rain reminded us that the turn of season
was upon us once again. Thank God, this time we were not heading for the front!

Strangely, our company came closer to representing the roster
that had made that first attack than at any time over the past year.

Since hostilities had ended in May, the hospitals in Paris and England had returned healed men to their original units; even seriously wounded men had gone through rehab therapy and were pronounced fit for duty again. Over two dozen Able Company men evacuated during the first two days of fighting came back to the company after combat was over. Those who had held noncom jobs found them filled by "kids" who had been promoted under fire in the field. Others simply picked up the more menial jobs they left when they were wounded.

On the farm when you mix two strange herds of cows, there is a period of milling, butting, and turmoil, that soon settles into an understood pecking order within the new group, just as a similar hierarchy existed within the smaller herds. Older noncoms attempting to reassert privileges of rank and the dispensing of peacetime chickenshit learned soon enough that chevrons earned by soldiers in battle had special distinction and recognition. They took crap from no one. Battle had made them strong peckers. Proud peckers.

Of course the five dozen men killed in Able Company were not all from the roster that jumped off initially. We were continually diluted by replacements as men left for reasons other than death: wounds, battle fatigue, missing in action, prisoners of war, noncombat accidents, serious illnesses, weather-related foot injury, cowardice, and transfers to units that had suffered greater losses than our outfit. One rifle squad, for instance, had seven squad sergeants during combat, none of them killed. When one sergeant was evacuated, another man moved up in rank to replace him.

I looked back on our lives since our planes had dropped the Big One in Japan in August. We were profoundly grateful that the A-bomb had terminated plans for our shipment to the Pacific, but a huge vacuum of uselessness replaced pressure. The Army introduced "I&E" (information and education) programs, athletics, drill teams, shooting competitions, anything to keep restless, sex-deprived, healthy boys out of trouble.

We held battalion and division formations and passed in review before generals and visiting congressmen. As much as we loathed spit-and-polish, decked out in our new ETO Eisenhower jackets, shined shoes, and glistening arms, those reviews were pretty impressive. I defy any veteran foot soldier, whether or not he liked the Army, to deny a tingle in the back of his neck when a John Phillips Sousa march is joined by the shouted command "Eyes right," as a snap-shit combat unit passes in review. It ranks right up there with a bugle sounding taps.

I had taken on the "E" in I&E and had a goodly number in my basic English class. Classes were sparse at first, but as more and more men admitted their shortcomings in "readin' and ritin'," more volunteers showed up "just to have something to do." Some had been so good at disguising their illiteracy that I was totally surprised to see them in class. A number of those nonreading noncoms and privates had demonstrated a special facility for communicating with the Germans. They compensated for illiteracy with a discriminating ear for meaning in the spoken word. But in class, they were strictly at the Dick-and-Jane and See-Spot-Run level.

Taking shape even before the division went to Berlin was a far different military unit than had endured the pitched battles that took us to and over the Rhine. Some replacements who had tasted only limited action during the final cleanup in central Germany, and most of the new replacements, had developed what, fifty years later, would be called an "attitude." They were unwilling simply to accept authority. They questioned it, often scornfully. It widened the persistent division between combat-hardened veterans and the johnny-come-latelys.

Once we settled in Berlin, the slow-grinding wheels of the system finally devised criteria by which men would be returned home. Length of service was a big qualifier. That whittled away the Regular Army old-timers, including those returned from hospitalization. Because our division was in for long-haul occupation of Berlin, ranks were quickly restored with noncombatants with brief service records. It was not long before half the company was not qualified to display the Combat Infantryman Badge.

Those of us with "only" two or three years in the Army wanted to go home in the worst way. We counted and recounted extra qualifying points such as Bronze Stars, Purple Hearts, and theater battle stars. Many of us still wound up short.

Trying to commiserate with Rube about going home, I found him vague and indecisive. He had fallen for a fraulein in the British zone. He wangled a transfer to the military police, accepted rewards for early reenlistment, and re-upped to spend three years in Germany. I never heard from him after the war. I guess he married the girl and learned to like the people we had been so earnestly killing all those months.

Sergeant Imo was an even greater enigma. During early occupation, he became listless and disinterested. He brightened up temporarily when we arrived in Berlin and his machine gun was resurrected to occupy the gun mount of our command jeep. Imo rode shotgun, eyes sweeping the horizon with customary vigilance. Soon he realized that a fire mission was pretty much out of the question. A machine gun without purpose equaled an Imo without mission.

Imo again became withdrawn, noncommunicative, moody. He shipped out before I did. Because he lived near my hometown, I did make an effort to visit him a few years after the war. We met in a crumb car (diner), inquired about each other's families, stirred our coffee in uncomfortable silence, and parted. Not a word about the war. No promise to get together soon. That was it. Peace estranged us as unconditionally as war had bonded us.

Two hospital returnees from the old outfit became my best buddies: my old teacher and boss, Sergeant Foote, and Mitchel, a PFC rifleman I had known back home. As first mole, I could billet friends near me, and of course, keep them off duty roster. I used the privilege of rank and know-how for us pals to get around the rapidly recovering American zone. We spent a few nights at the Resi nightclub, playing with their unique table-to-table phone system to flirt with pretty girls across the huge room. If we were finally invited to their tables, they usually turned out less attractive on closer inspection. We leered at the frauleins and got sick on weak beer and green wine. This close to going home we didn't want to get burned by VD, which was rampant. Berlin was the pits.

We had relieved a bunch of Airborne guys in Berlin. Word was that the supply trucks ordinarily accompanying their troop movements left the city with little aboard. Except for their weapons and ammo, the troopers had sold everything they could lay hands on in the bottomless black market. As a measure of inflation, a pack of smokes sold for the equivalent of a dollar. They had been free during combat, but now cost soldiers all of a nickel a pack.

It didn't take our guys ten minutes to learn that the marauding Russian soldiers, dirty, smelly, and disheveled, were on the prowl, armed, mean, and short tempered. When they took a notion to eat, they simply went to the head of the long line at a bakery, bludgeoned or shot the clerk and toted off what they wanted. Maybe that wasn't true throughout the city, but around the huge railroad terminal we guarded in the Russian zone, crime was virulent.

We discovered Russian soldiers' weakness for American drugs—penicillin or sulfa to treat prevalent venereal disease. We'd put aspirin, even salt tablets, in a bottle labeled "Sulfa" and sell the individual pills for invasion marks, which the Russians had by the pocketful.

Early on, our men converted the invasion money to dollars by having the military deposit them in home banks, converted to dollars; that is, until limits were imposed ruling that no one could send back home in any month more than his pay. Before that new rule, however, some unscrupulous rascals built hefty U.S. bank accounts with black-market money.

We were part of a security force at a railroad station with a bombed-out roof in the Russian zone that was as big as Grand Central in New York City. Floodlights allowed those on guard to discover some of the pillage and robbery of American supplies, and it was shoot and ask questions later. In the station itself, just a few passenger trains a day departed through the Russian zone. Destitute men and women waited days in line, some expiring where they stood. So desperate were they to escape the ruins of Berlin that our biggest, burliest guards were forced to fire at sandbag piles on either side of the main doors to shut off the flow of would-be passengers for the few trains allowed out each day.

Our quarters were in the less damaged rooms of a bombed-out five-story apartment building. Nearby, we watched the daily roundup by rowboat of corpses floating in the canal. To slow the Russian advance into Berlin, the German army had flooded the subways with canal waters to deny underground access to the enemy. They didn't bother to tell the civilians who had relied on underground stations as air-raid shelters. The bodies of the drowned gradually worked their way through the destroyed walls, out into the canals.

Accustomed as we were to death, we were nonetheless aghast to witness how cheap life was in the big city. You could be stabbed or shot for a loaf of bread, a pair of boots, a warm coat. After each long night, the shadows in the bahnhof yielded in daylight the stiffened bodies of hiding children, women, old men. To add insult to the misery of seeking escape by train, from time to time a couple of drunken Russian officers would stride to the platform and clear an entire car of passengers so they could sprawl out in the worn coach by themselves, totally unconcerned for the displaced refugees.

Former mortar section leader Leo Foote retained a slight limp after his long hospitalization. Face lined, temples graying, he was an old man of twenty-nine. Changing guard at the bahnhoff one evening, the detail ended one man short. Foote was riding with me, and I asked him if he'd fill in while I rounded up a supernumerary. He wasn't crazy about the detail, but as a favor, loaded a carbine and took the post, partly wrapped in the shelter of a large, vertical I-beam that had once supported the station roof.

When I came back with his replacement a little while later, Leo had just shot and killed at point-blank range a drunken Russian soldier who had given him grief. The citizens who had observed his act from their interminable lines where shouting joyfully, cheering and flashing V-for-victory signals. We placed the dead Russian in the passenger seat of the jeep, held him erect from the rear by his collar, and drove away quickly, the delighted cheers of the German bystanders echoing behind us.

The "report of incident" we wrote up worried us that it might kick off World War III against the Russians. When our Russian interpreter informed them of the mishap, however, their curt response was that we had to bury the man; they didn't want the extra work. As for Foote, he was found guilty of the shooting, fined one dollar, given a carton of cigarettes (worth a dollar at the PX), and transferred out to be shipped home.

The two themes played by every German we encountered, military or civilian were: (1) We are not and never have been Nazis, and (2) The real enemy is Russia; you should drive right on through Berlin to Moscow. We had our doubts about point number one; as to their advice about the Russians, they had a point. Despite orders to remain unarmed except on guard duty, I kept my looted, .25-caliber pistol loaded and ready in my shirt pocket.

In a few weeks, the required number of service credits for shipment home were lowered to my level, and I received orders to report to the German seaport of Bremerhaven along with a truckload of other first sergeants. Before departing, I oriented the soldier our new CO had promoted to replace me on to how to run the company. His name? Sgt. Oscar Fay, Second Mortar Squad, now First Sergeant Fay. He was the same former Private First Class Fay, who, during heavy fighting, escaped by a whisker being shot by Section Leader Foote for dogging it because of fatigue and blistered feet. Like a bad penny, he had showed up back at his old company, all healed-up from combat wounds, happy that he had been spared further combat.

I would have protested the promotion, but then, I was leaving for good. I am sure, as in my case, that first sergeants think of themselves as okay, good guys; real good guys. In helping install Fay as top kick, I did my bit to preserve the conventional wisdom, however, that all first sergeants are pricks.

Immortal Youth

━━━━━━━━━━━━━━━━━━ «(●)» ━━━━━━━━━━━━━━━━━━

W hen our troopship passed the Statue of Liberty and docked in New York on New Year's Day 1946, the brass bands that had greeted boatloads of triumphant, returning ETO servicemen had themselves been disbanded. The ongoing chore of welcoming troops was left to the ever-loving Red Cross ladies with their trademark maternal cheer and donuts. But even their smiles seemed slightly distracted and vapid; they'd been at it a long, long time, and the profusion of goodwill that distinguished their presence everywhere had worn thin several disembarkments ago. Hell, the war was over. Hell, the hell was over. The heroes who'd done the fighting were all back home doing what they were supposed to do back in civilian life; except for us and a few hundred thousand other GIs.

That spring I made good on a foxhole promise to myself, and set off in a freshly Simonized, prewar, maroon Dodge business coupe to see the good old US of A that we had saved from enslavement. I wanted to gather my thoughts and find a direction for the future. My pockets were loaded with back pay. Or actually, my money belt was loaded. No use taking chances flashing a roll.

I had gotten as far as a small town in Indiana and an inexpensive motel, made even cheaper because just before arrival I stopped by the roadside and shed work pants and sweat shirt to don my GI uniform. Even at this late date, showing up at hotel reception counters in military garb still qualified for a deep discount on the room rate. No one wanted to be first to terminate this widely adopted gesture to the heroic warriors.

My recently issued uniform was clean, pressed, and topped off by a brand new Eisenhower jacket. I had carefully arranged authorized award and battle ribbons over my breast pocket, right below my Combat Infantryman Badge. The gold-framed, blue Presidential Unit Citation was balanced opposite, over the right breast. My mother had proudly and neatly sewed on my first sergeant's chevrons; above them on the left shoulder, my colorful division patch; and on the lower sleeve, overseas service stripes. I didn't know quite how to display the stripe on my sleeve indicating a battle wound. One stripe seemed a little chintzy. Anyway, the Purple Heart ribbon next to the red Bronze Star took care of that. The bright blue piping and regimental pin on my folding cap topped it off. Returning hero? Bet your ass!

But I was becoming bored with my soldier suit, and uniforms were getting to be old hat to others. Motels being new on the scene, this was my first experience at one and I liked having my car parked in plain sight outside the bedroom window. The old duffer signing me in, however, grimaced as he spied my uniform. He skipped the warm welcome bit to inquire whether I had a job or not. He carped that too many guys in uniforms were hanging around bars and spending money like there was no tomorrow.

The free spending was mostly by discharged servicemen who had joined the "52-20" Club. The government provided a cash allowance of $20 per week for up to a year, while newly made civilians supposedly hunted for jobs. After picking up their weekly stipend, many veterans simply cashed the check, grabbed a buddy, and headed for the nearest bar.

The motel decor was strictly wartime: skimpy material, knotty pine, with linoleum floors, oil cloth curtains, and a tin shower stall so confining I had to step out and reach back in to recover a dropped soap bar. I lay awake late that night, naked, flat on my stomach on the utilitarian bed, still luxurious by military standards, soothed by the soft Hoosier nighttime air wafting through the screened window. As a tourist, I savored not sleeping with an unwashed crowd of snoring, farting, loud-talking, and largely inconsiderate lummoxes, which pretty well described my nighttime companions for the past three years, however fond I may have been of them.

Surging engines and shouting in the gravel parking lot outside the motel, until then all but empty on a Friday night, pulled me up on my elbows to see what was going on.

A half dozen high-school-age boys in yellow-lettered, blue athletic jackets piled out of three cars and were arguing, pushing, yelling, being teenage pains in the ass. The drivers remained in place, goosing their motors, flicking dimmer switches up and down, and hurling taunts at each other. The bystanders piled in one car or another. The family chariots lined up on the gravel, and one by one, jack-rabbited off the line to roar to the other end of the lot, skid into a 180-degree "whirly," and return, engines still surging, to the starting line. The fastest chariot was a 1939 Ford with straight exhausts that sounded like some earthbound buzz bomb.

Unintelligible jabbering between open car windows persisted for a few minutes and the drivers signaled a fresh start by pumping up increasingly rapid engine revs. Jockeys peaked rpms on the raging engines, popped clutches, and fishtailed out onto the asphalt highway where tires bit with a screech. Off they went, engines recovering maximum turnover as they disappeared, finally out of earshot.

Off to play chicken. I shook my head. Great way to get killed. Great way to make Pop wonder why his clutch was turning mushy and why the old family boat was starting to eat even more thirty- or forty-weight oil. Takes one to know one, I ruefully concluded.

I flopped over on my back, hands back of my head, a posture typical of a soldier zoning-out on rest and recreation.

There is no time in life, I pondered, when a guy is more at the peak of his bravado and self-confidence than at eighteen or nineteen years. He's old and strong enough to live out the acts of daring and physical prowess that frustrated him during earlier growing years, but still too young to weigh the consequences. At eighteen years, six months, I decreed to myself, a guy achieves the zenith of his own immortality. He'll walk jauntily through the Valley of Death bouncing a softball in one hand, the other holding a lighted Camel. Balls and gall.

Brash kids make great cannon fodder. Initial draft procedures in World War II sought to preserve our nation's flower of youth, but the increasing requirements of global war made dipping deep into teenage ranks a harsh necessity. As it turned out, the innocent belief of these raw American recruits in their own ability to live forever provided much of the balance of effectiveness in winning final battles in Germany and elsewhere. Near the end the enemy, in contrast, were weary, older, cynical veterans. We fought a lot of old codgers because virile German youngsters had long ago been chewed up in battle. Those older soldiers were only too aware of their vulnerability, not anxious to embrace the inevitability of their own demise.

As surely as the body produces antibodies to fight various infections, we young American infantrymen cultivated defense mechanisms to sustain our sanity and ability to face death. Our preservation depended on pulse-quickening adrenaline, which flows ever-refreshing and stronger as the reaction to fear is practiced with ever-increasing frequency and in greater measure. In my case, will-to-live was aided and abetted by sleep, my narcotic of choice.

In mortal combat, personal conviction of immortality is finally dashed, broken, erased, no matter your age. You can't watch people around you getting killed without recognizing your own vulnerability. You test and retest your own capacities, humbled by firsthand knowledge of what might happen to you.

Without war to do it for them, young men that night in Indiana still had to test their nerve. The Old Man's jalopy was the vehicle. Well, if they wanted to get killed, and couldn't wait for the next war, screw 'em all! I added an old first sergeant's familiar tag line: just save four for KP.

The next morning I pulled on my blue jeans, crammed my uniform in the back of the car trunk, and proclaimed that, for me anyway, the "Good War" was over.

ABOUT THE AUTHOR

Born and raised in Ithaca, New York, John B. Babcock entered the Army in 1943 and saw combat in the European theater of operations with the Seventy-eighth Infantry Division. He earned a Bronze Star, a Purple Heart, and the Combat Infantryman's Badge during his service. His battalion received the Presidential Unit Citation with gold frame and blue ribbon. After the war he embarked on a career in the broadcasting and communications industries. Married over fifty years and with three daughters, he is now retired and lives in his boyhood home of Ithaca, New York.